dinosaur friendship

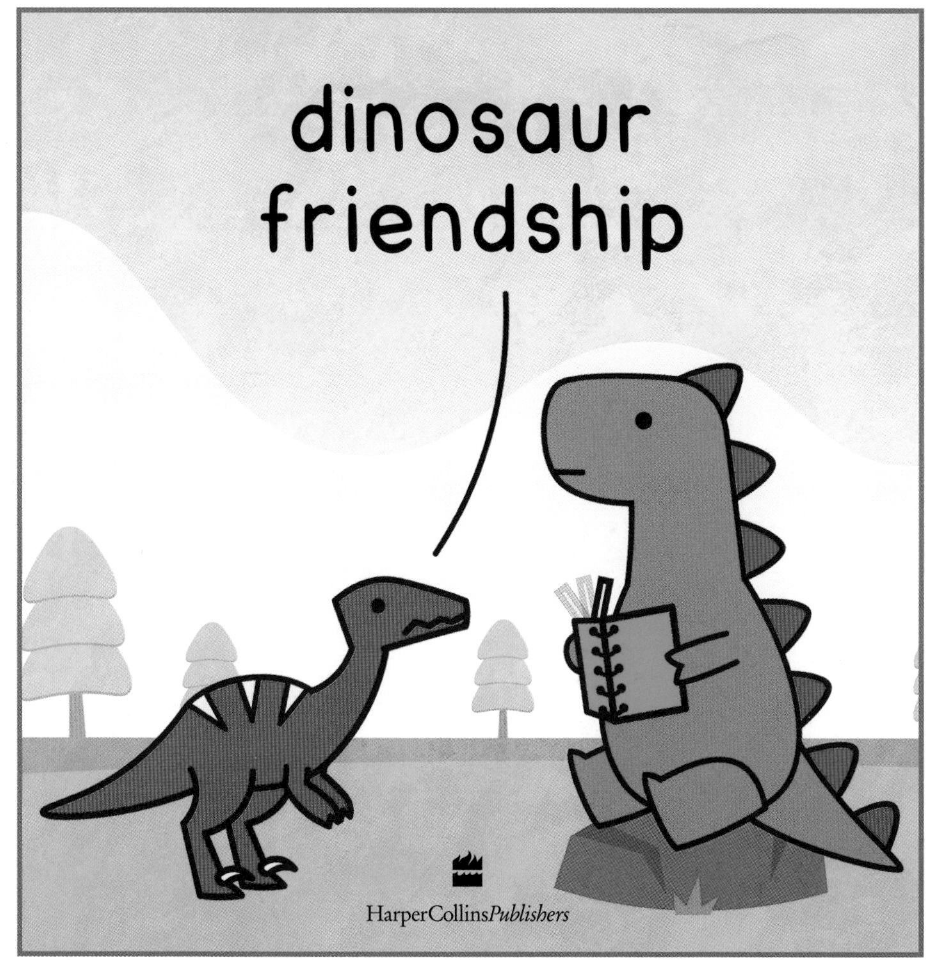

HarperCollins*Publishers*

HarperCollins*Publishers*
1 London Bridge Street
London SE1 9GF

www.harpercollins.co.uk

HarperCollins*Publishers*
Macken House, 39/40 Mayor Street Upper
Dublin 1, D01 C9W8 Ireland

First published by HarperCollins*Publishers* 2023

1 3 5 7 9 10 8 6 4 2

A catalogue record of this book is
available from the British Library

ISBN 978-0-00-857894-7

Printed and bound in Latvia

This book is produced from independently certified FSC™ paper to
ensure responsible forest management.

For more information visit: www.harpercollins.co.uk/green

contents

introduction

The very first description we wrote of dinosandcomics was 'a comic about depressed dinosaurs, who find hope in each other'. Over the few years I've been writing, the focus of the comic has shifted slightly from depression to hope, both because I've got my depression more under control and because I've come to realize that hope is far more important and fulfilling to write about.

dinosaur friendship

The title *dinosaur friendship* is both fitting and not: fitting because our friends are often those we find hope in, but also not, because friends are by no means the entirety of what can give us that hope. Consequently, this book has comics not just on friendship, but on family, lovers, professional acquaintances, and perhaps the most important people we have to look to for hope, ourselves.

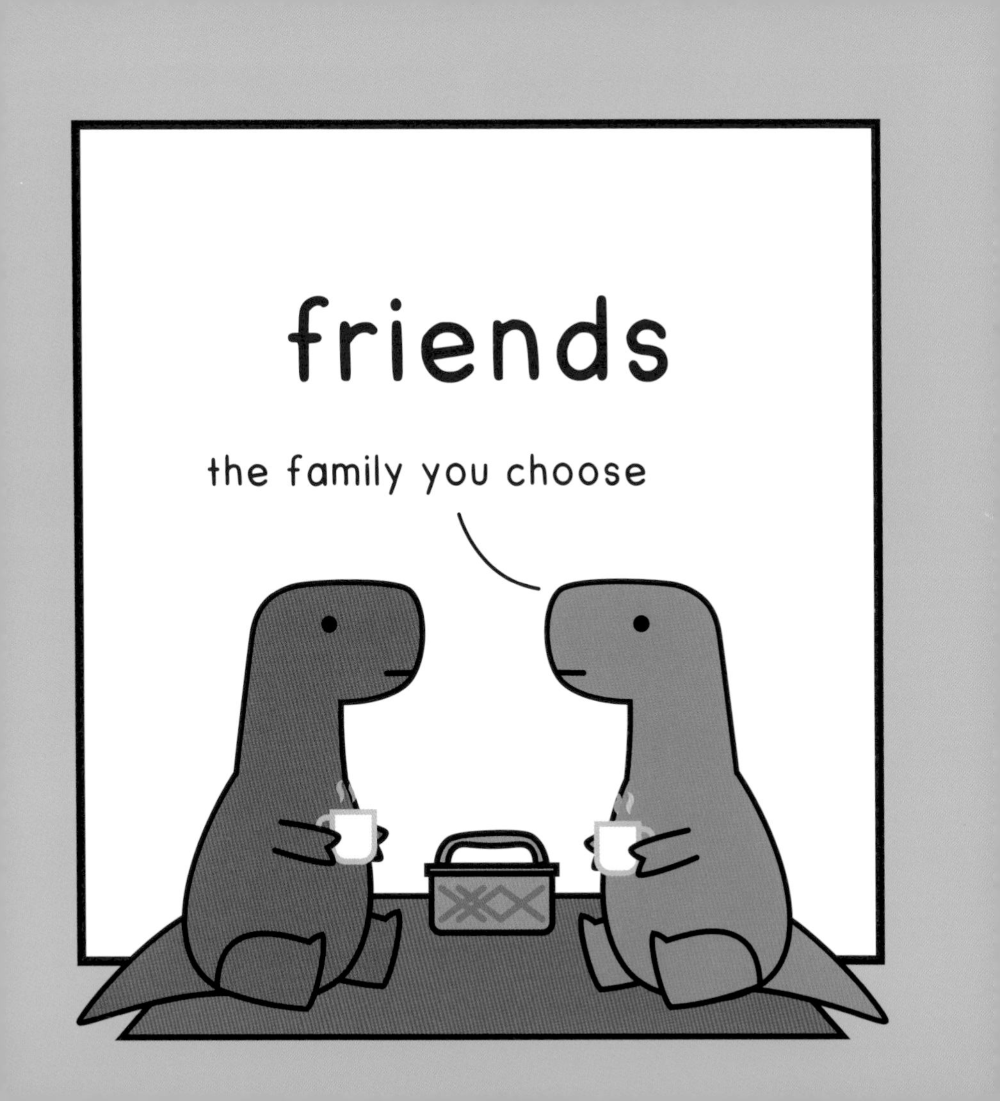
friends
the family you choose

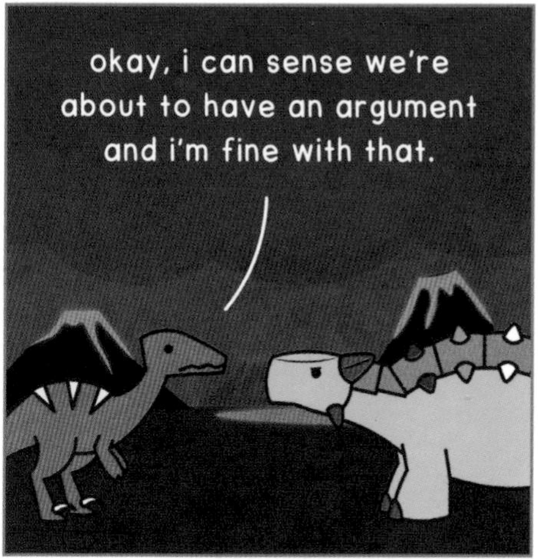
okay, i can sense we're about to have an argument and i'm fine with that.

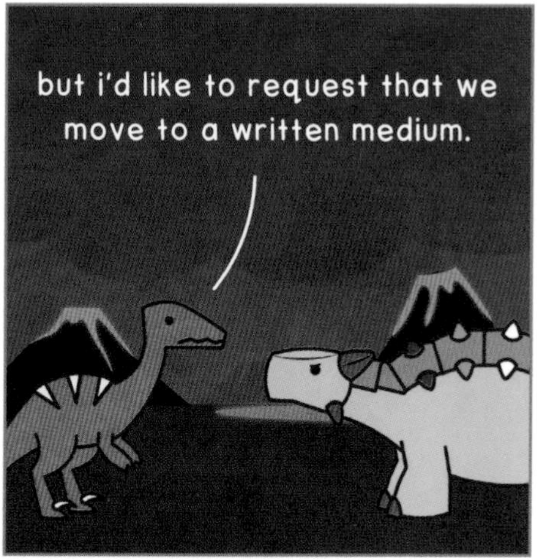
but i'd like to request that we move to a written medium.

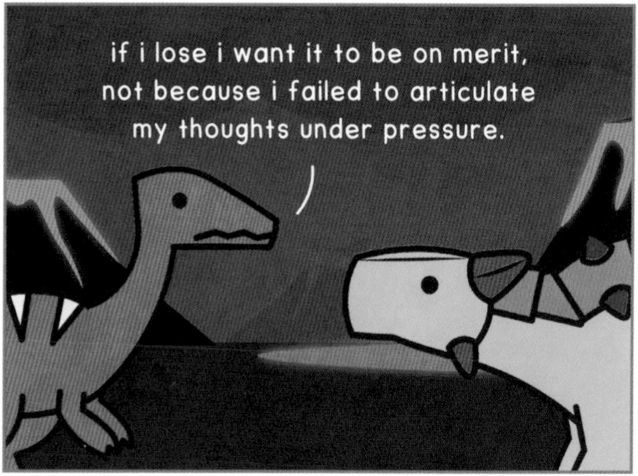
if i lose i want it to be on merit, not because i failed to articulate my thoughts under pressure.

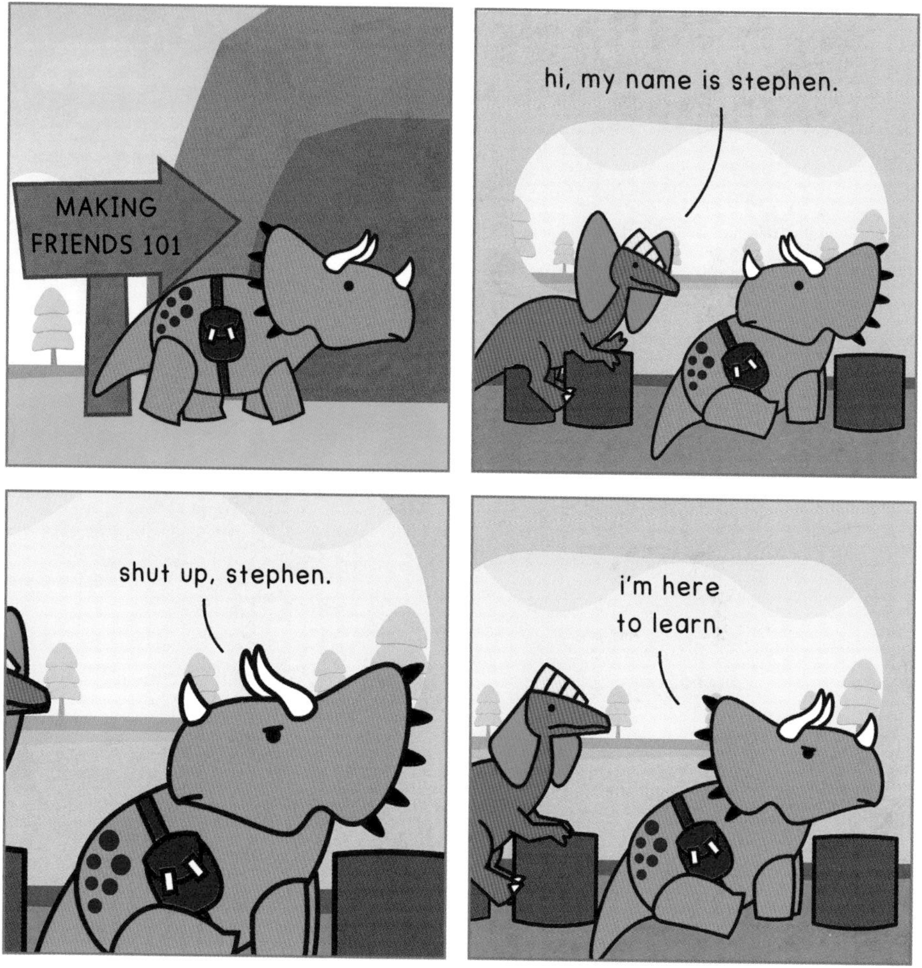
MAKING FRIENDS 101
hi, my name is stephen.
shut up, stephen.
i'm here to learn.

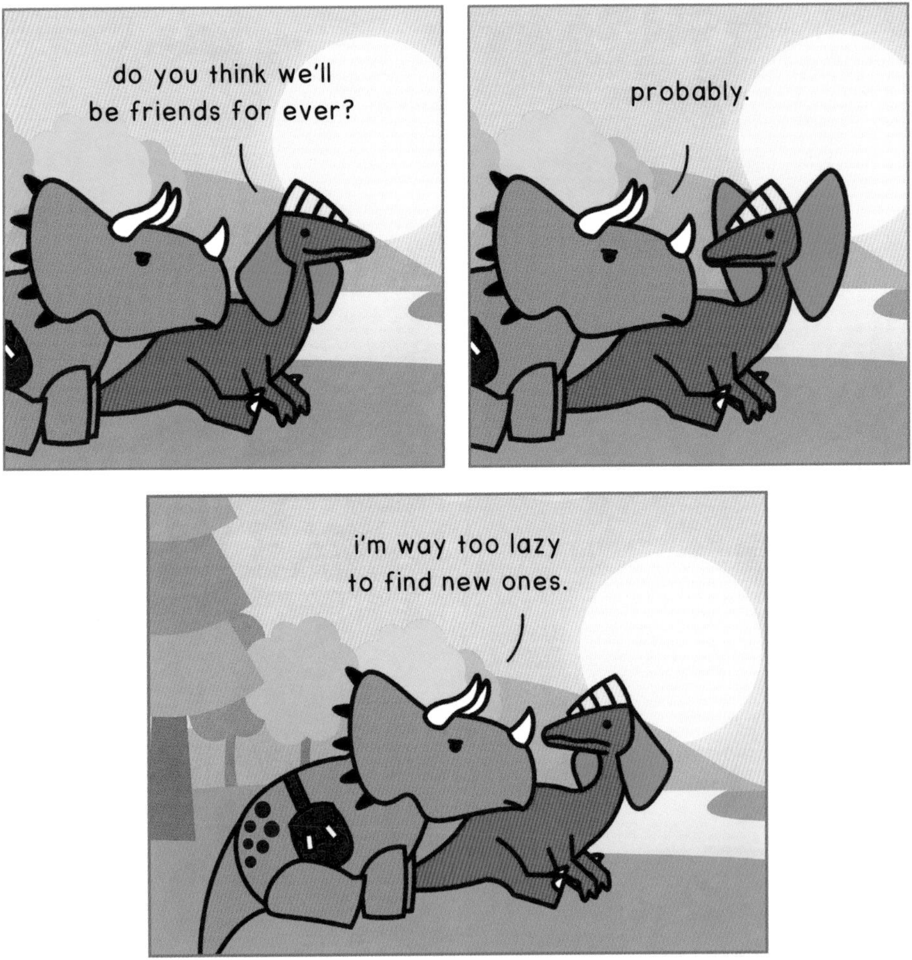
do you think we'll be friends for ever?
probably.
i'm way too lazy to find new ones.

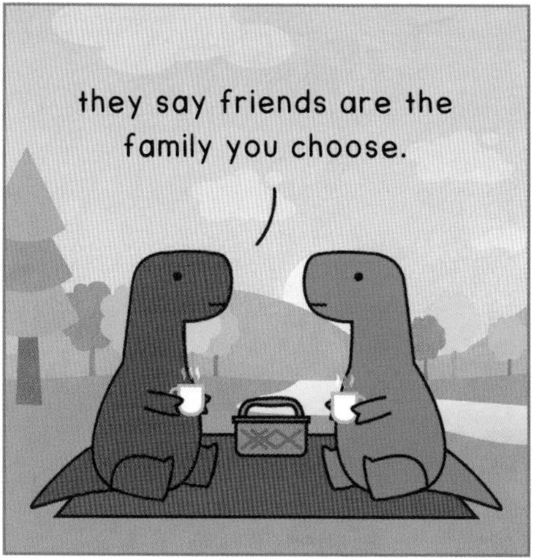
they say friends are the family you choose.

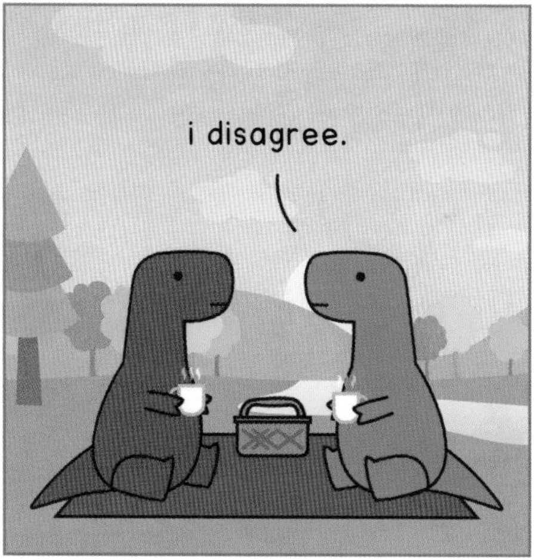
i disagree.

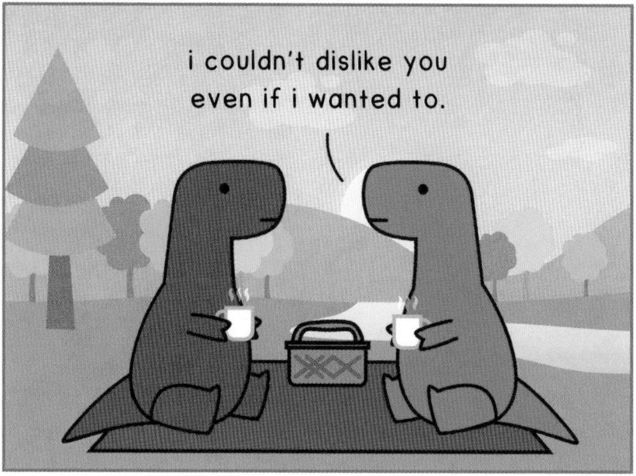
i couldn't dislike you even if i wanted to.

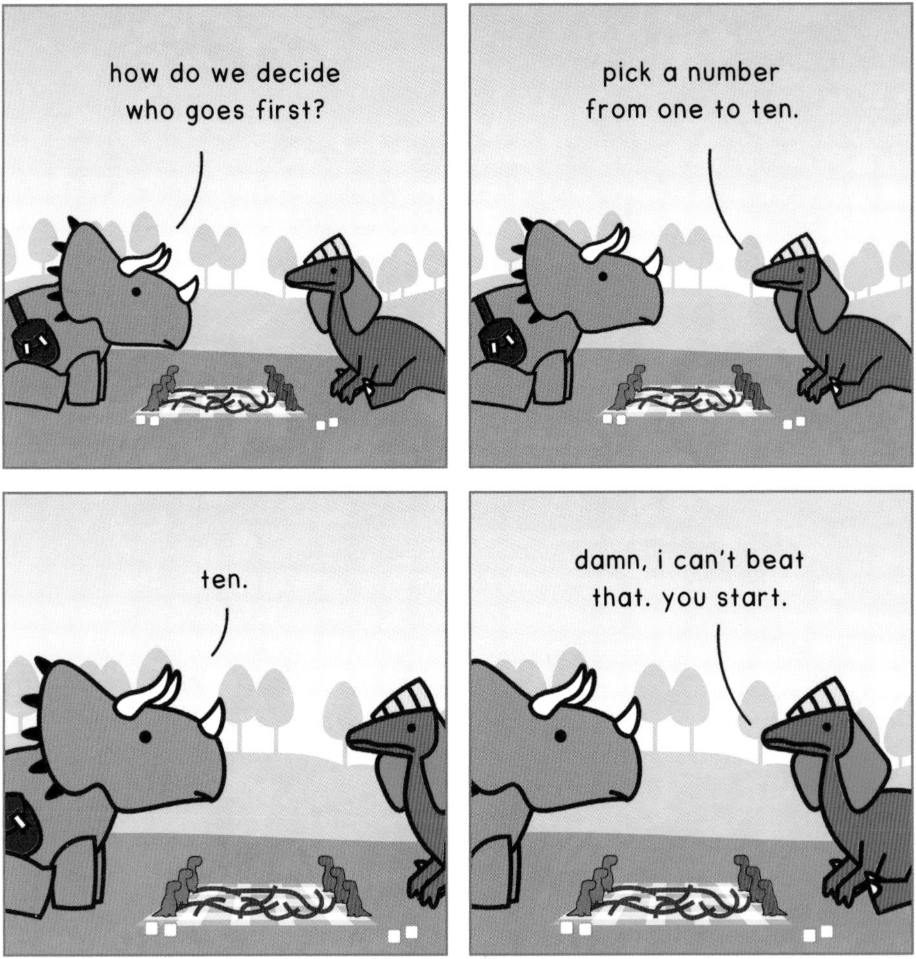
how do we decide who goes first?
pick a number from one to ten.
ten.
damn, i can't beat that. you start.

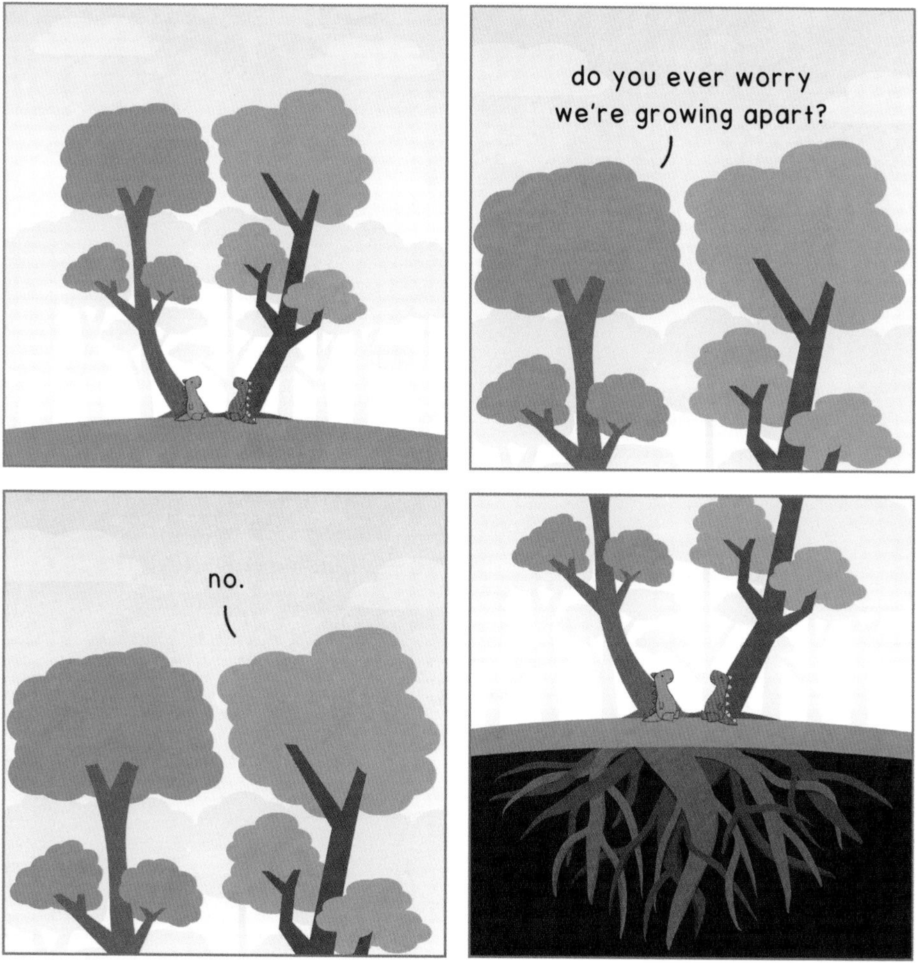
do you ever worry
we're growing apart?
no.

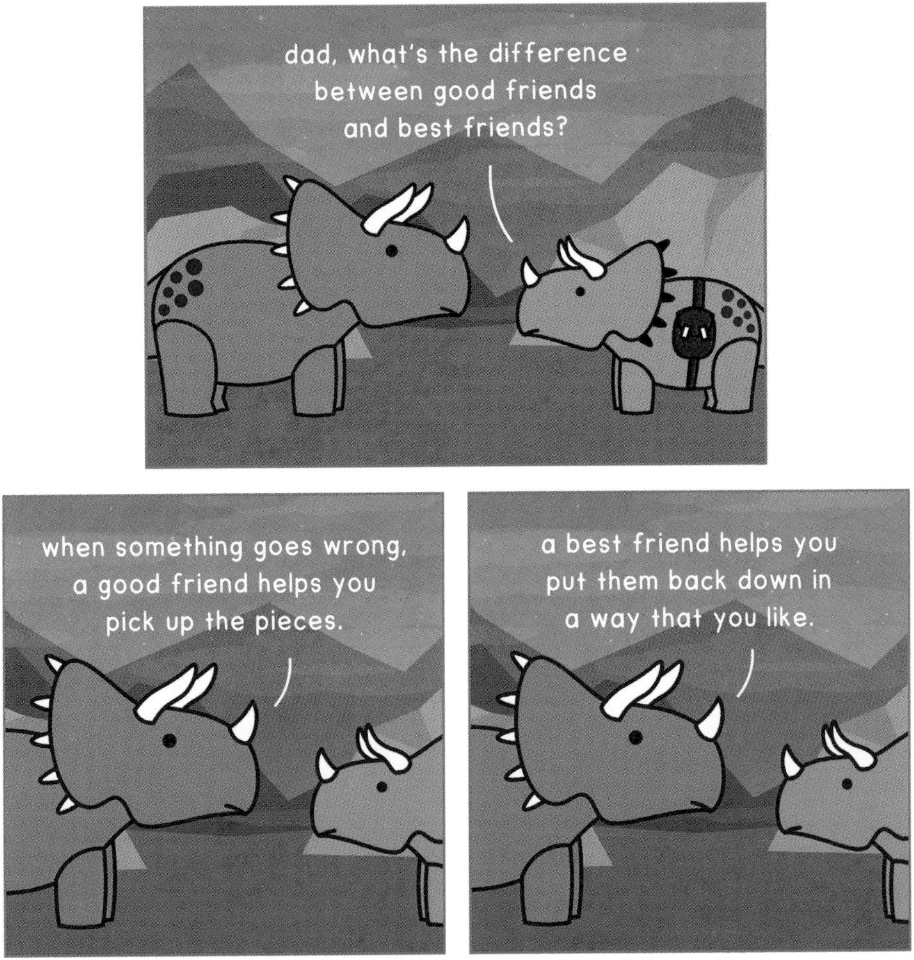
dad, what's the difference between good friends and best friends?
when something goes wrong, a good friend helps you pick up the pieces.
a best friend helps you put them back down in a way that you like.

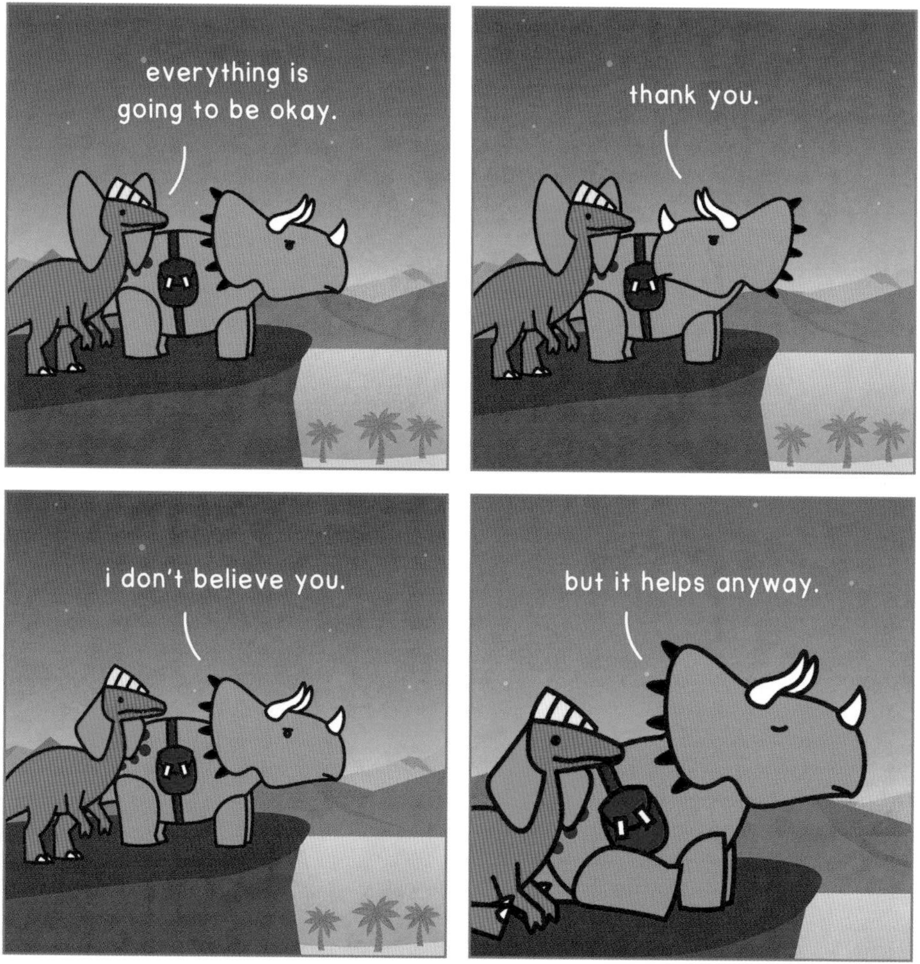
everything is going to be okay.
thank you.
i don't believe you.
but it helps anyway.

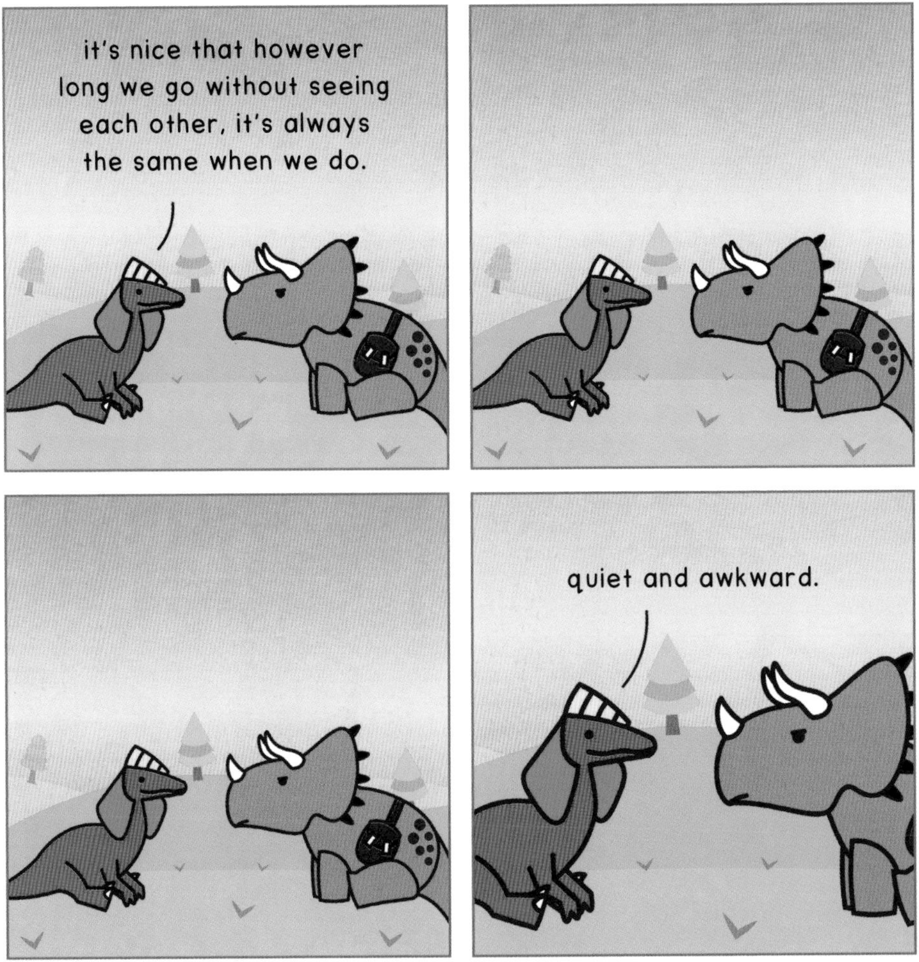
it's nice that however long we go without seeing each other, it's always the same when we do.
quiet and awkward.

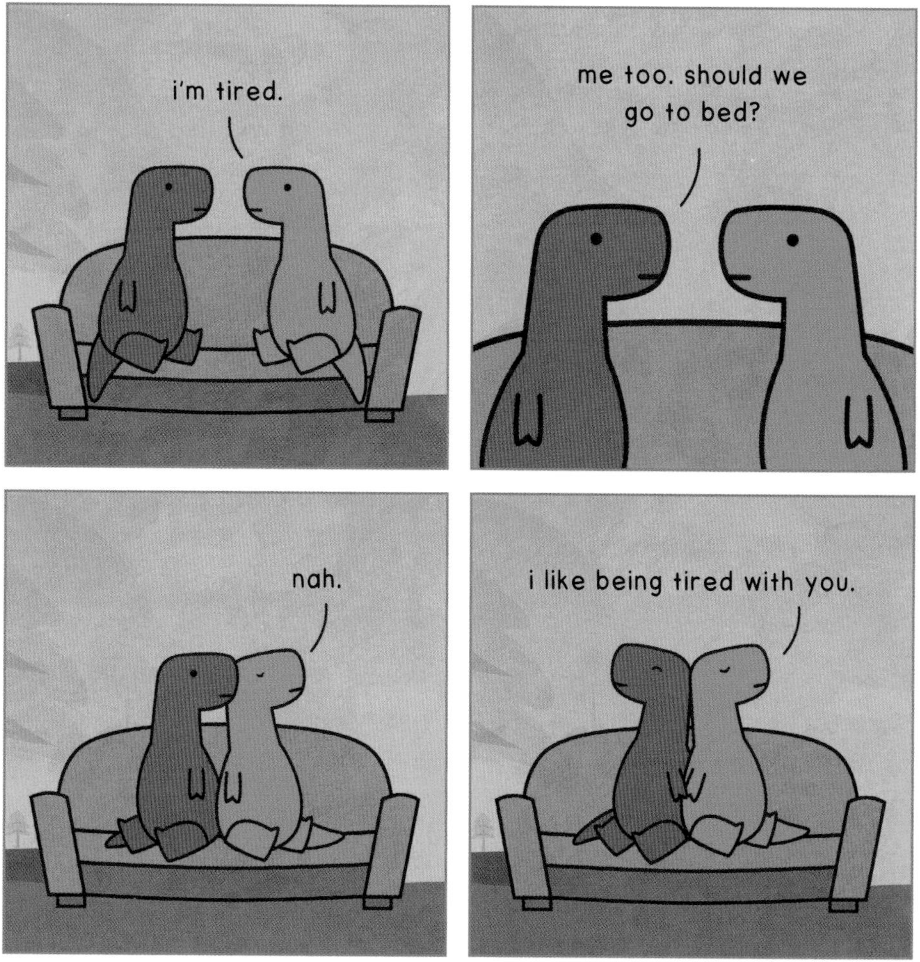
i'm tired.
me too. should we go to bed?
nah.
i like being tired with you.

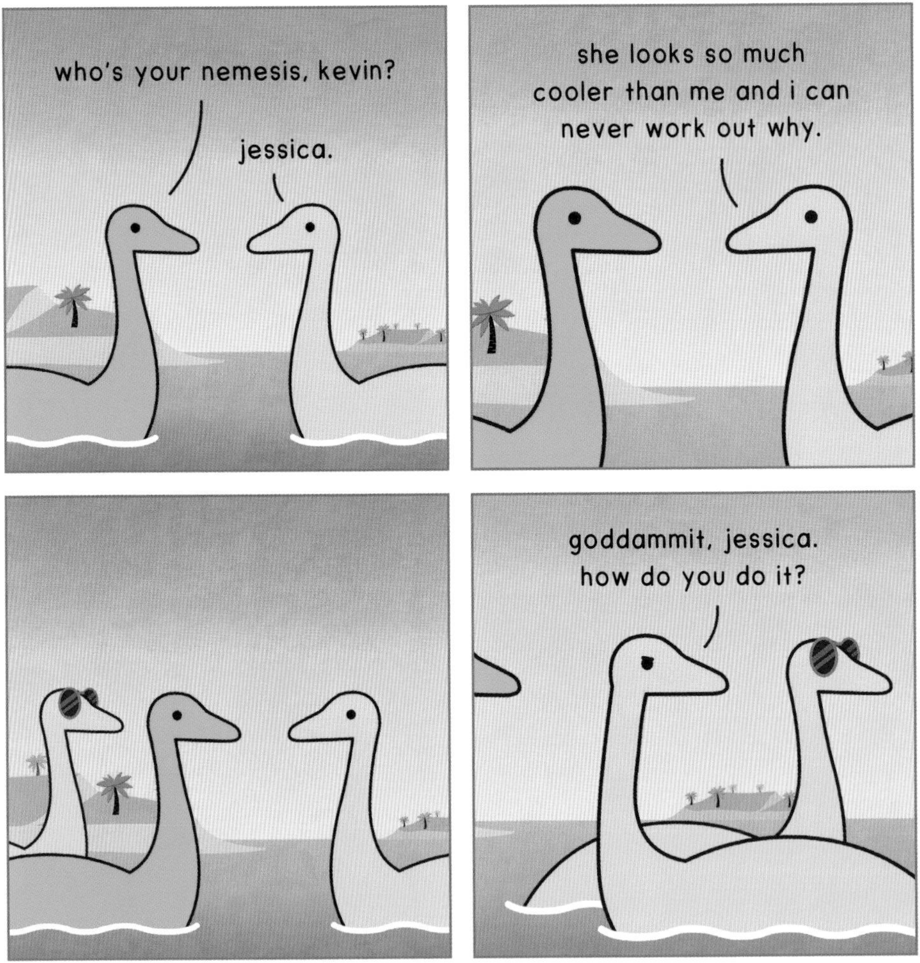
who's your nemesis, kevin?
jessica.
she looks so much cooler than me and i can never work out why.
goddammit, jessica. how do you do it?

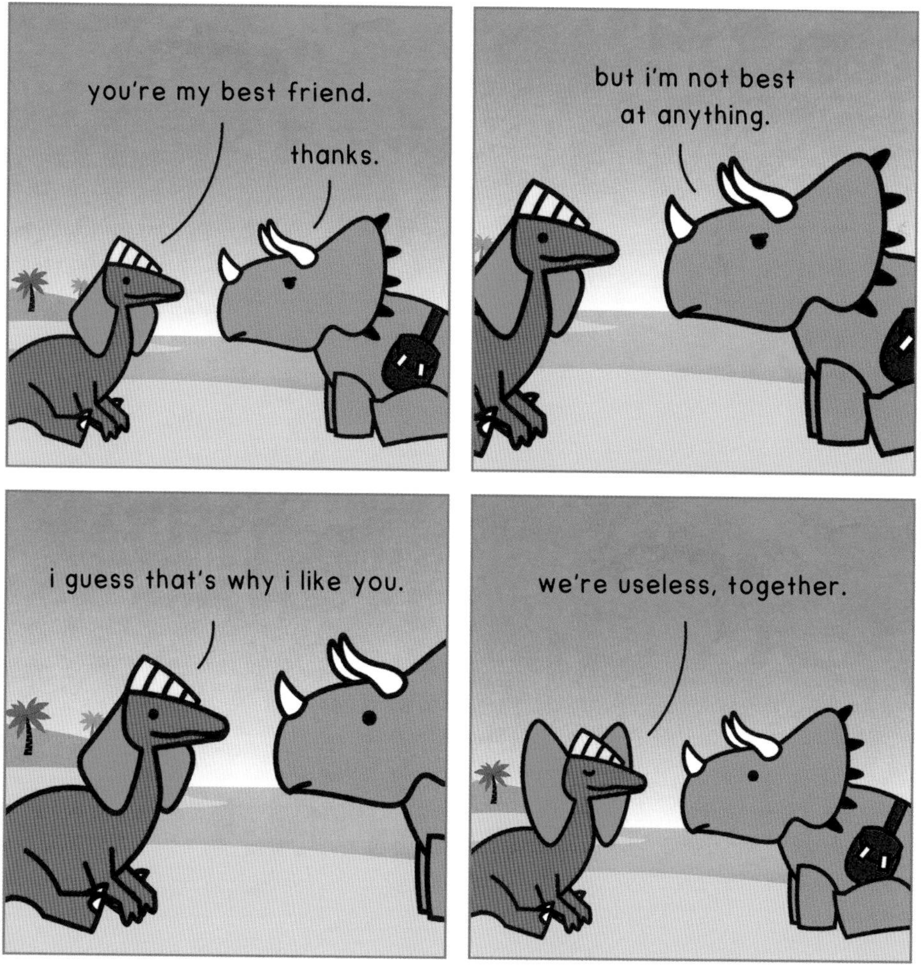
you're my best friend.
thanks.
but i'm not best at anything.
i guess that's why i like you.
we're useless, together.

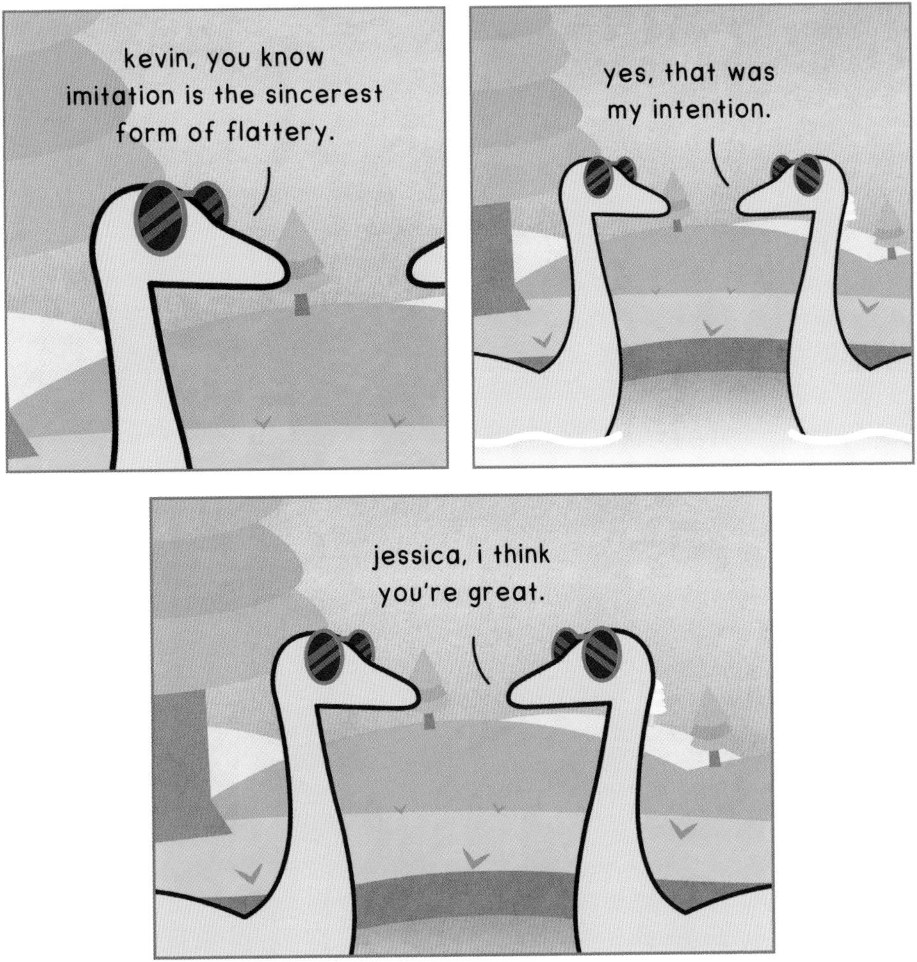
kevin, you know imitation is the sincerest form of flattery.
yes, that was my intention.
jessica, i think you're great.

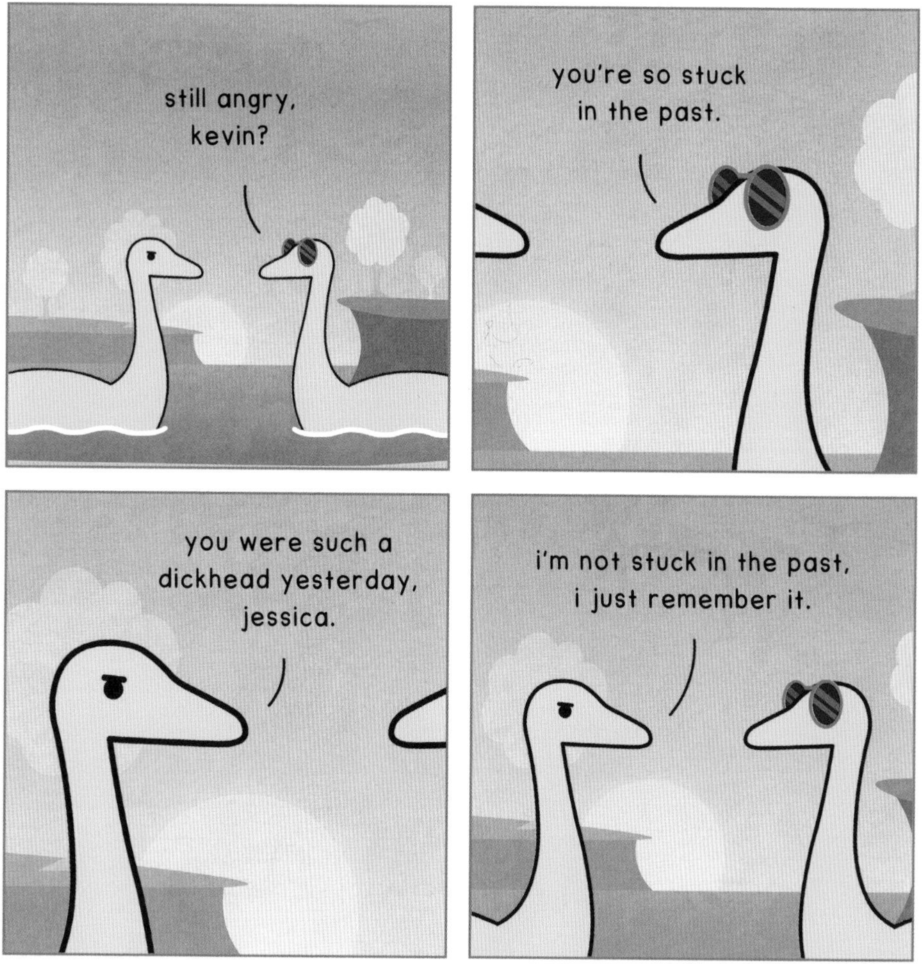
still angry, kevin?
you're so stuck in the past.
you were such a dickhead yesterday, jessica.
i'm not stuck in the past, i just remember it.

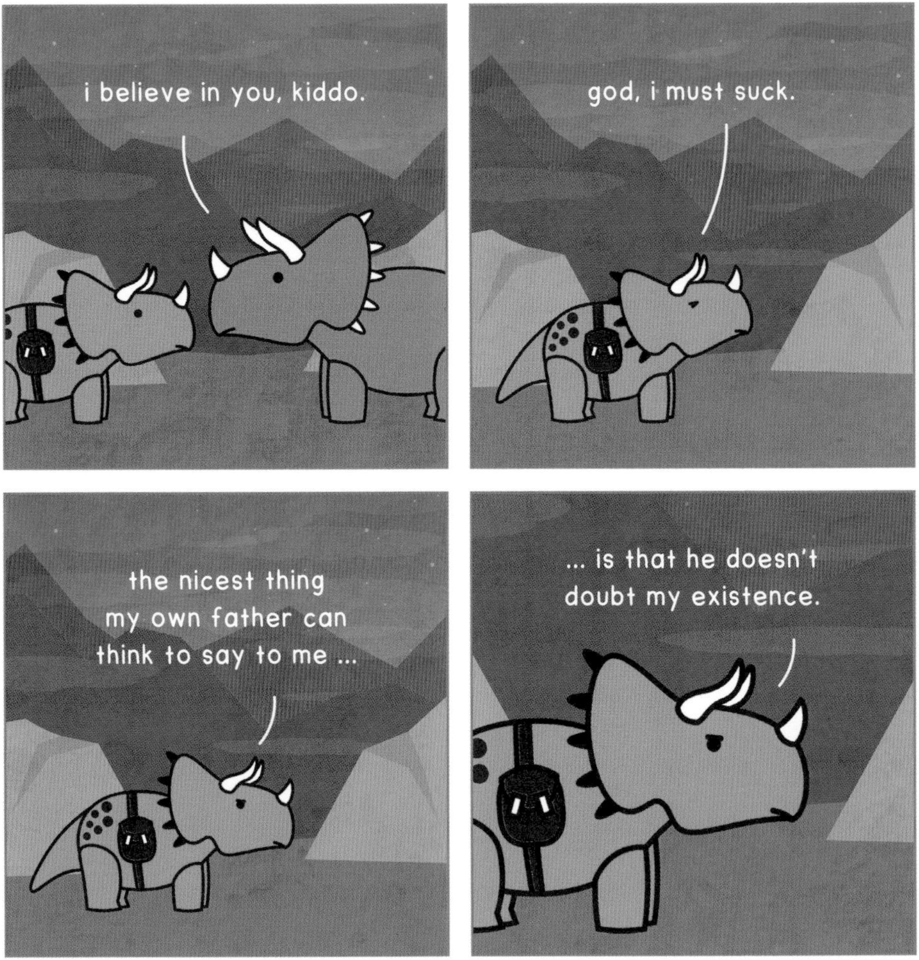
i believe in you, kiddo.
god, i must suck.
the nicest thing my own father can think to say to me ...
... is that he doesn't doubt my existence.

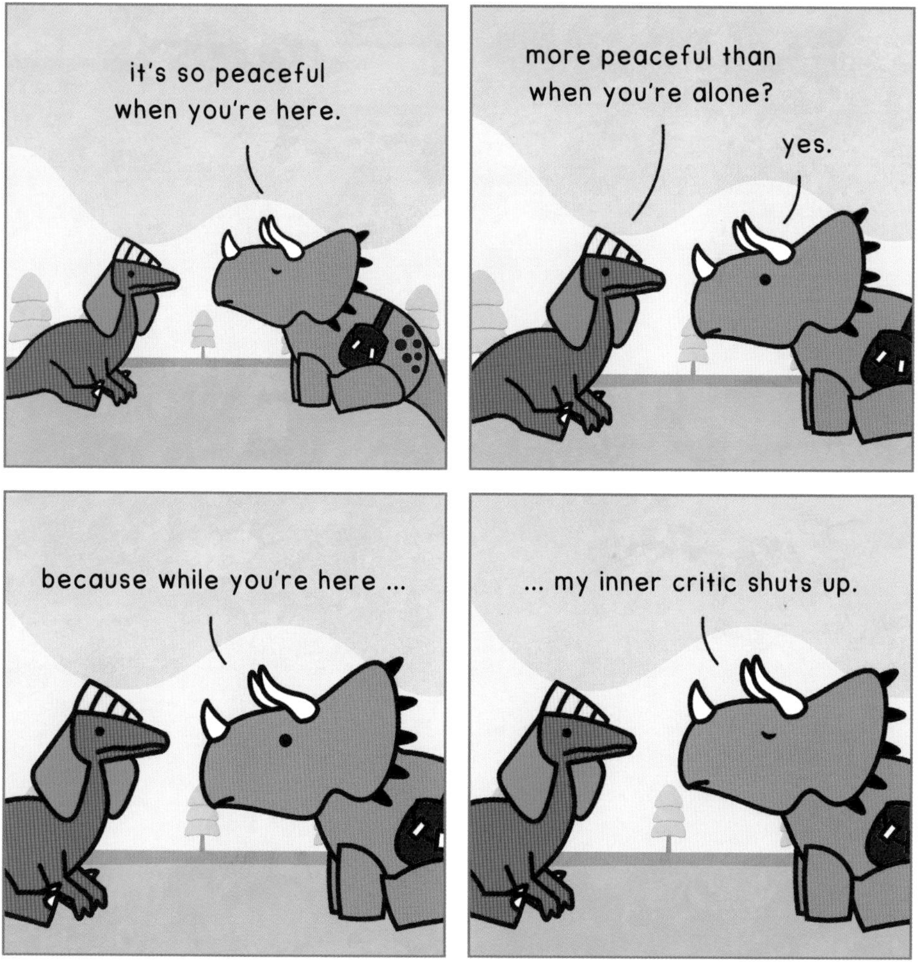
it's so peaceful when you're here.
more peaceful than when you're alone?
yes.
because while you're here ...
... my inner critic shuts up.

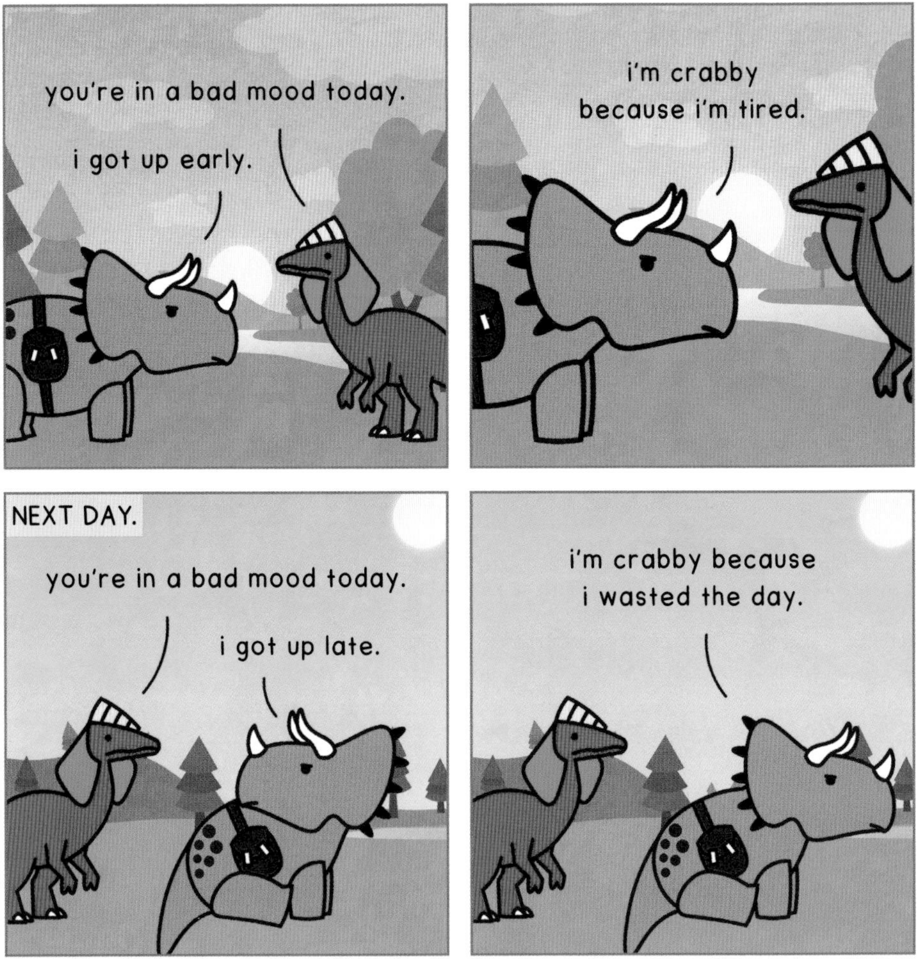
you're in a bad mood today.
i got up early.
i'm crabby
because i'm tired.
NEXT DAY.
you're in a bad mood today.
i got up late.
i'm crabby because
i wasted the day.

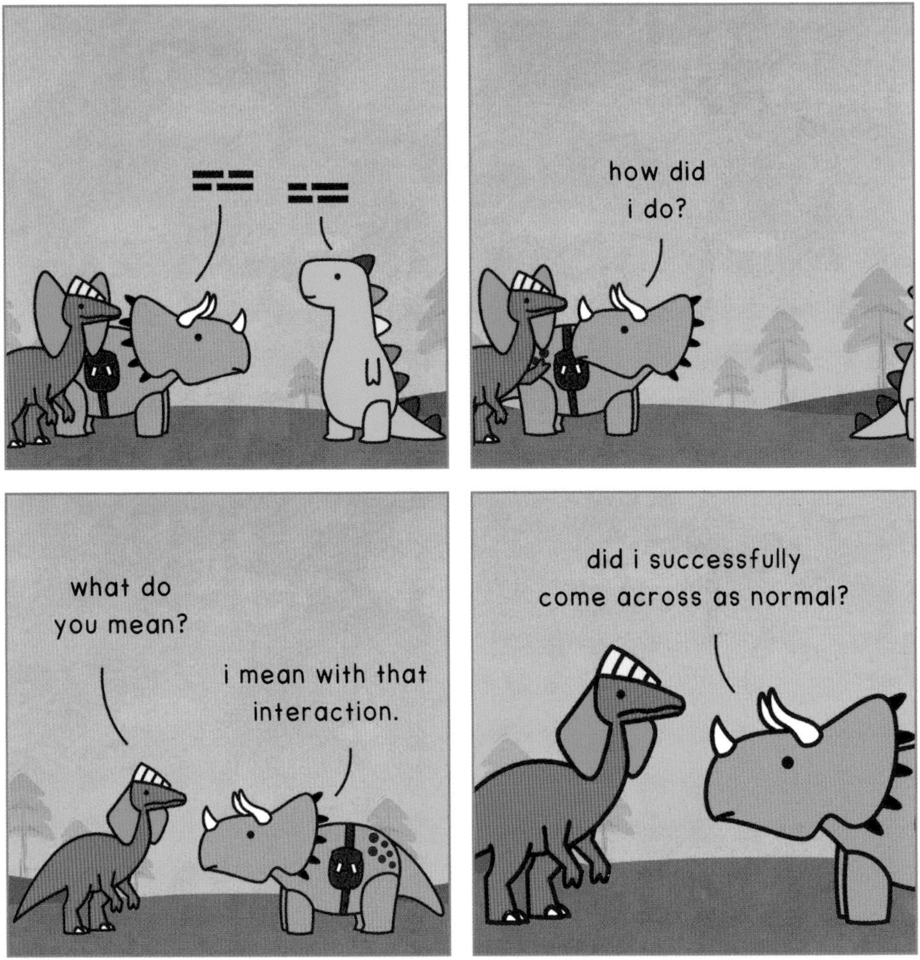
how did
i do?
what do
you mean?
i mean with that
interaction.
did i successfully
come across as normal?

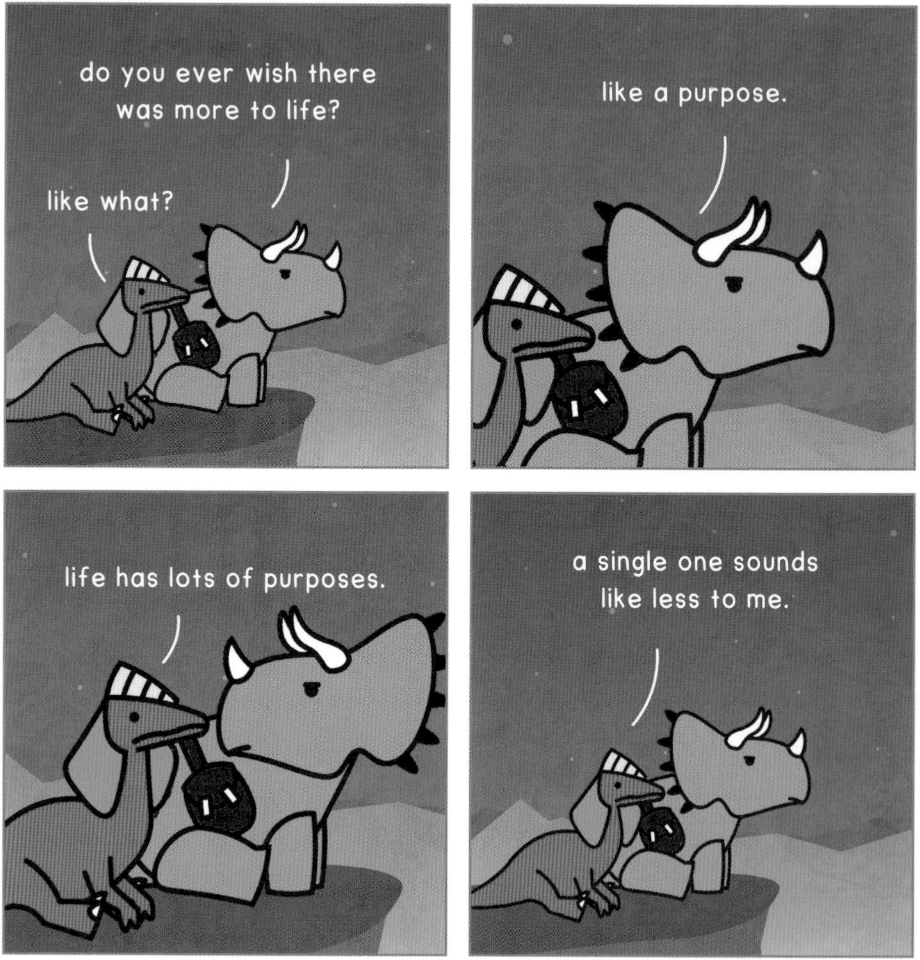
do you ever wish there was more to life?
like what?
like a purpose.
life has lots of purposes.
a single one sounds like less to me.

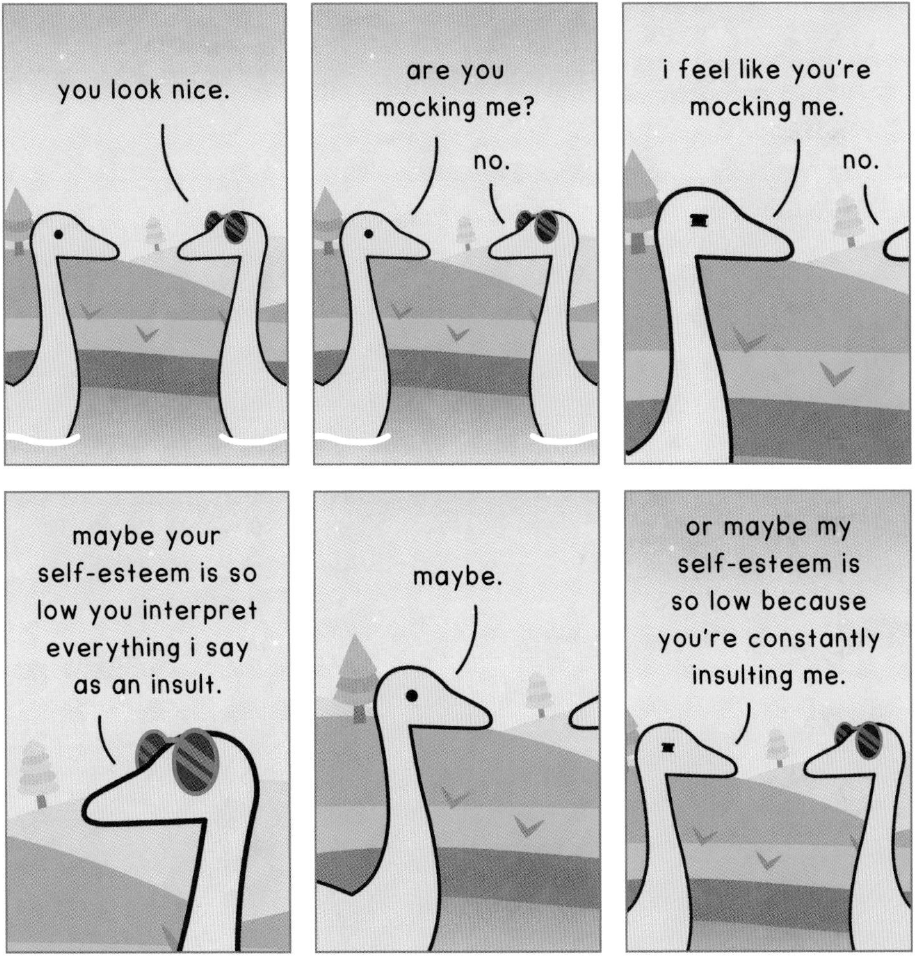
you look nice.
are you mocking me?
no.
i feel like you're mocking me.
no.
maybe your self-esteem is so low you interpret everything i say as an insult.
maybe.
or maybe my self-esteem is so low because you're constantly insulting me.

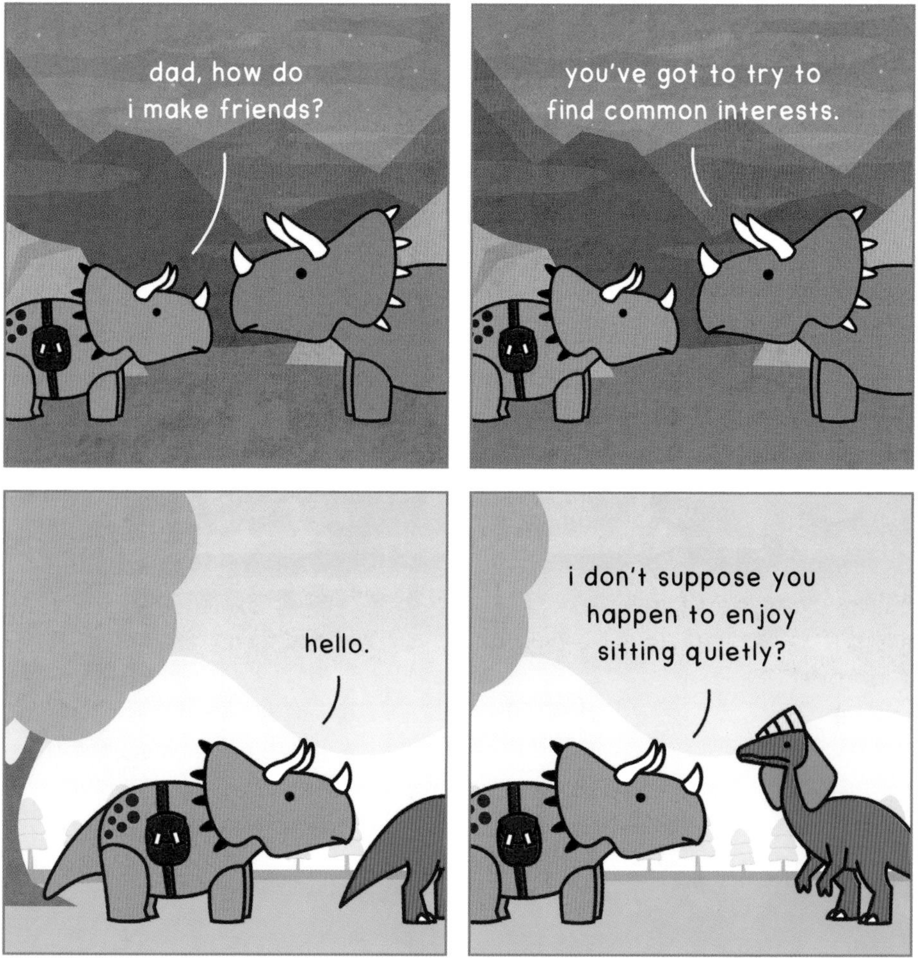
dad, how do
i make friends?
you've got to try to
find common interests.
hello.
i don't suppose you
happen to enjoy
sitting quietly?

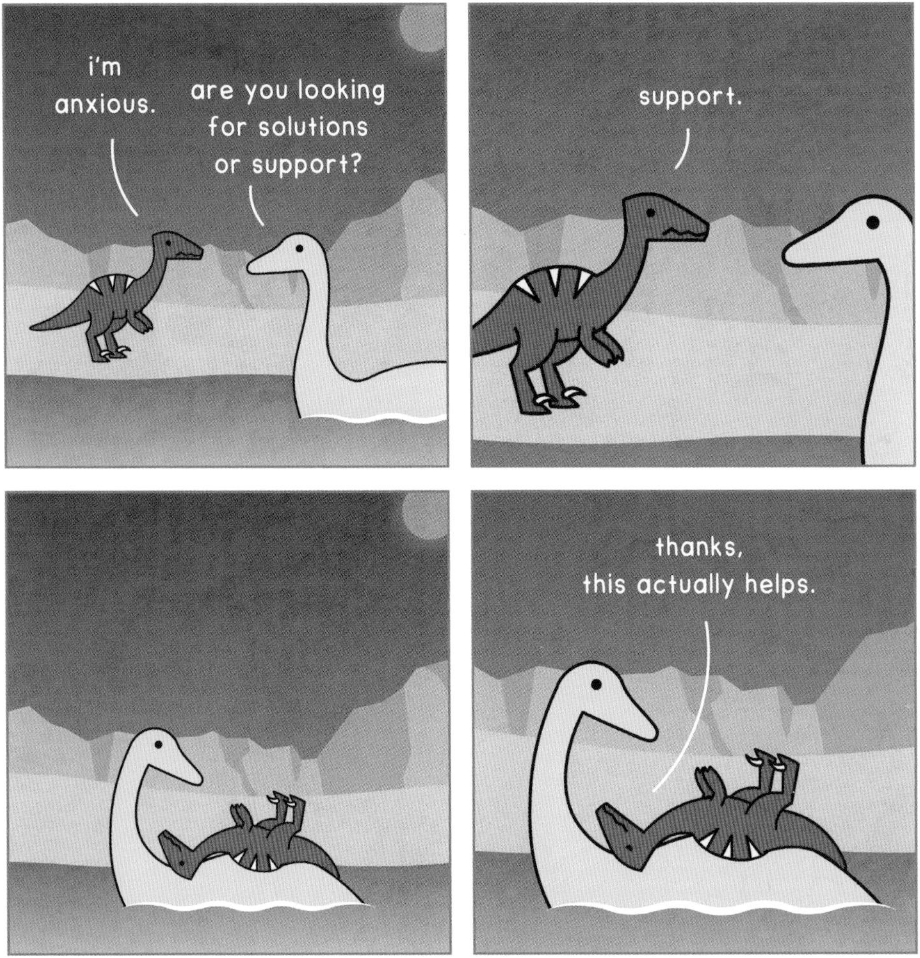
i'm
anxious.
are you looking
for solutions
or support?
support.
thanks,
this actually helps.

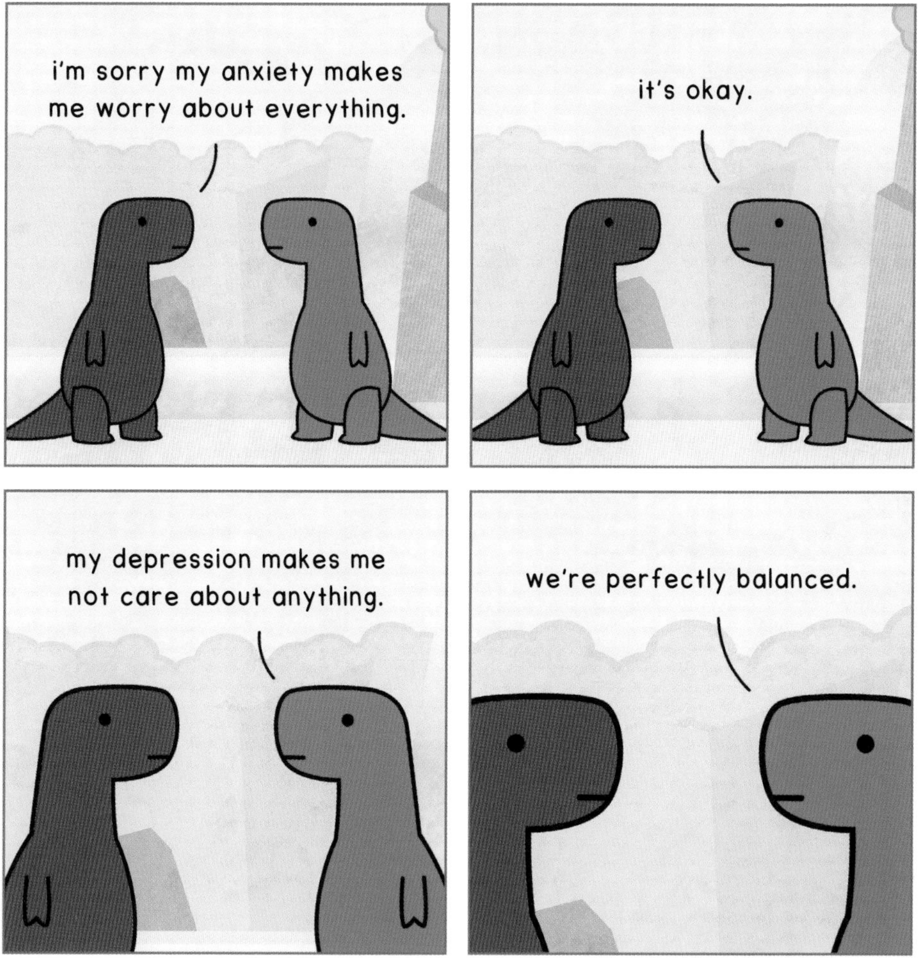
i'm sorry my anxiety makes me worry about everything.
it's okay.
my depression makes me not care about anything.
we're perfectly balanced.

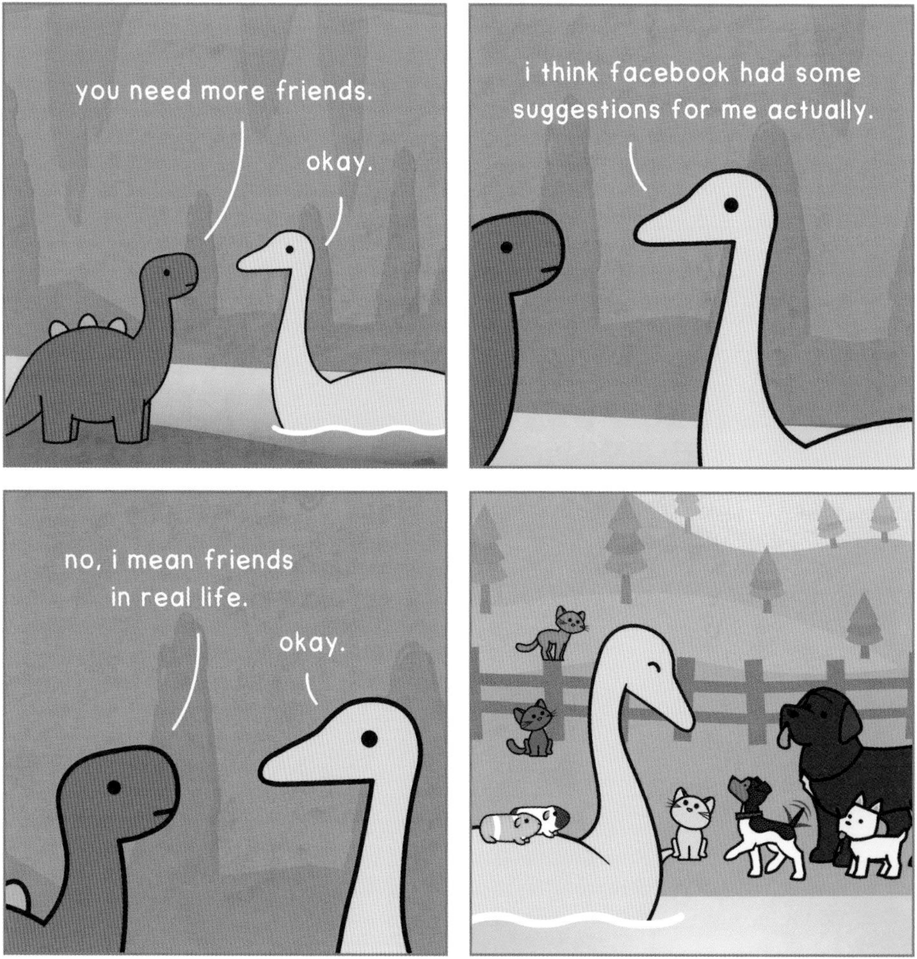
you need more friends.
okay.
i think facebook had some suggestions for me actually.
no, i mean friends in real life.
okay.

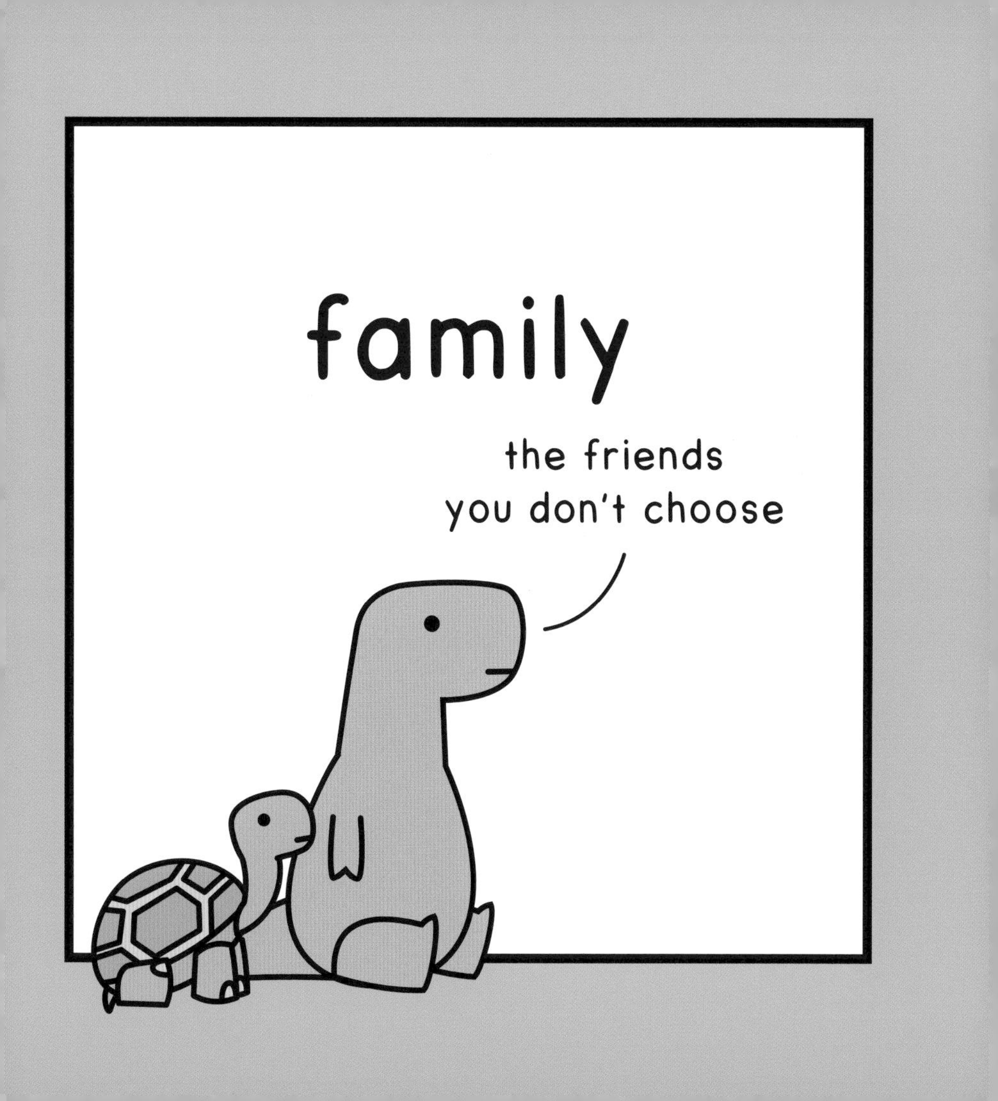
family
the friends
you don't choose

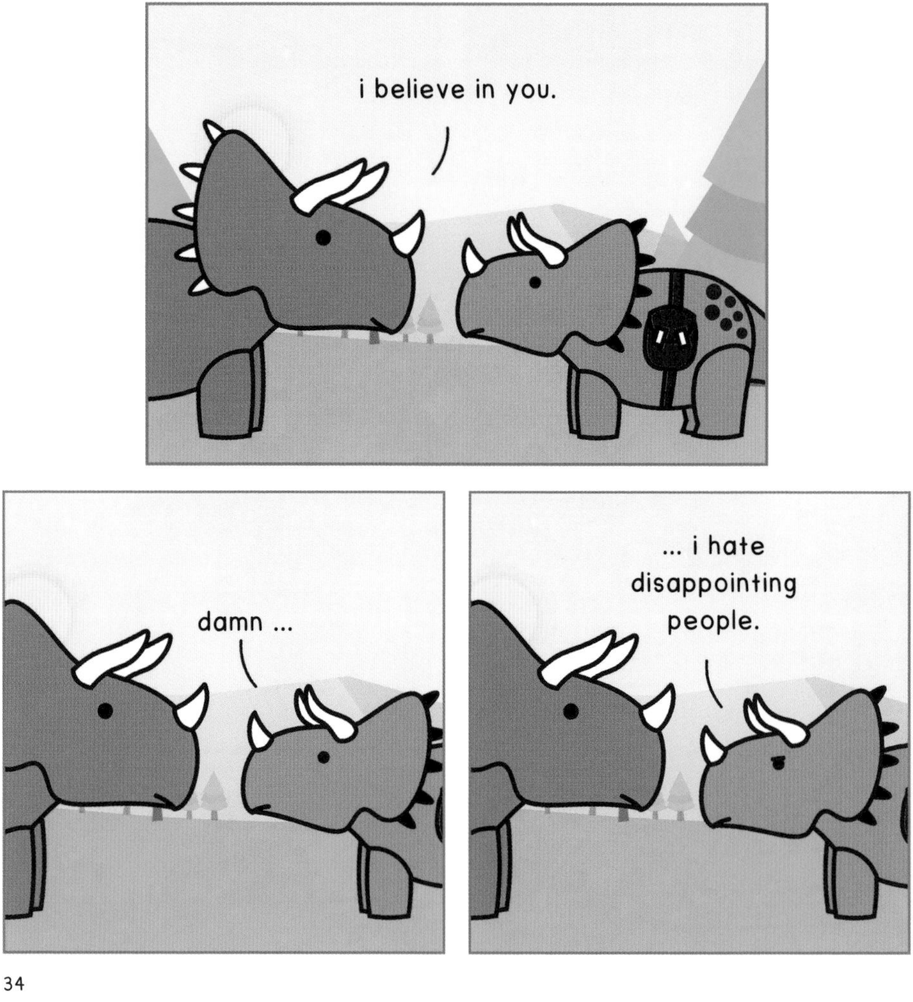
i believe in you.
damn ...
... i hate
disappointing
people.

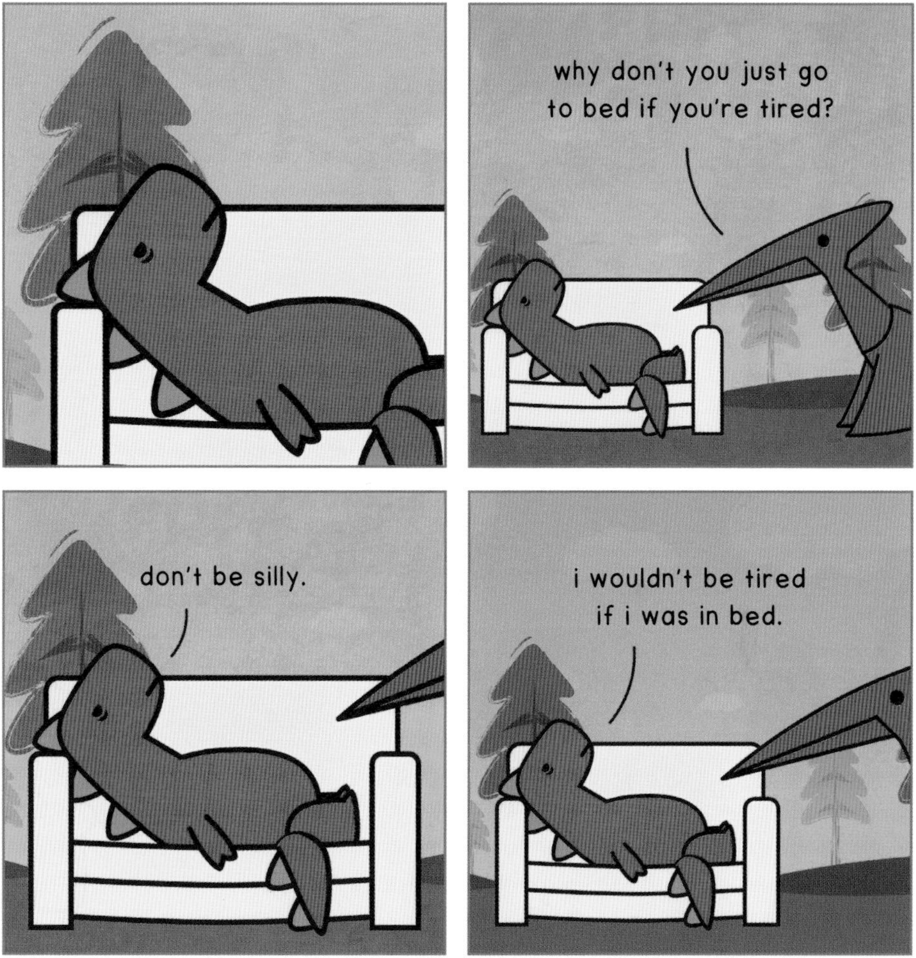
why don't you just go to bed if you're tired?
don't be silly.
i wouldn't be tired if i was in bed.

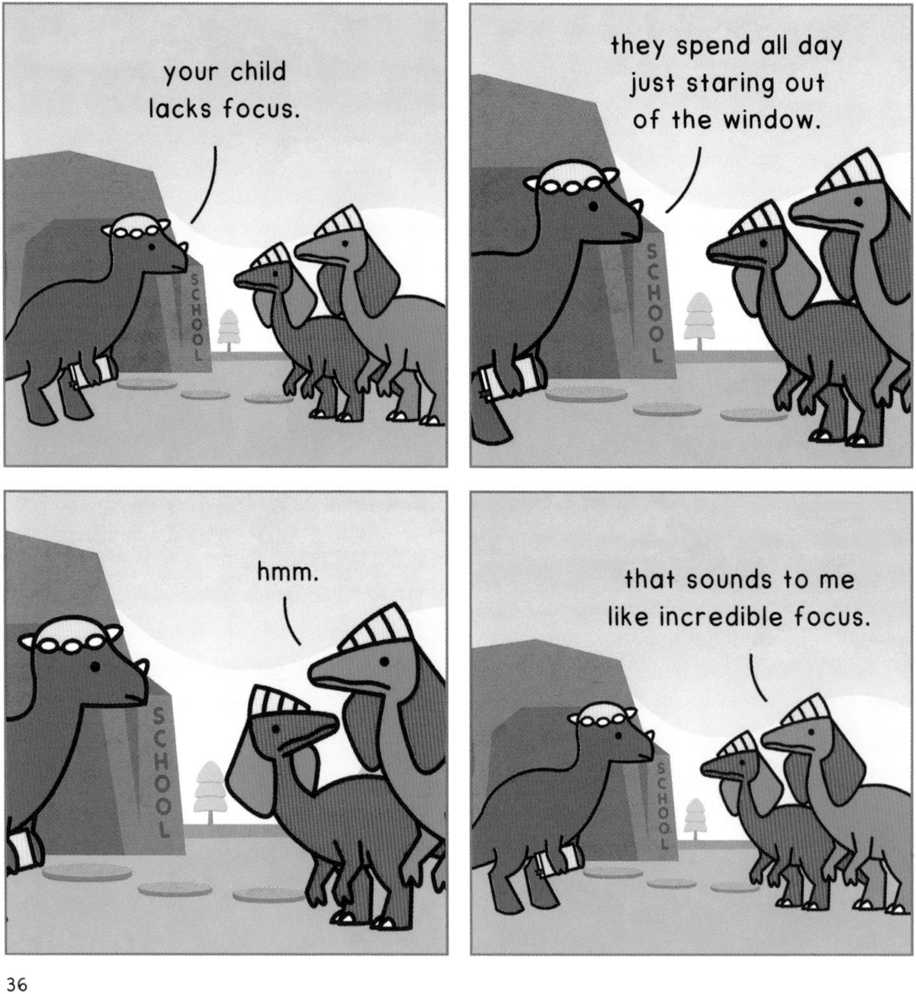
your child
lacks focus.
SCHOOL
they spend all day
just staring out
of the window.
SCHOOL
hmm.
SCHOOL
that sounds to me
like incredible focus.
SCHOOL

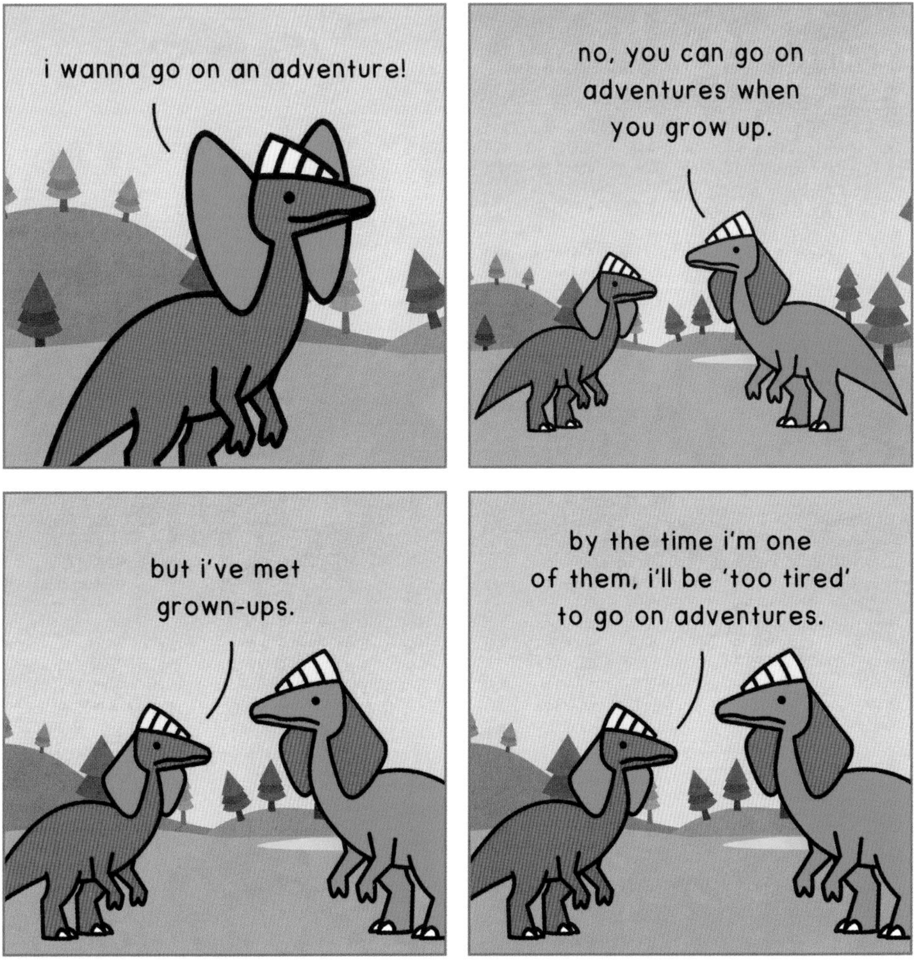
i wanna go on an adventure!
no, you can go on adventures when you grow up.
but i've met grown-ups.
by the time i'm one of them, i'll be 'too tired' to go on adventures.

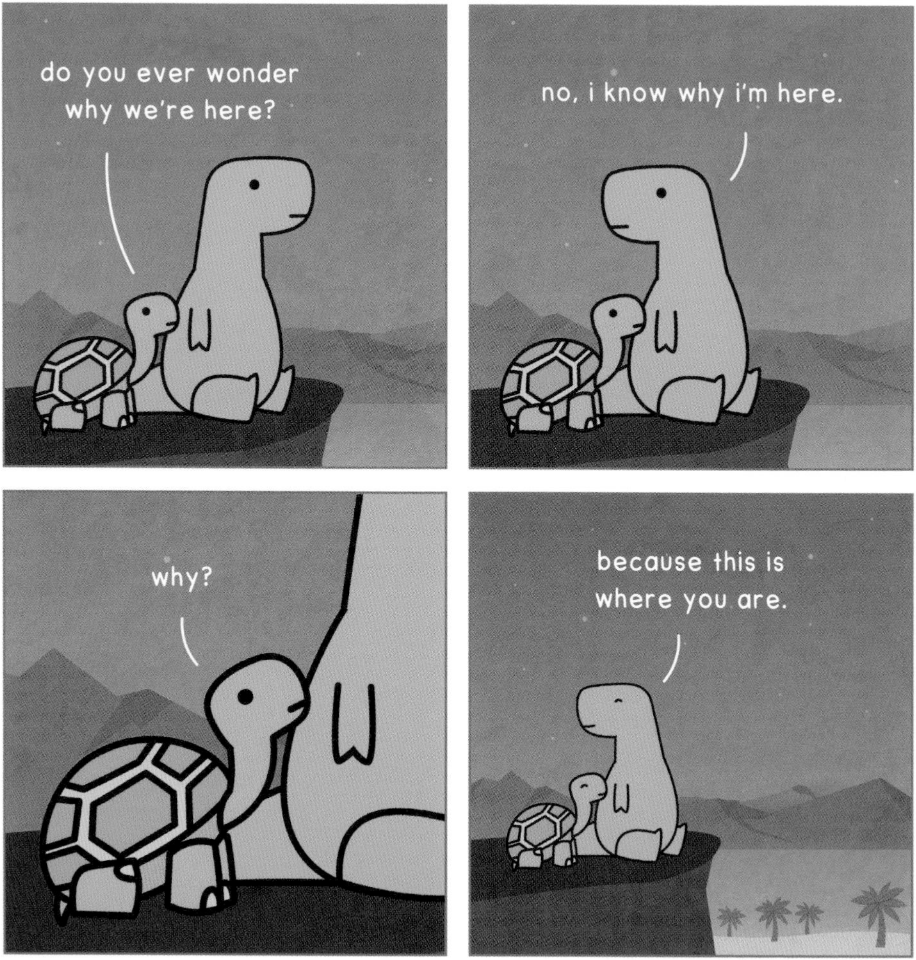
do you ever wonder why we're here?
no, i know why i'm here.
why?
because this is where you are.

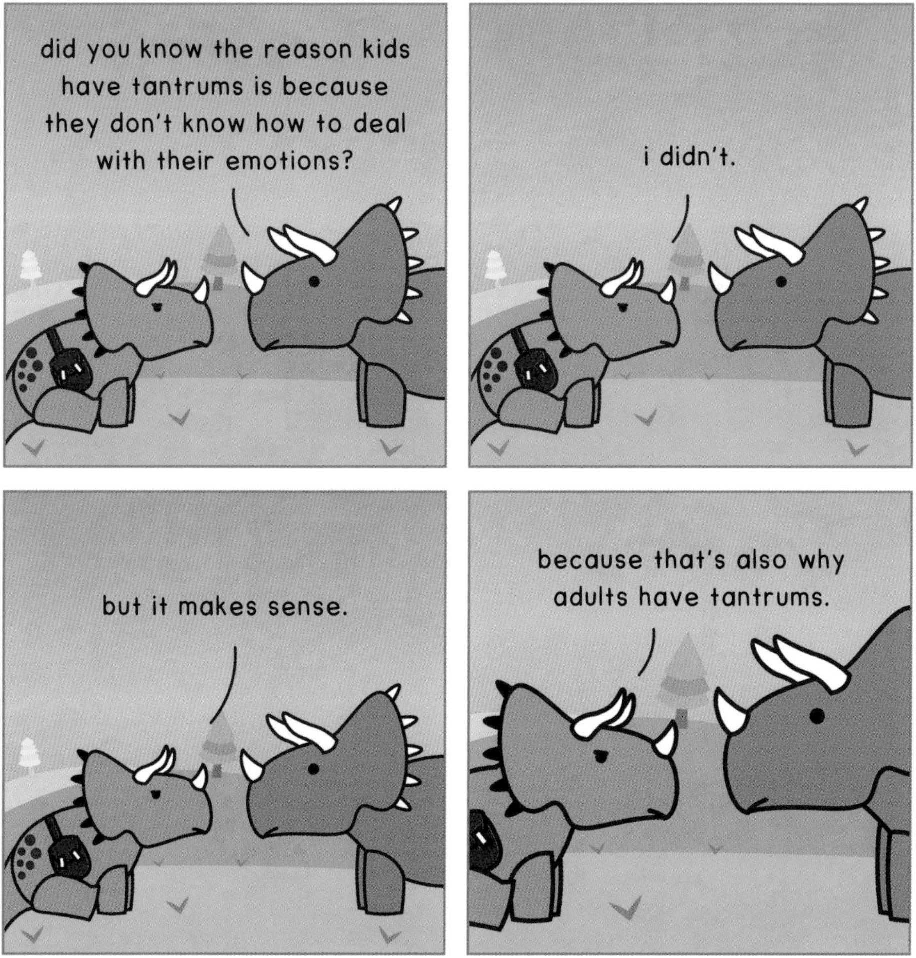
did you know the reason kids have tantrums is because they don't know how to deal with their emotions?
i didn't.
but it makes sense.
because that's also why adults have tantrums.

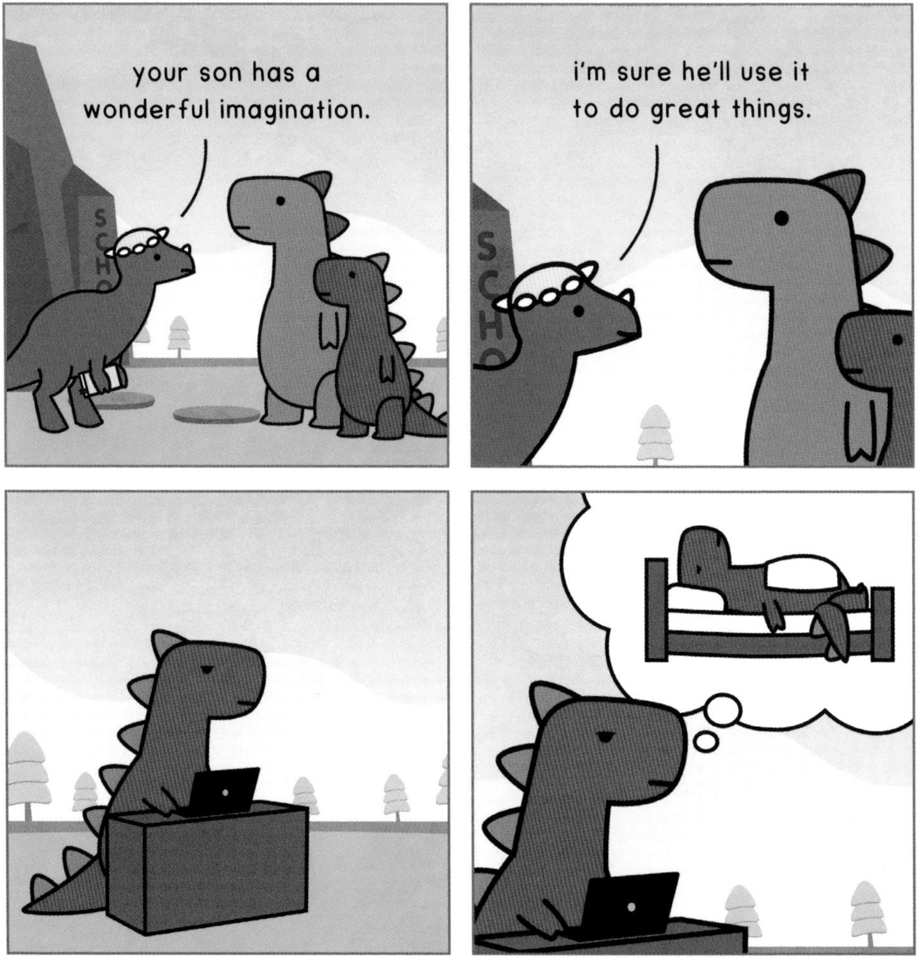
your son has a wonderful imagination.
SCHO
i'm sure he'll use it to do great things.

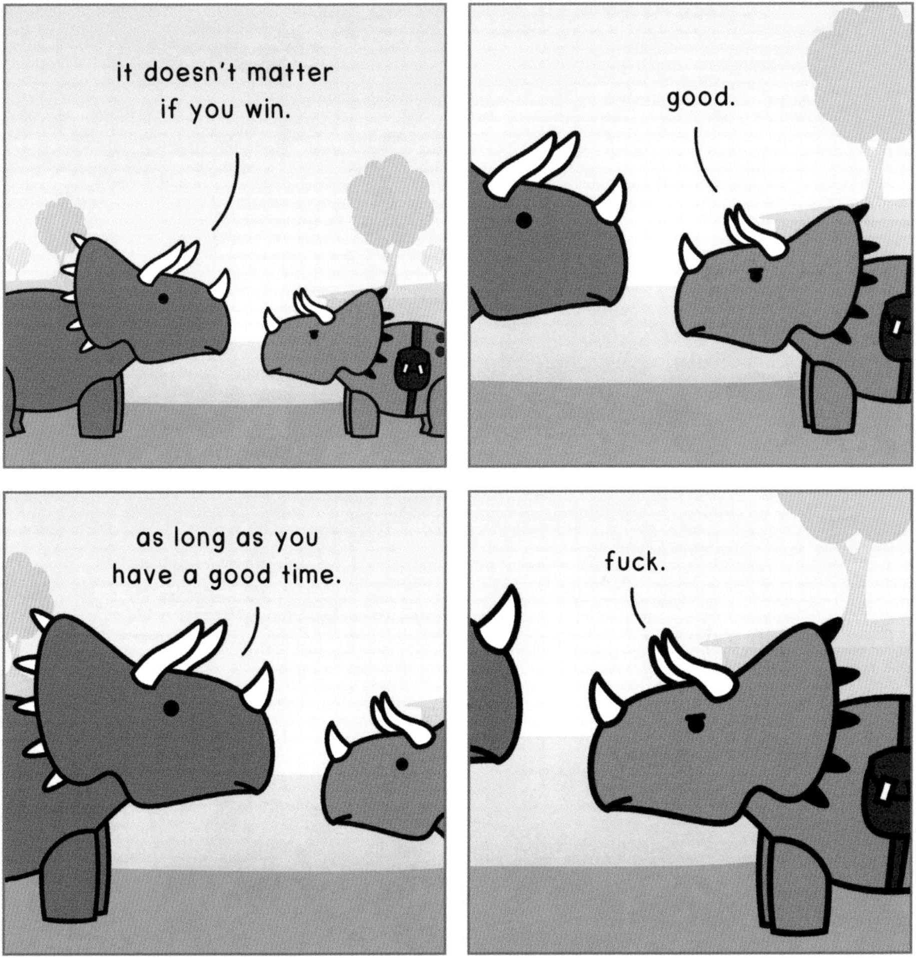
it doesn't matter if you win.
good.
as long as you have a good time.
fuck.

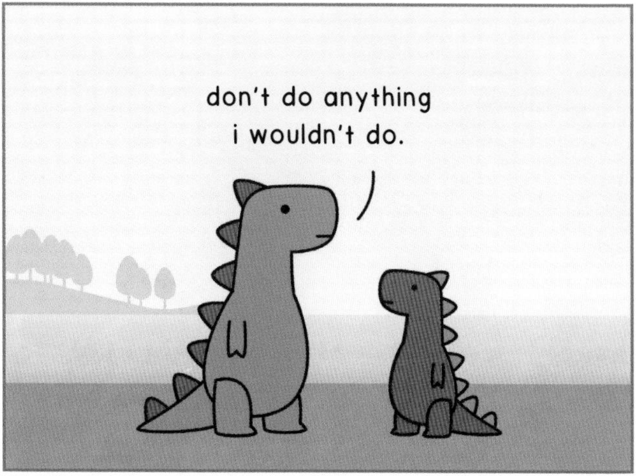
don't do anything
i wouldn't do.

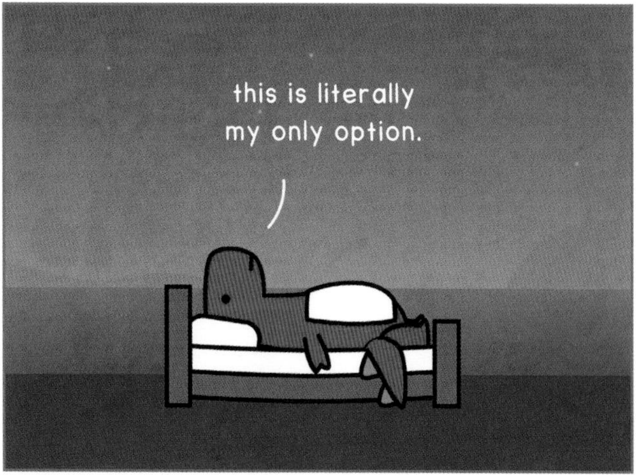
this is literally
my only option.

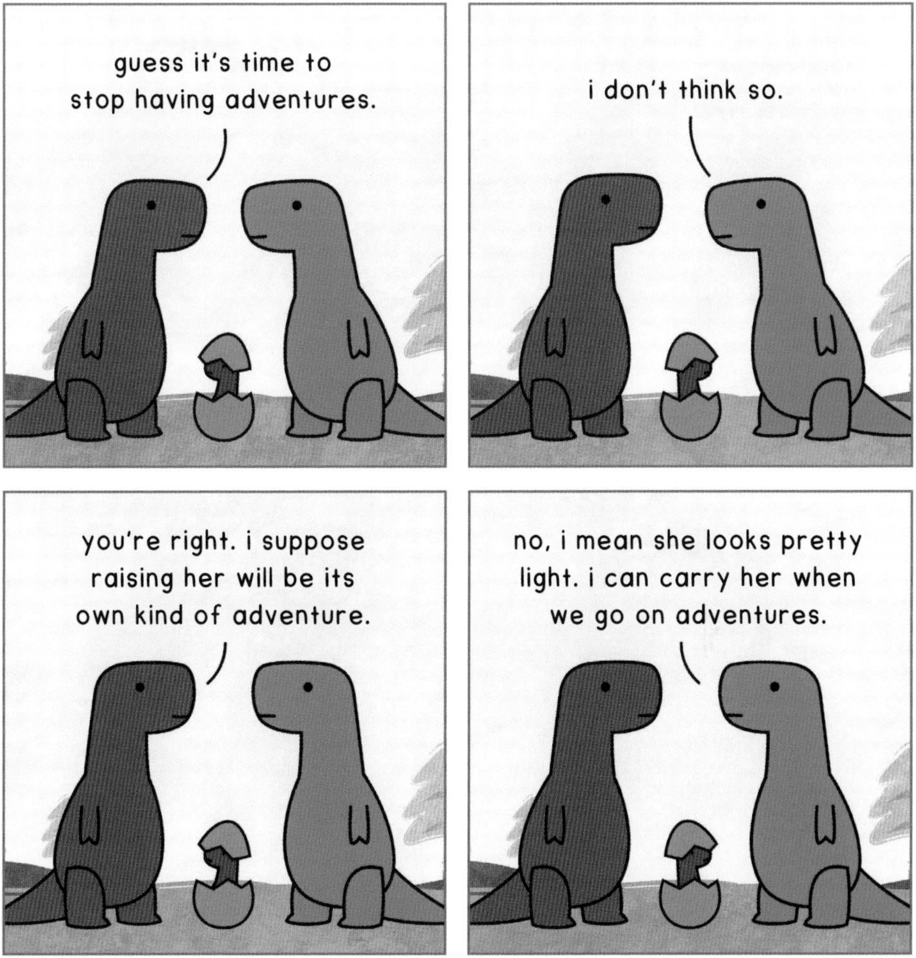
guess it's time to stop having adventures.
i don't think so.
you're right. i suppose raising her will be its own kind of adventure.
no, i mean she looks pretty light. i can carry her when we go on adventures.

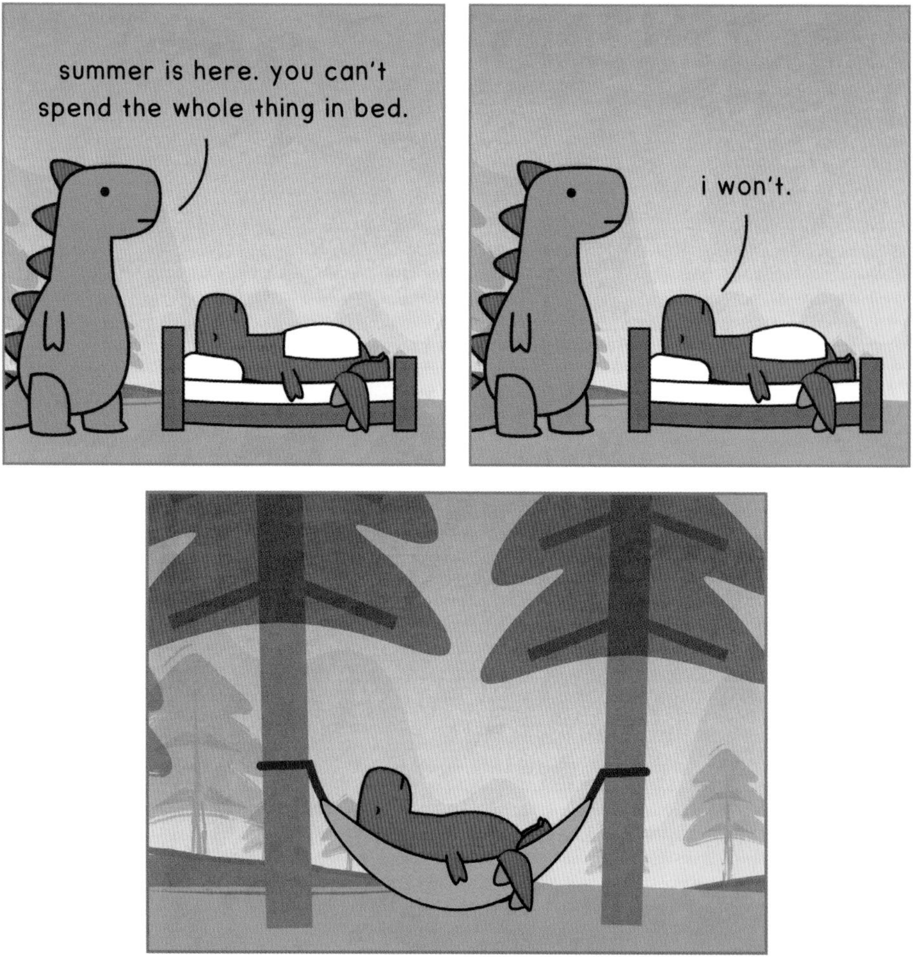
summer is here. you can't
spend the whole thing in bed.
i won't.

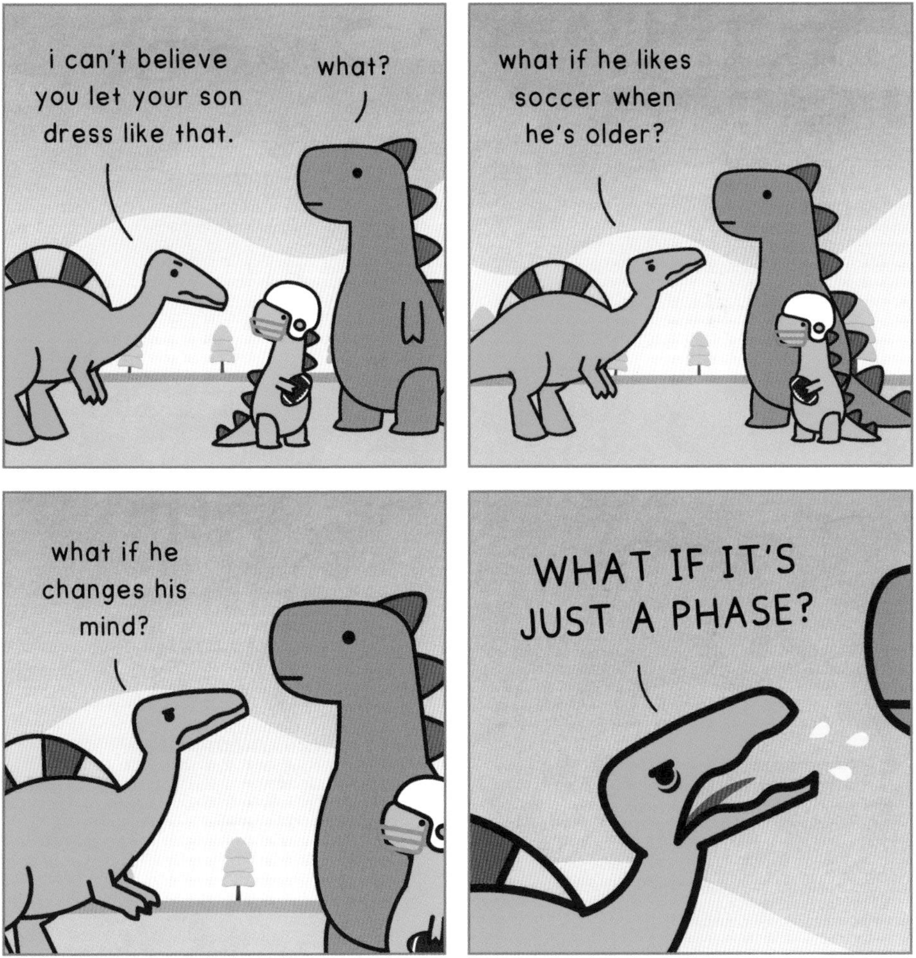
i can't believe you let your son dress like that.
what?
what if he likes soccer when he's older?
what if he changes his mind?
WHAT IF IT'S JUST A PHASE?

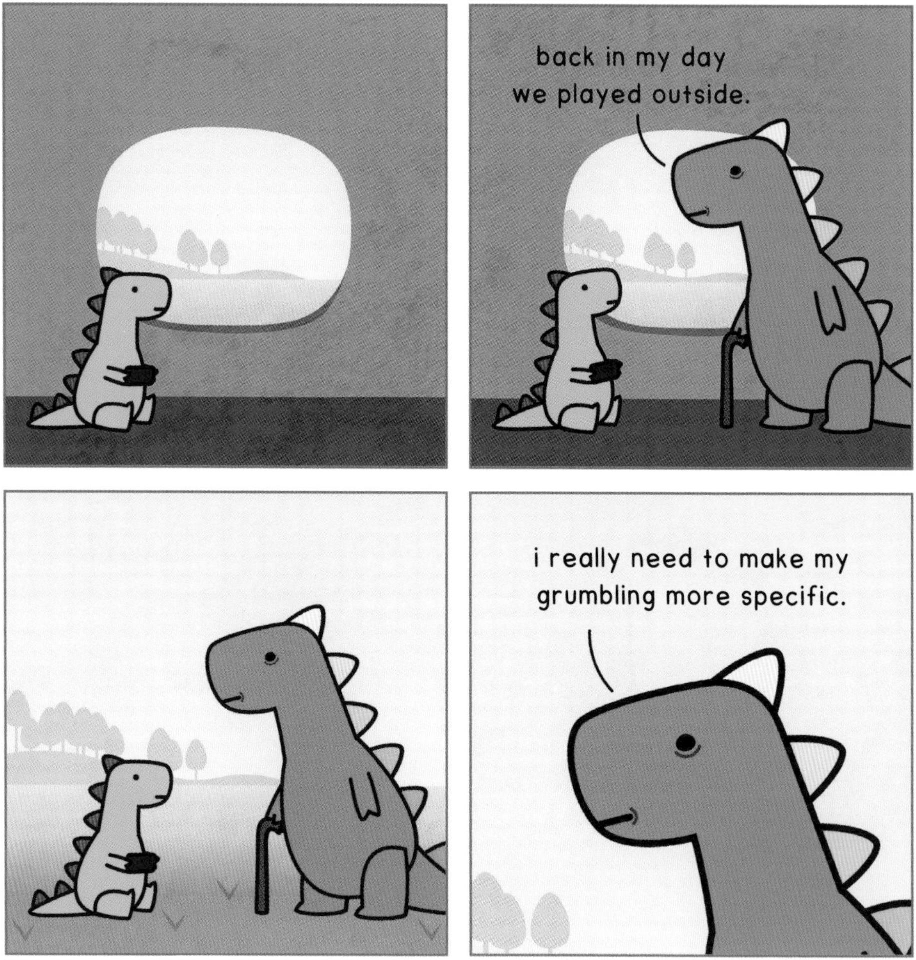
back in my day
we played outside.
i really need to make my
grumbling more specific.

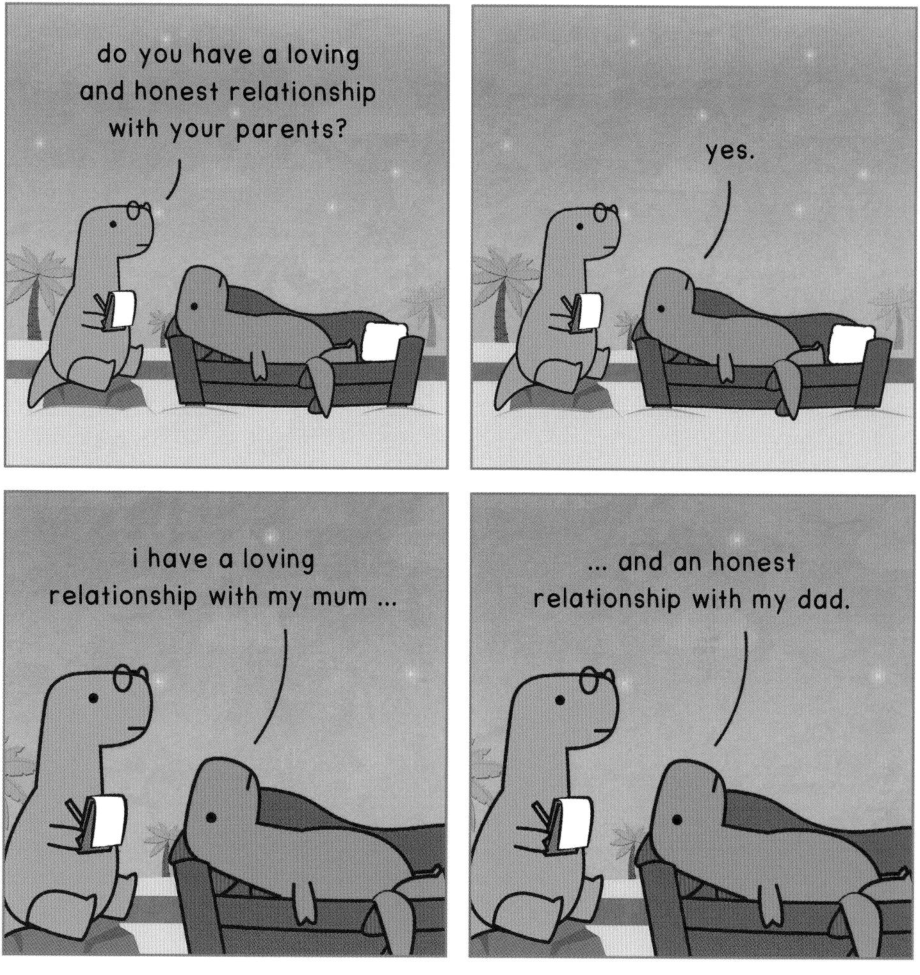
do you have a loving and honest relationship with your parents?
yes.
i have a loving relationship with my mum ...
... and an honest relationship with my dad.

love

really, really
good friends

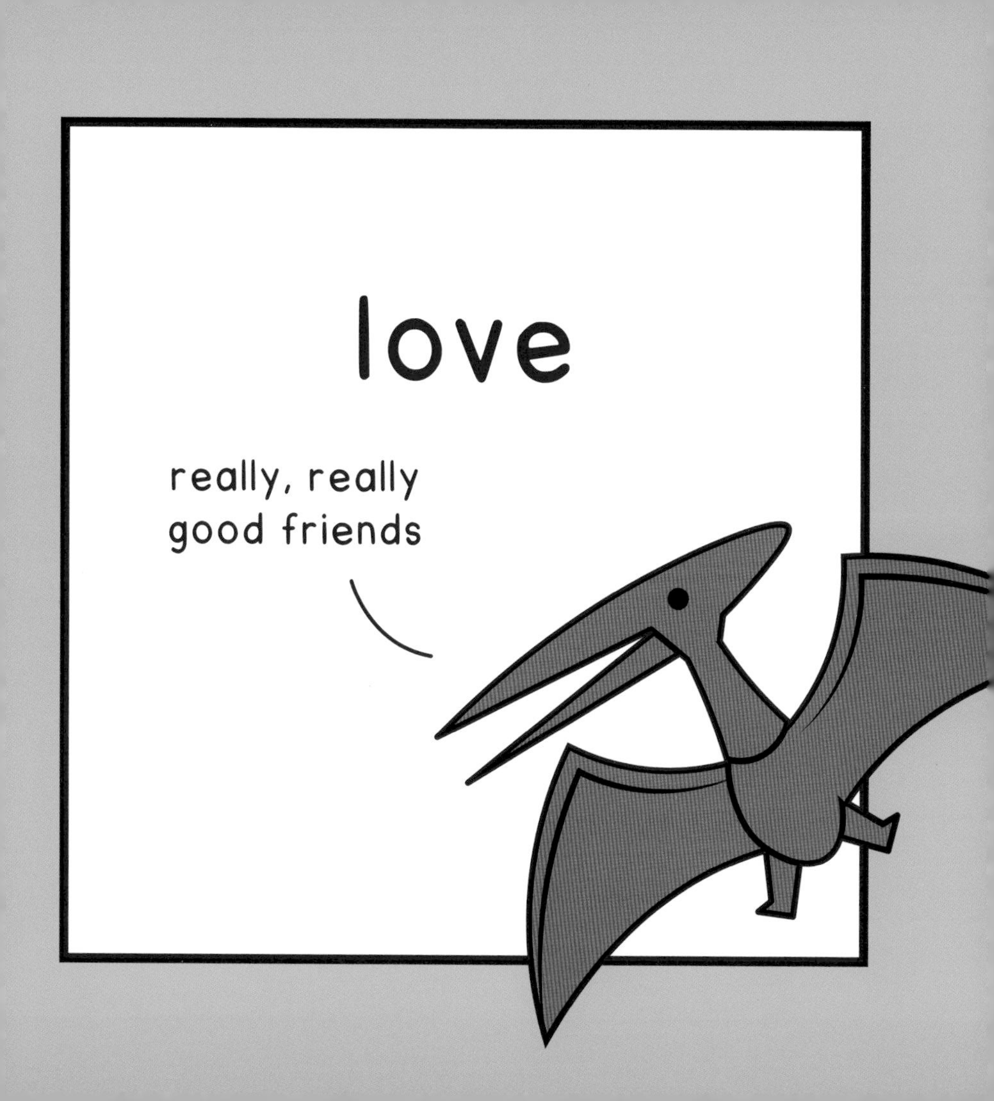

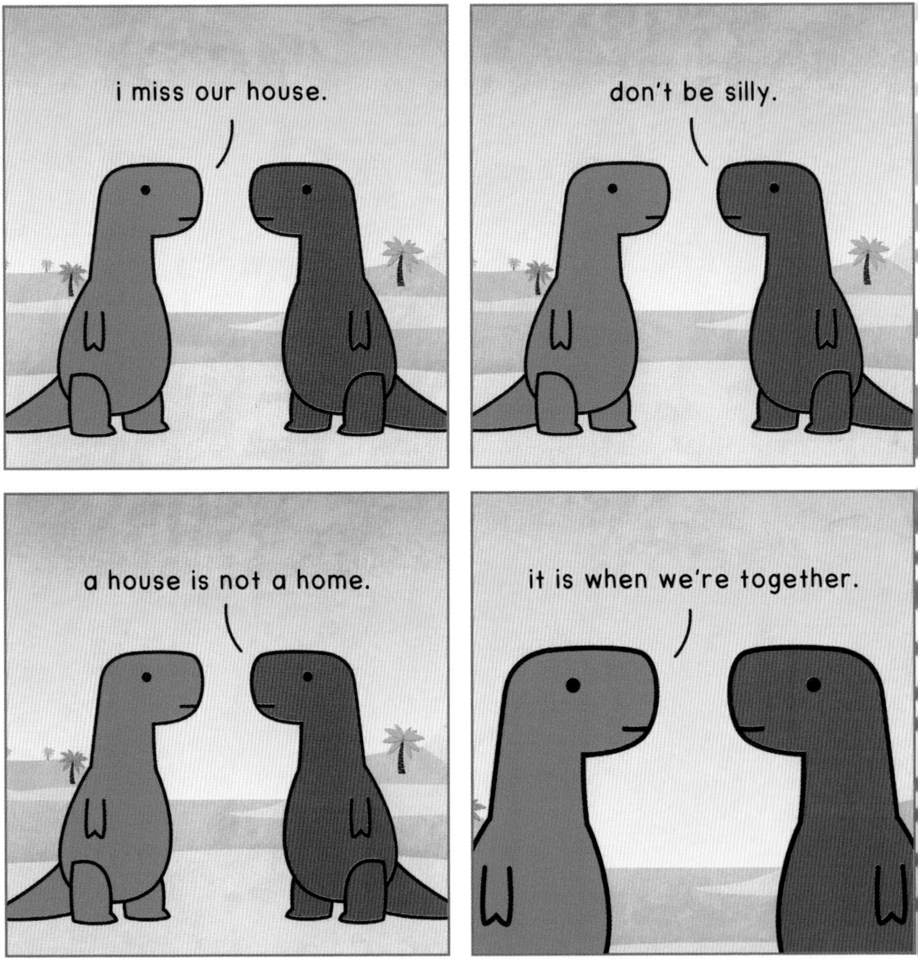
i miss our house.
don't be silly.
a house is not a home.
it is when we're together.

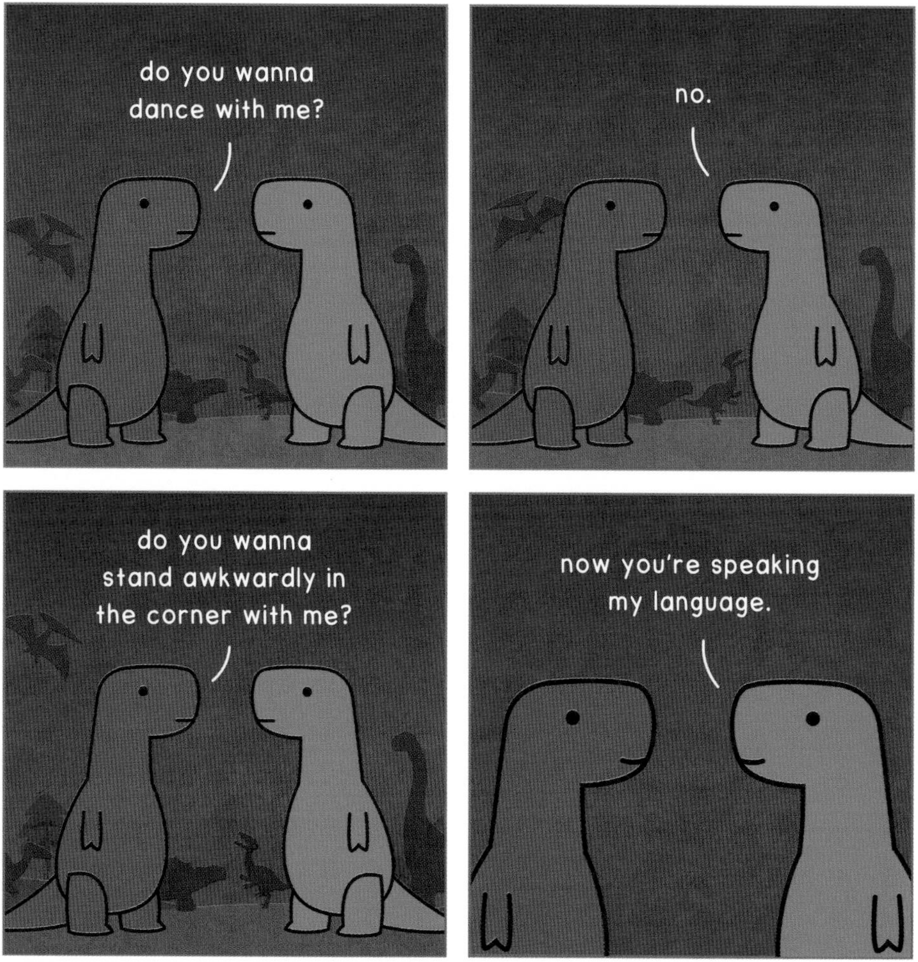
do you wanna dance with me?
no.
do you wanna stand awkwardly in the corner with me?
now you're speaking my language.

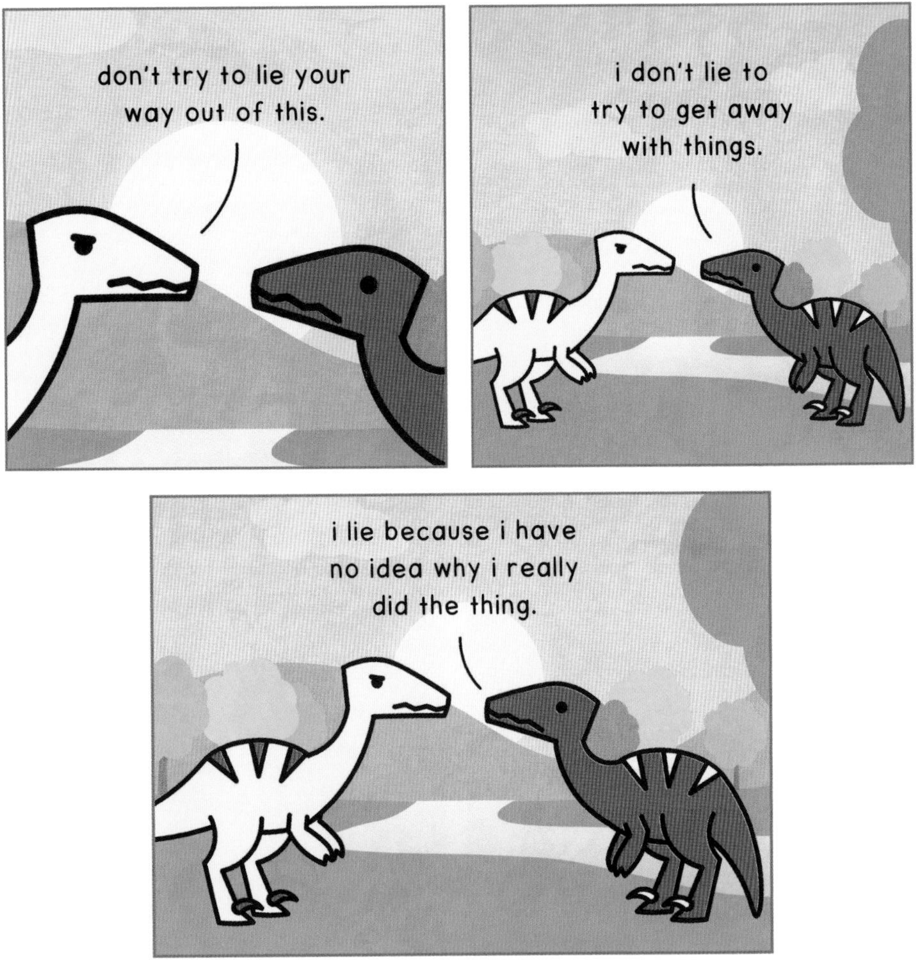
don't try to lie your way out of this.
i don't lie to try to get away with things.
i lie because i have no idea why i really did the thing.

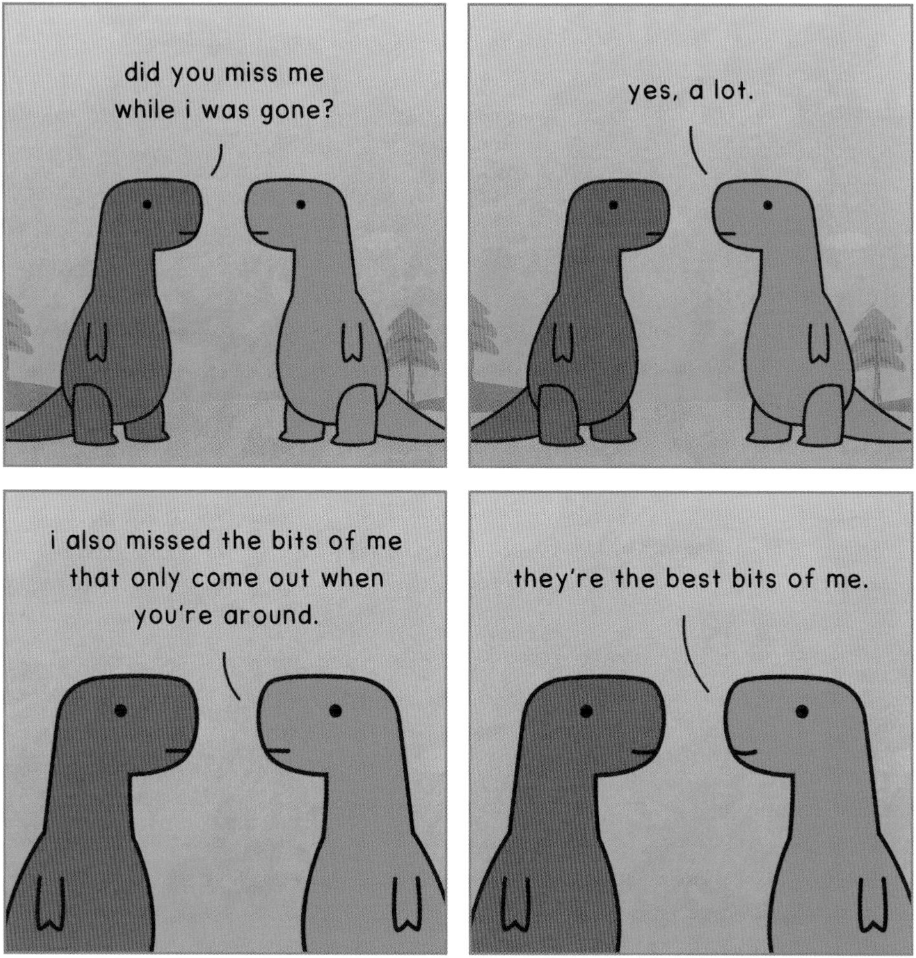
did you miss me while i was gone?
yes, a lot.
i also missed the bits of me that only come out when you're around.
they're the best bits of me.

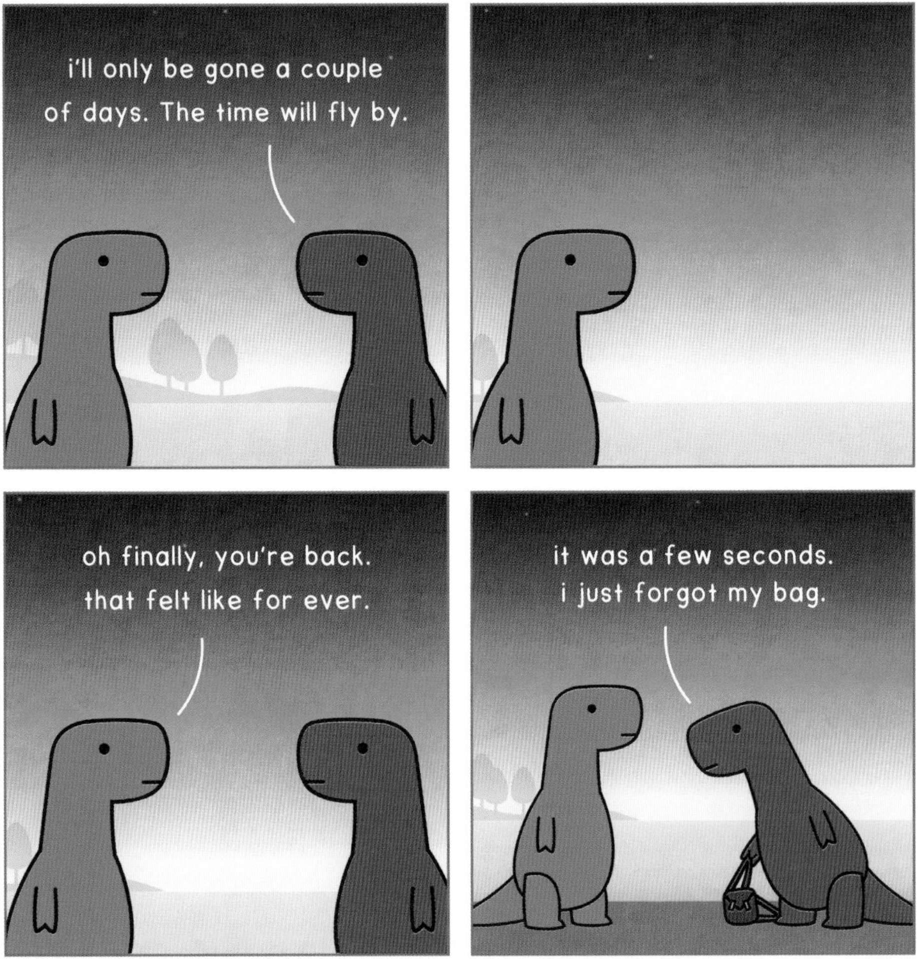
i'll only be gone a couple of days. The time will fly by.
oh finally, you're back. that felt like for ever.
it was a few seconds. i just forgot my bag.

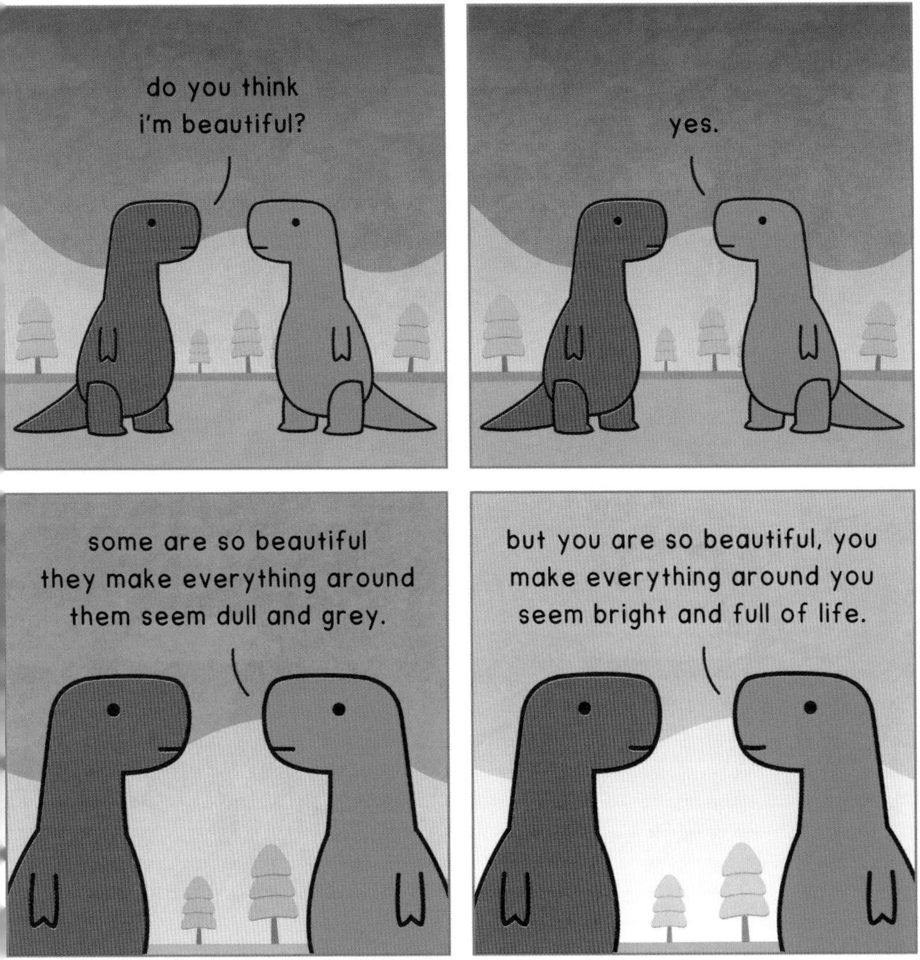
do you think
i'm beautiful?
yes.
some are so beautiful
they make everything around
them seem dull and grey.
but you are so beautiful, you
make everything around you
seem bright and full of life.

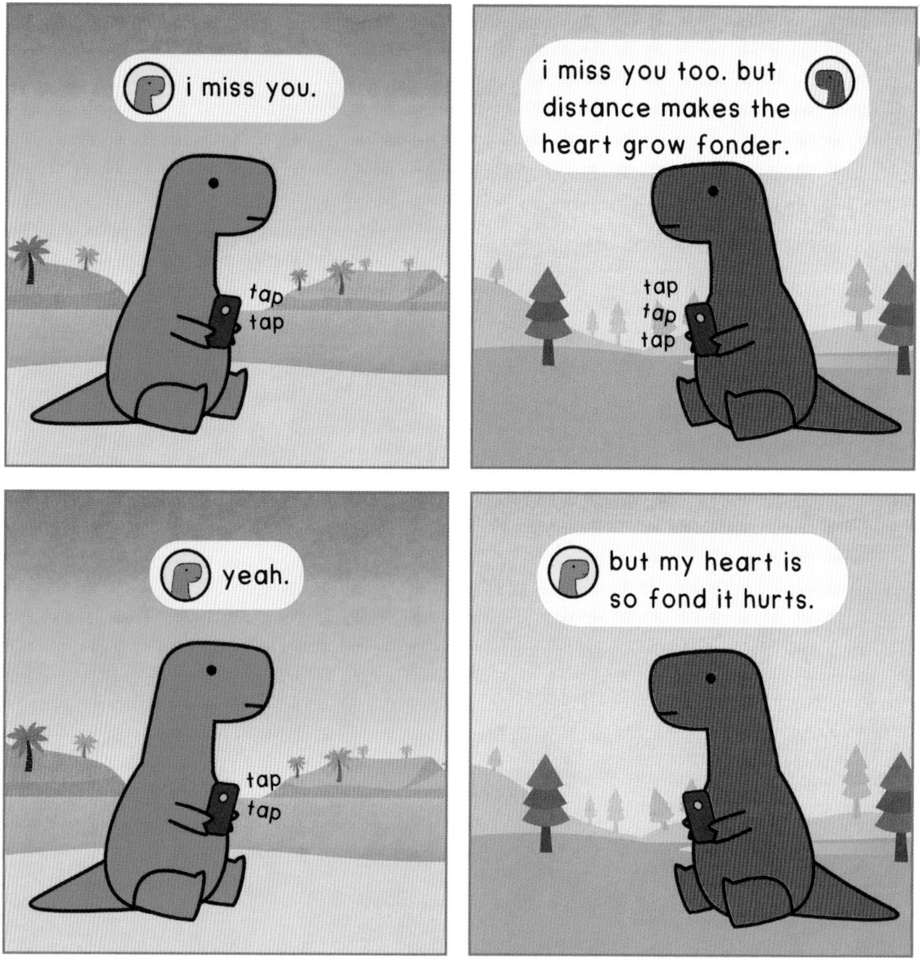
i miss you.
tap
tap
i miss you too. but distance makes the heart grow fonder.
tap
tap
tap
yeah.
tap
tap
but my heart is so fond it hurts.

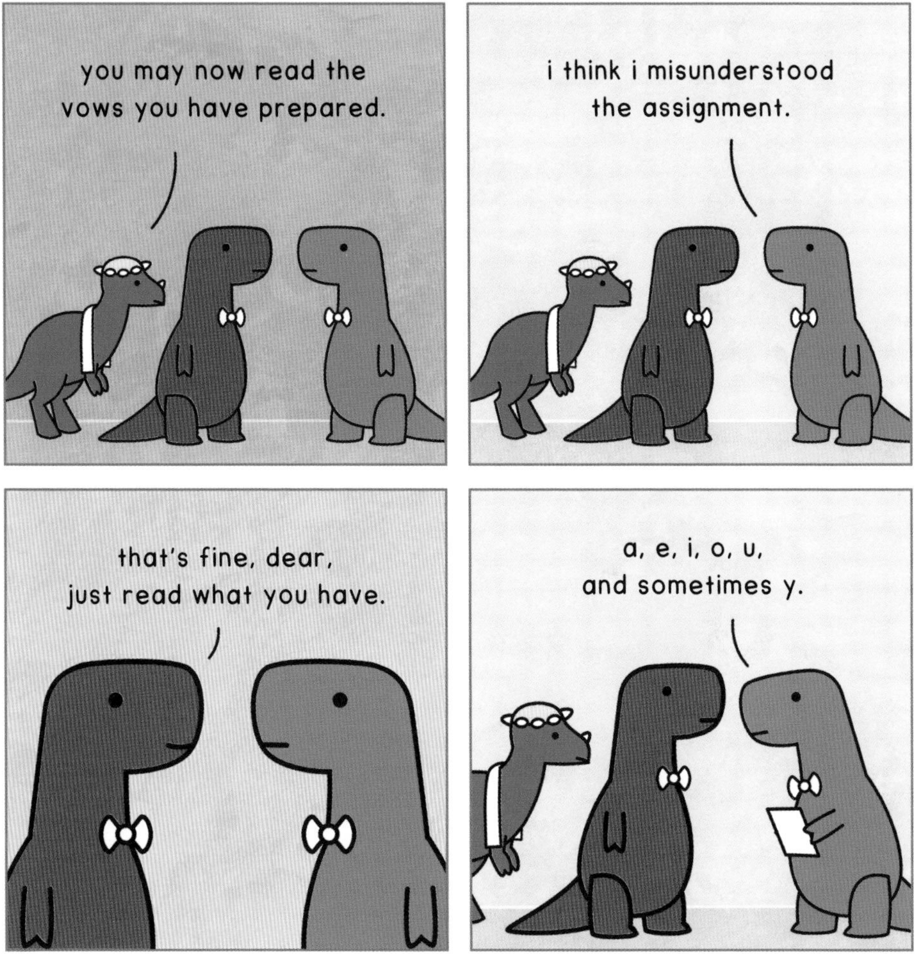
you may now read the vows you have prepared.
i think i misunderstood the assignment.
that's fine, dear, just read what you have.
a, e, i, o, u, and sometimes y.

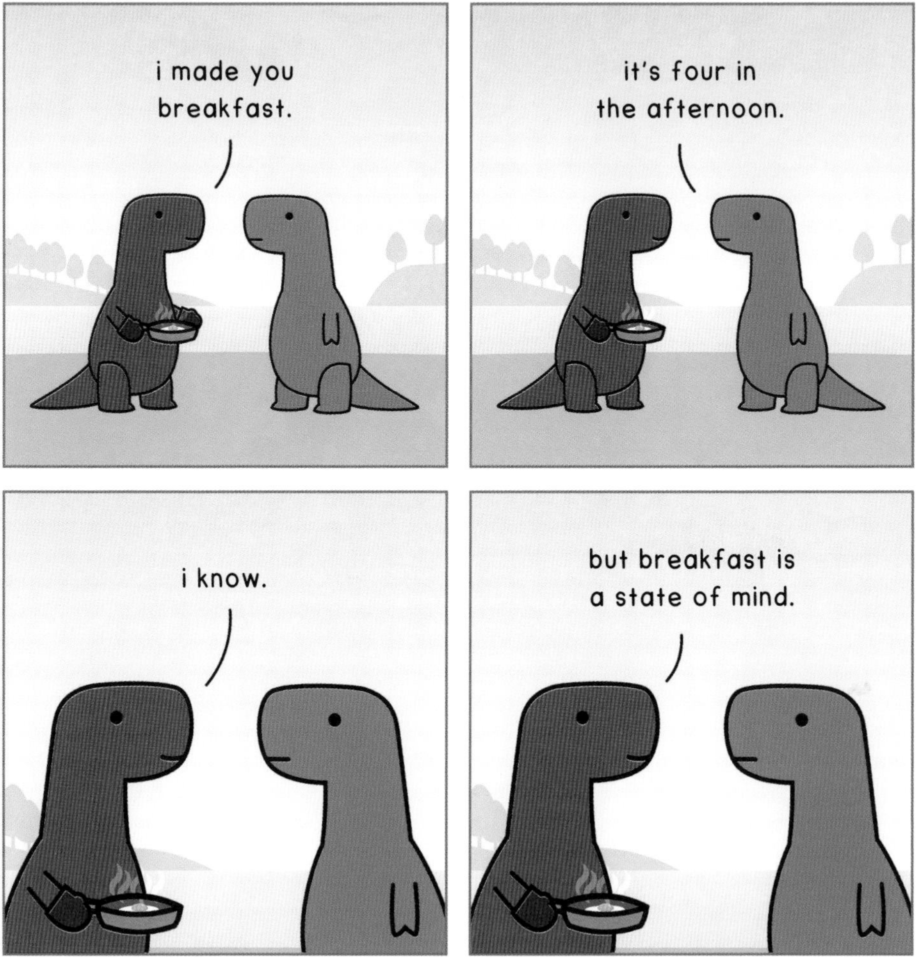
i made you
breakfast.
it's four in
the afternoon.
i know.
but breakfast is
a state of mind.

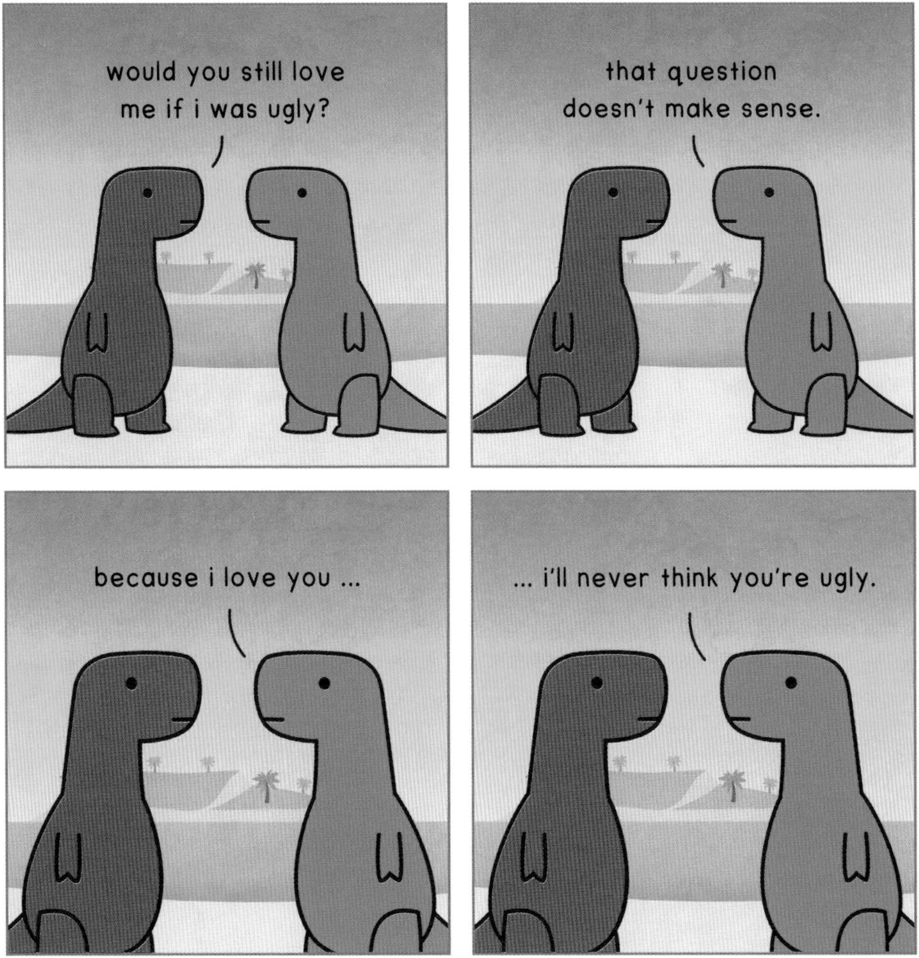
would you still love me if i was ugly?
that question doesn't make sense.
because i love you ...
... i'll never think you're ugly.

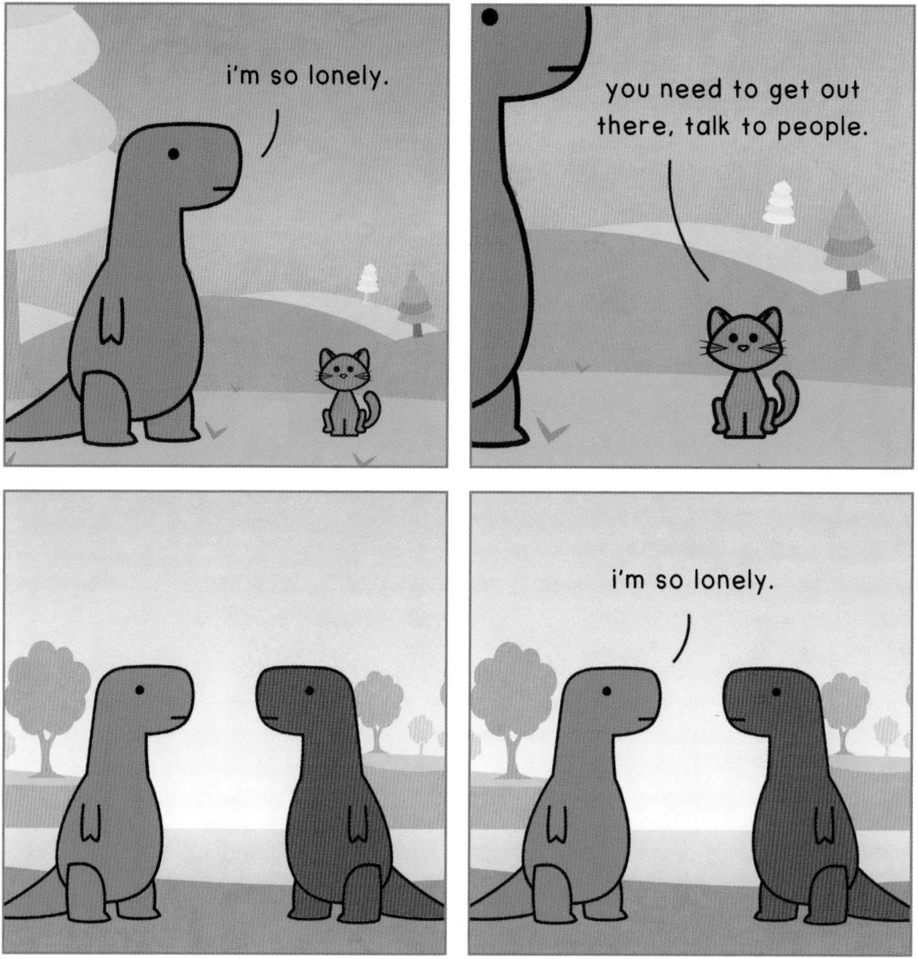
i'm so lonely.
you need to get out there, talk to people.
i'm so lonely.

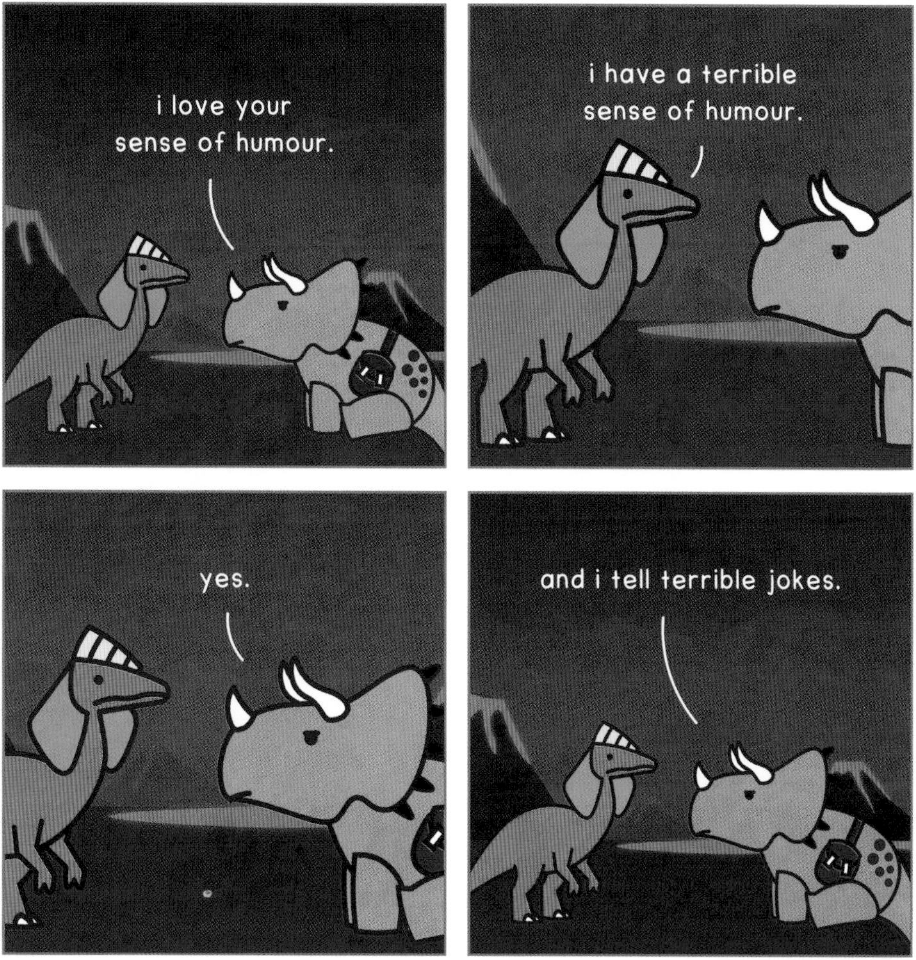
i love your sense of humour.
i have a terrible sense of humour.
yes.
and i tell terrible jokes.

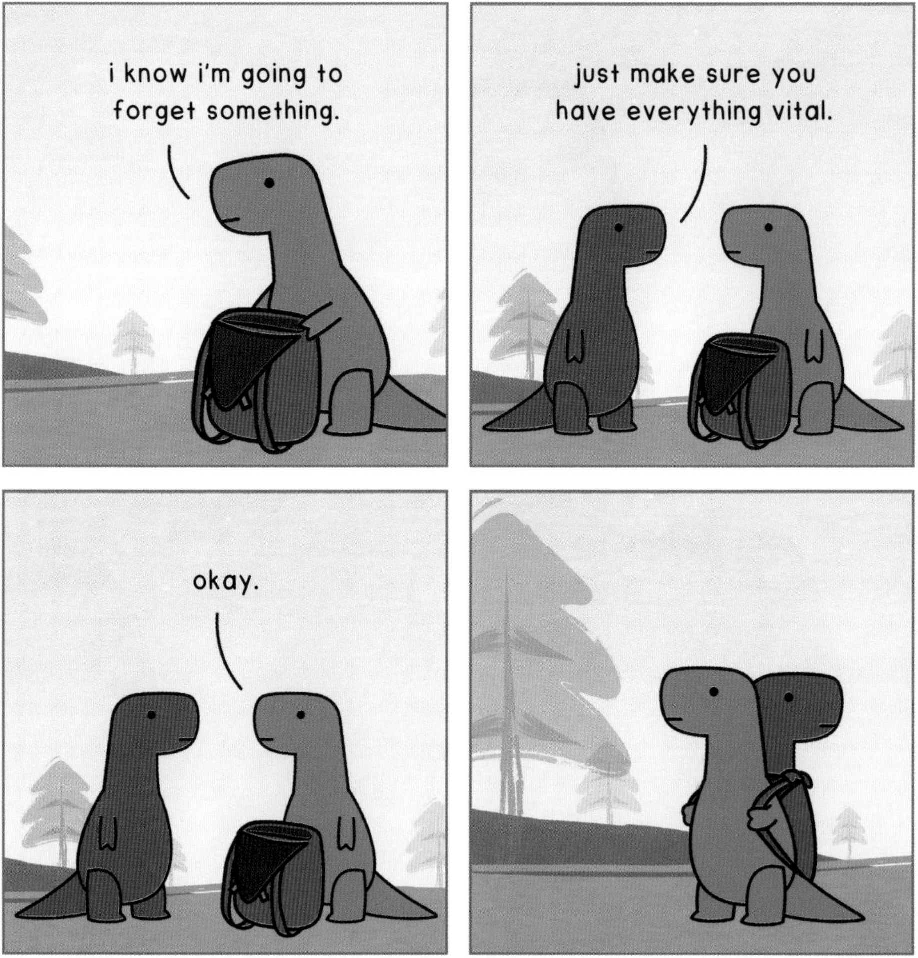
i know i'm going to forget something.
just make sure you have everything vital.
okay.

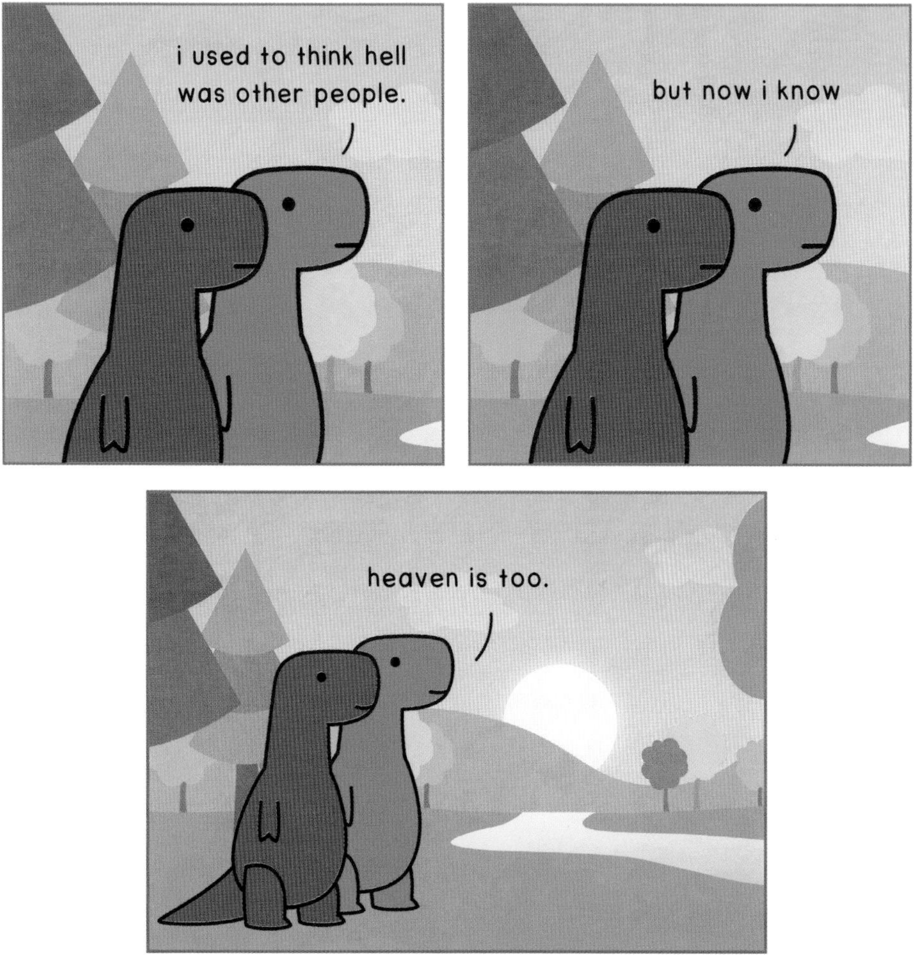
i used to think hell was other people.
but now i know
heaven is too.

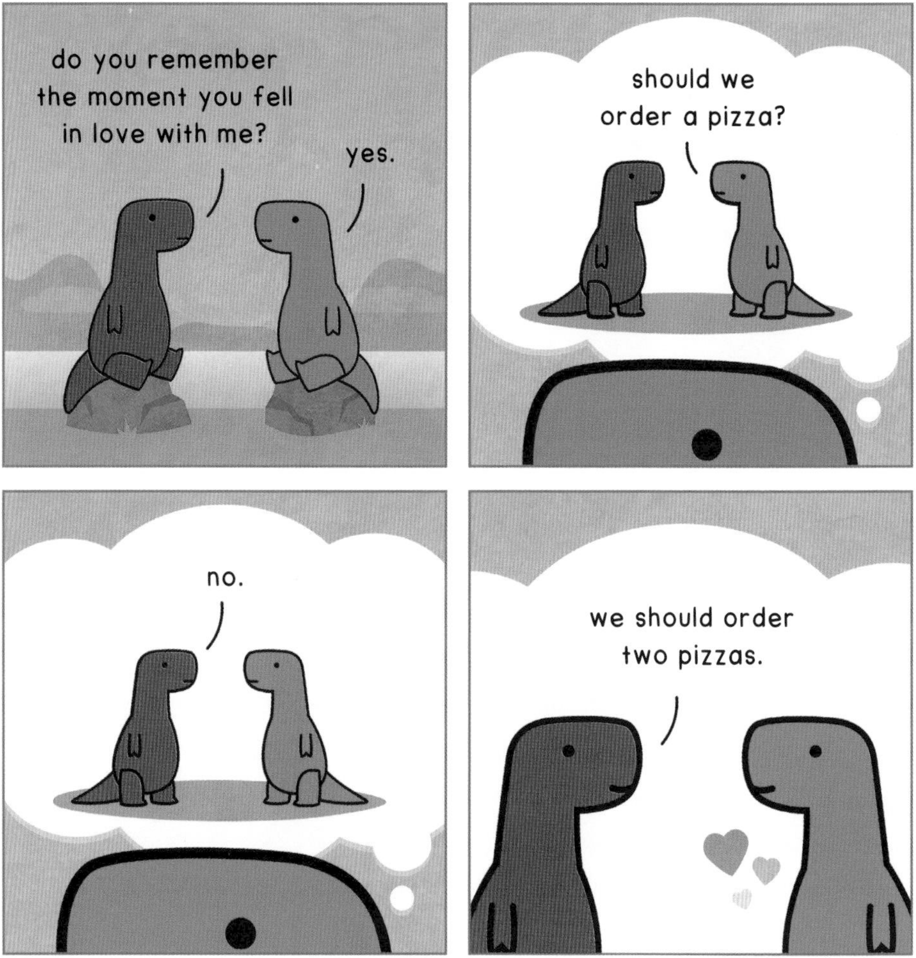
do you remember
the moment you fell
in love with me?
yes.
should we
order a pizza?
no.
we should order
two pizzas.

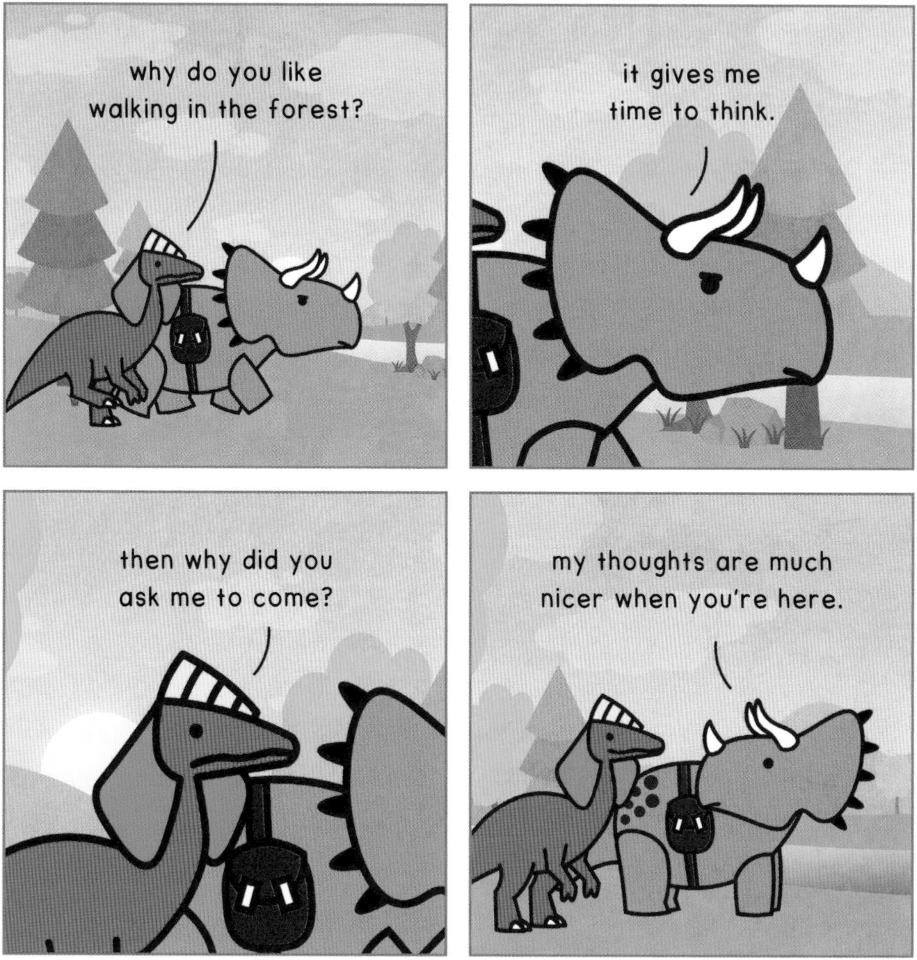
why do you like walking in the forest?
it gives me time to think.
then why did you ask me to come?
my thoughts are much nicer when you're here.

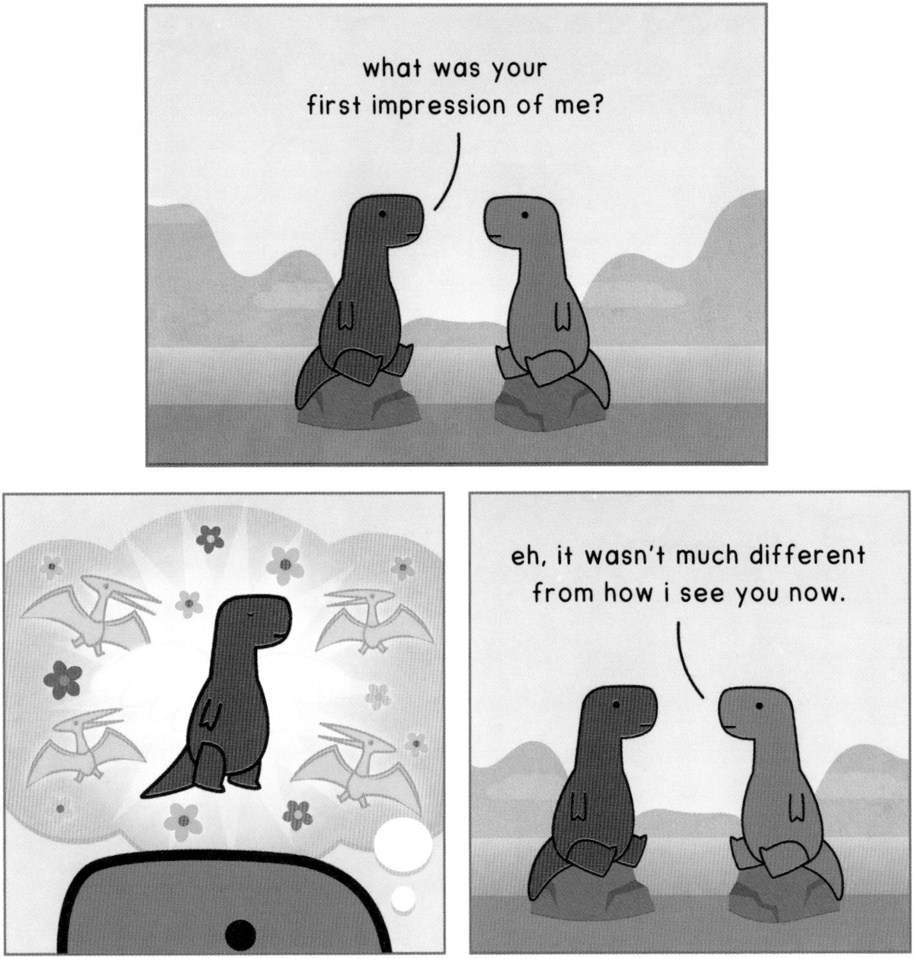
what was your first impression of me?
eh, it wasn't much different from how i see you now.

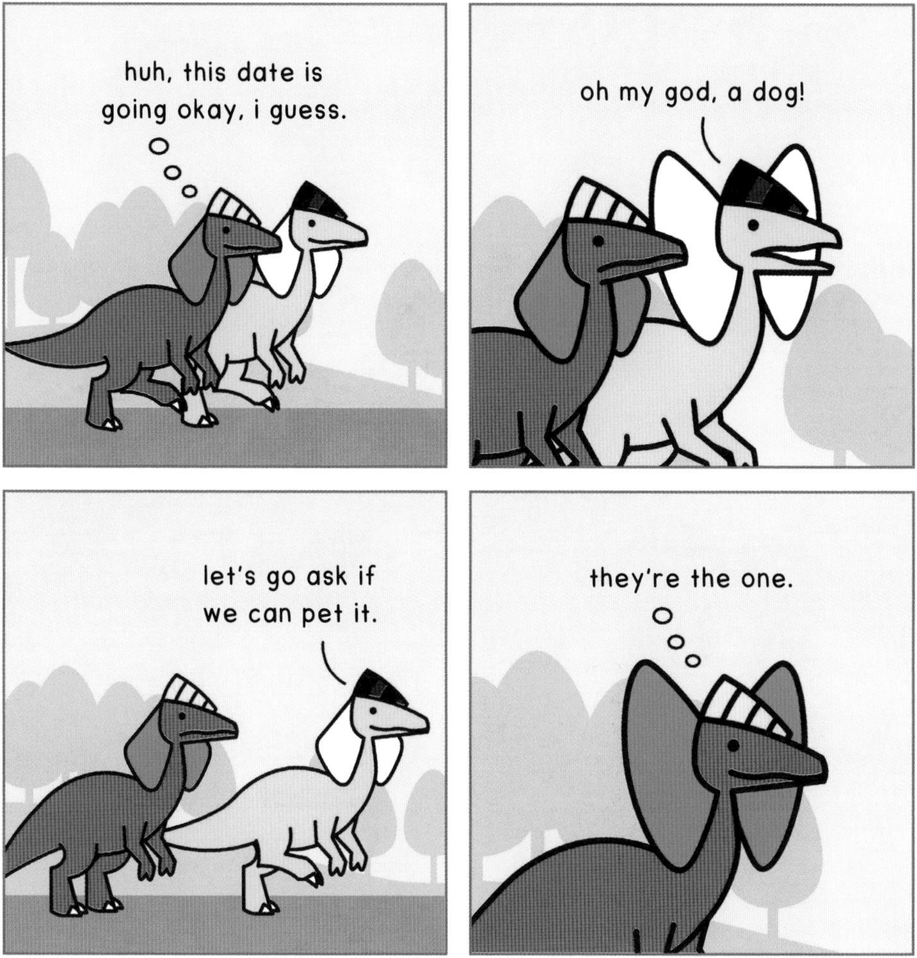
huh, this date is going okay, i guess.
oh my god, a dog!
let's go ask if we can pet it.
they're the one.

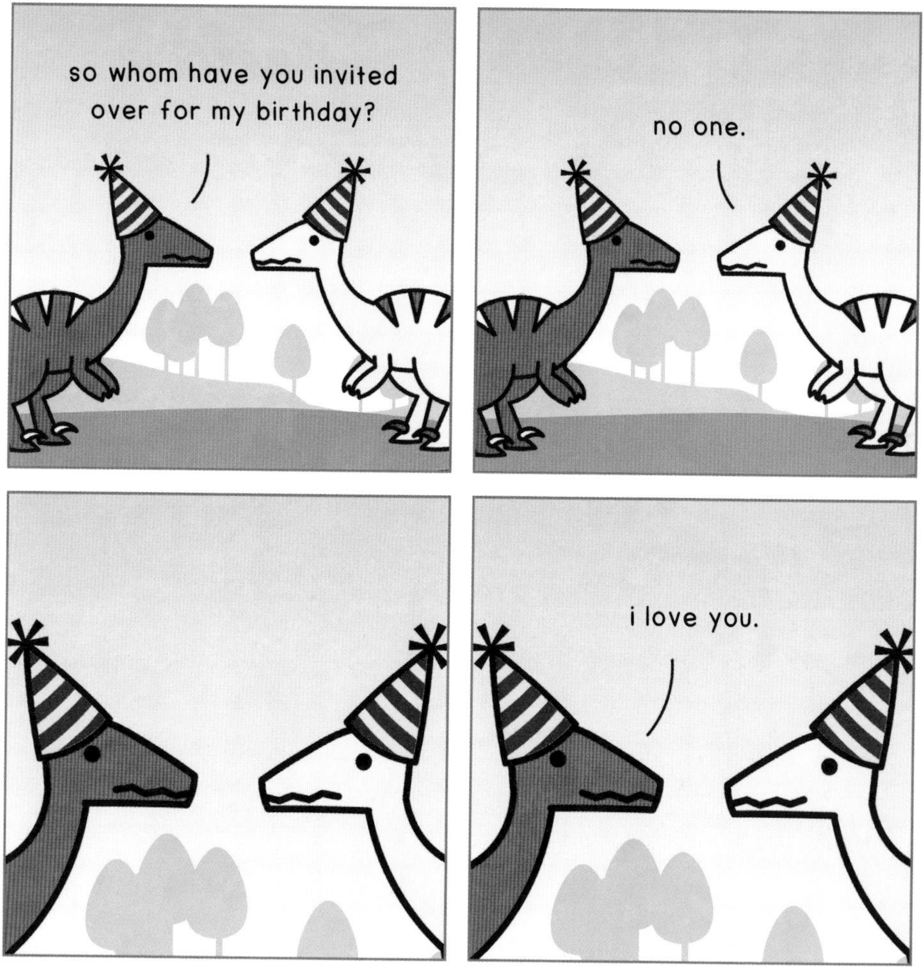
so whom have you invited over for my birthday?
no one.
i love you.

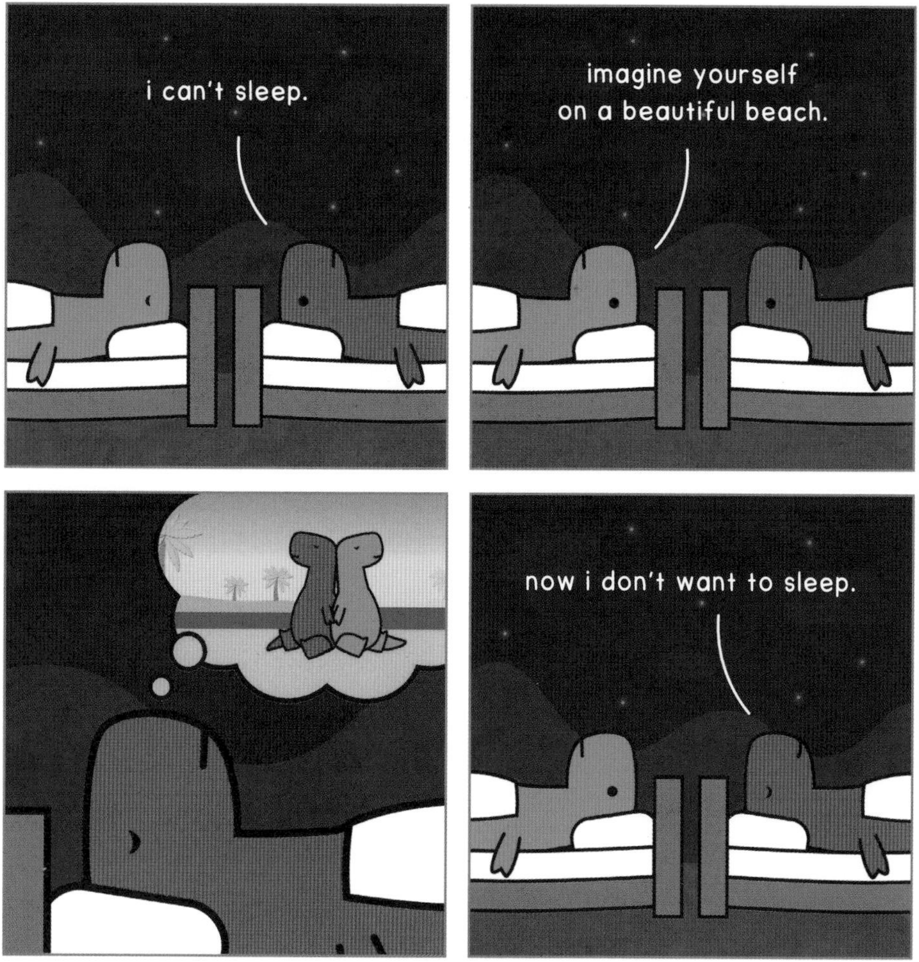
i can't sleep.
imagine yourself
on a beautiful beach.
now i don't want to sleep.

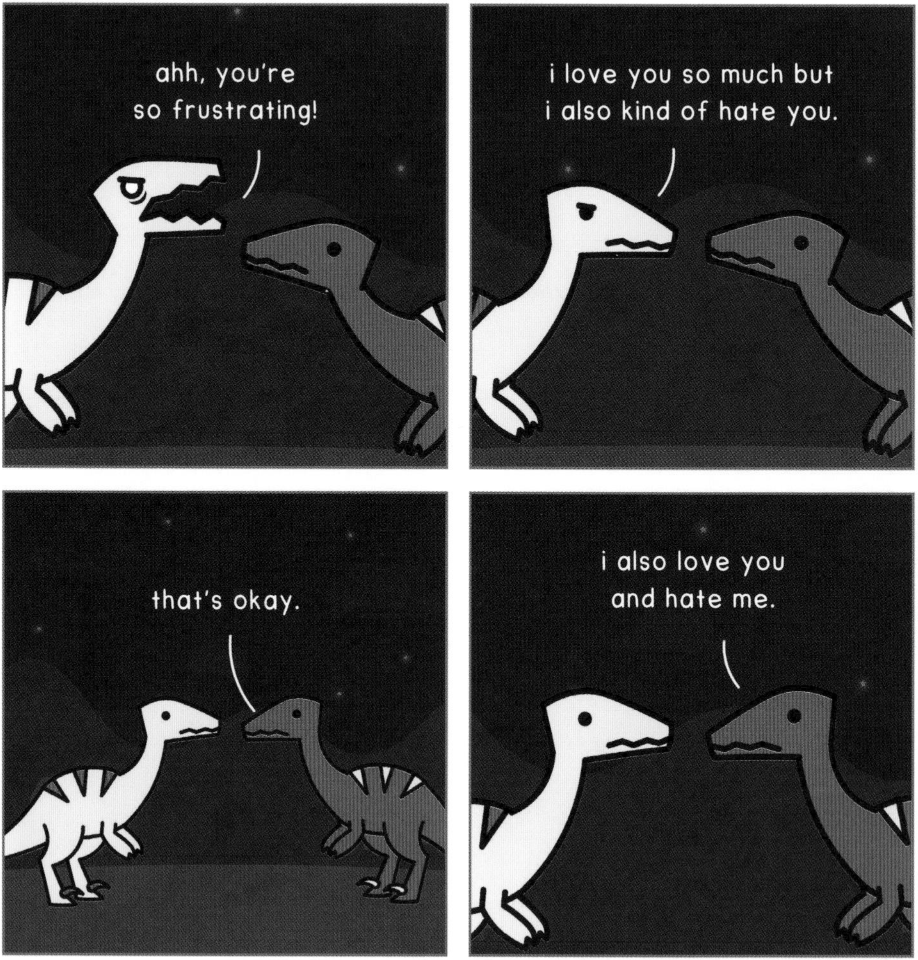
ahh, you're so frustrating!
i love you so much but i also kind of hate you.
that's okay.
i also love you and hate me.

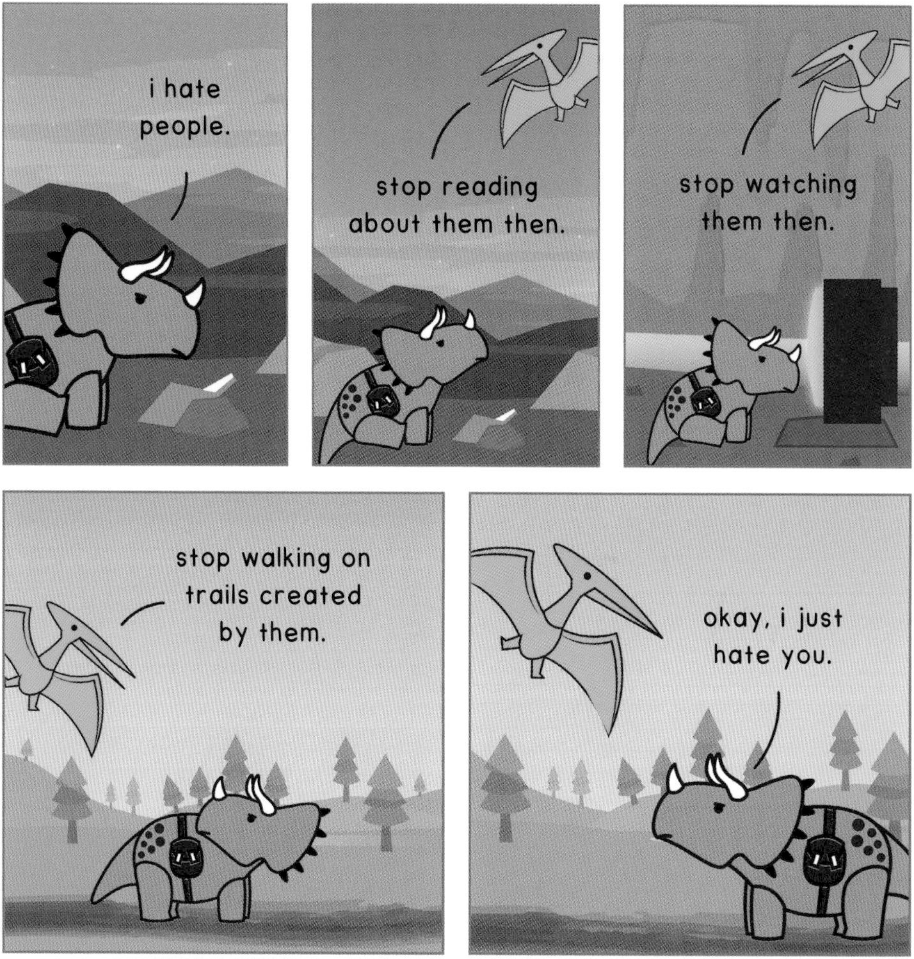
i hate people.
stop reading about them then.
stop watching them then.
stop walking on trails created by them.
okay, i just hate you.

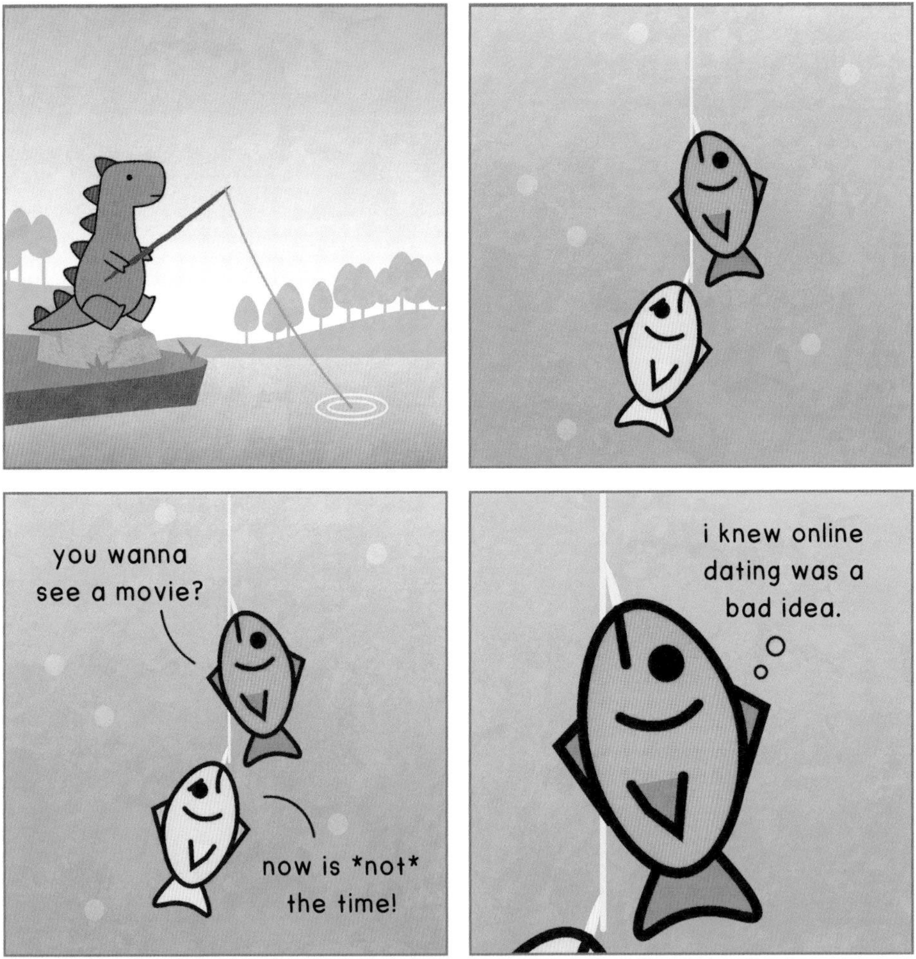
you wanna see a movie?
now is *not* the time!
i knew online dating was a bad idea.

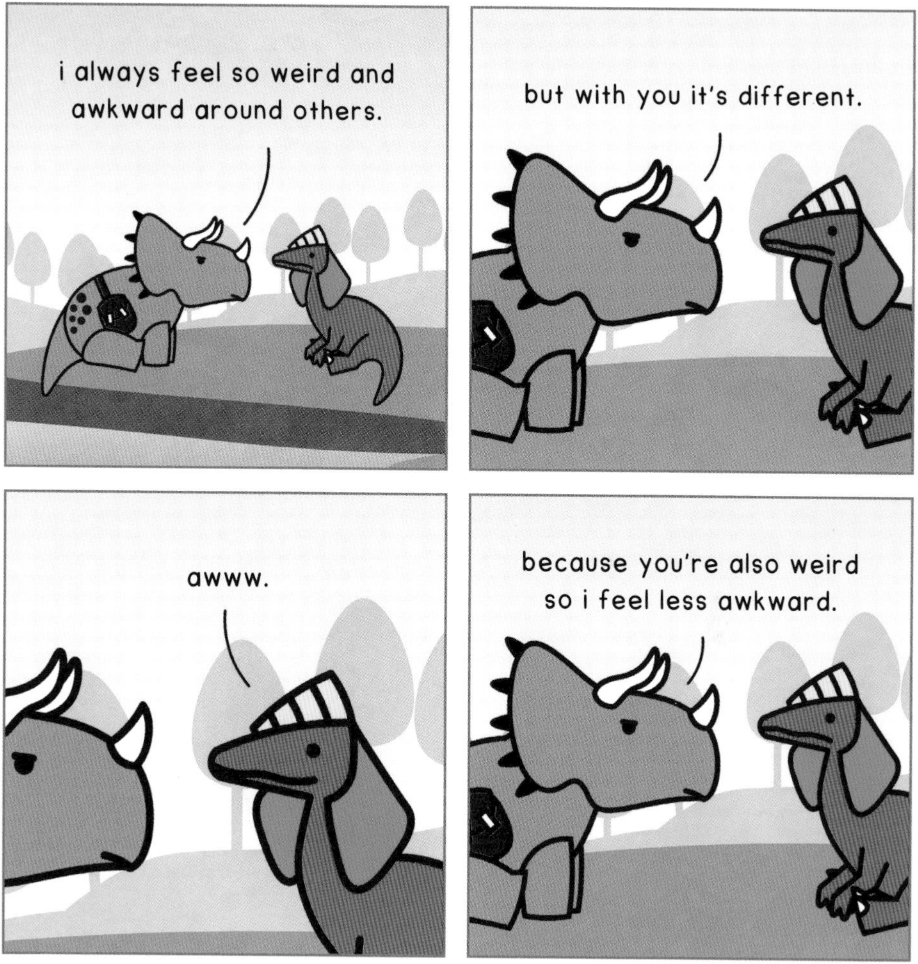
i always feel so weird and awkward around others.
but with you it's different.
awww.
because you're also weird so i feel less awkward.

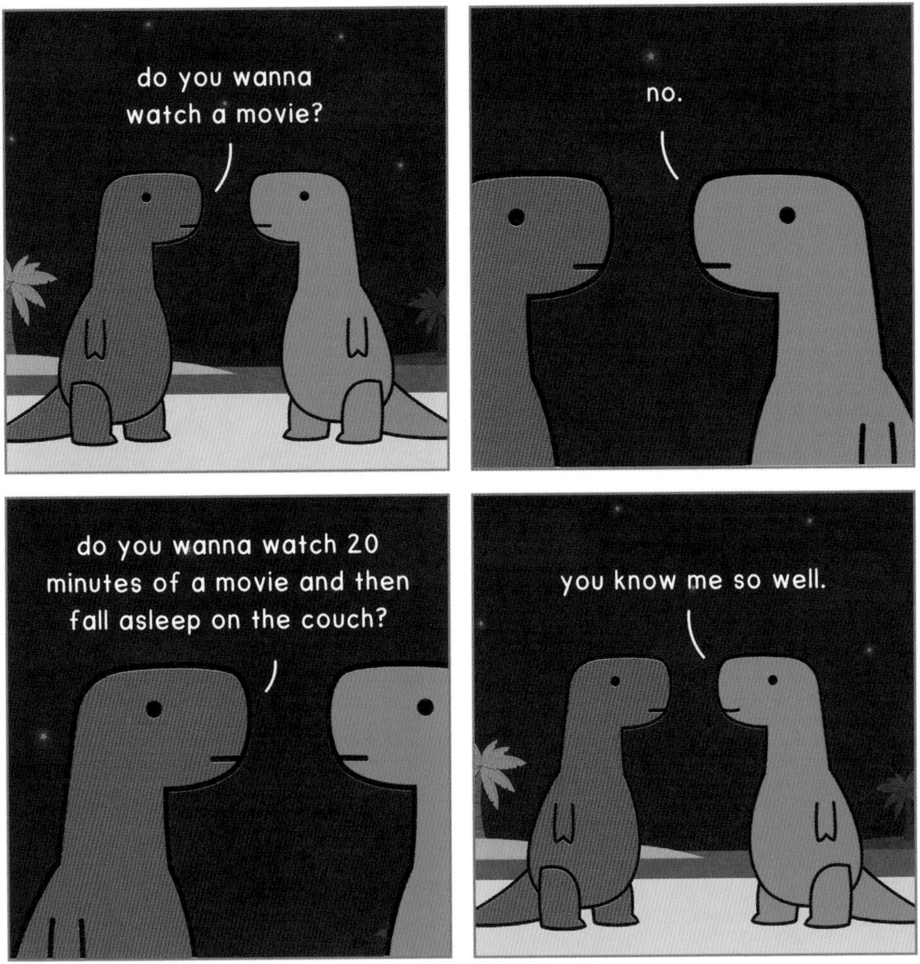
do you wanna
watch a movie?
no.
do you wanna watch 20
minutes of a movie and then
fall asleep on the couch?
you know me so well.

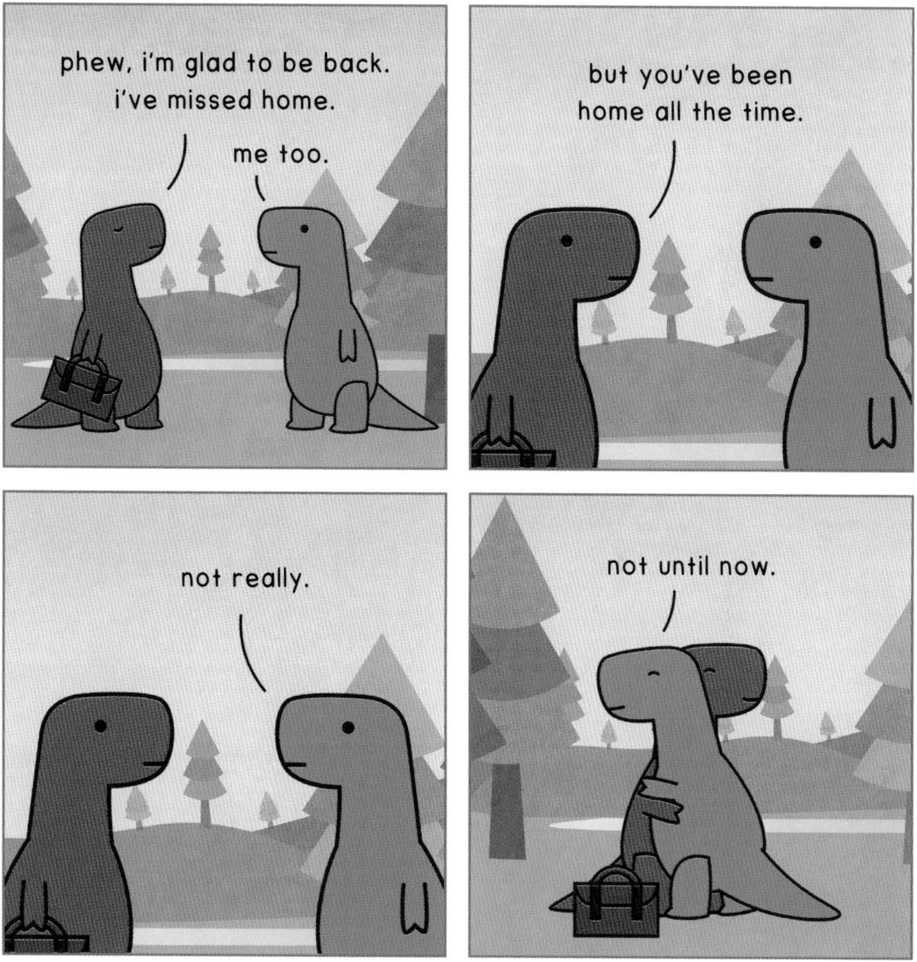
phew, i'm glad to be back.
i've missed home.
me too.
but you've been
home all the time.
not really.
not until now.

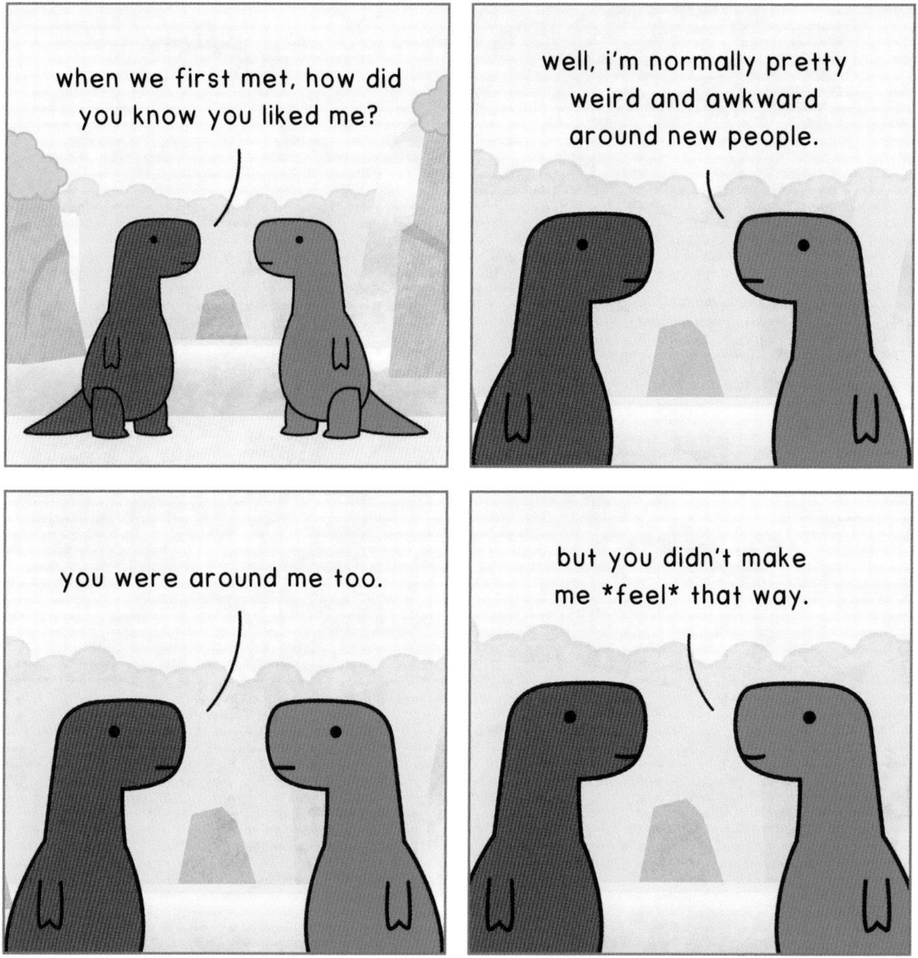
when we first met, how did you know you liked me?
well, i'm normally pretty weird and awkward around new people.
you were around me too.
but you didn't make me *feel* that way.

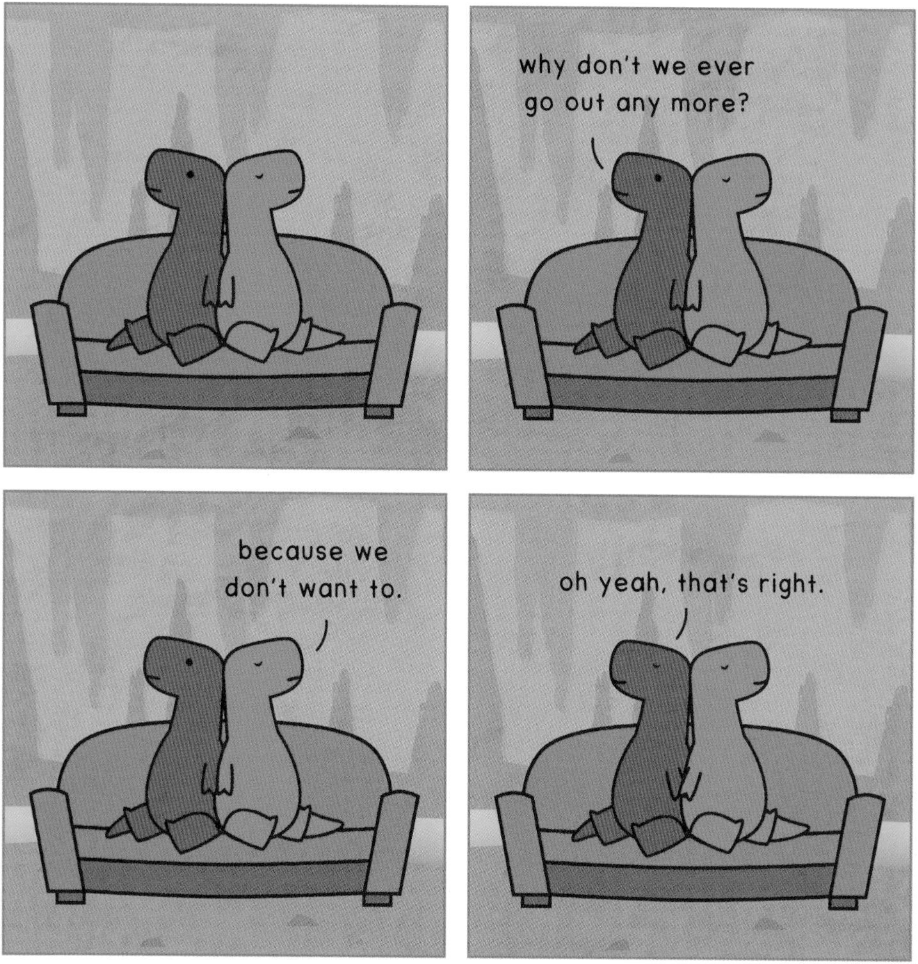
why don't we ever
go out any more?
because we
don't want to.
oh yeah, that's right.

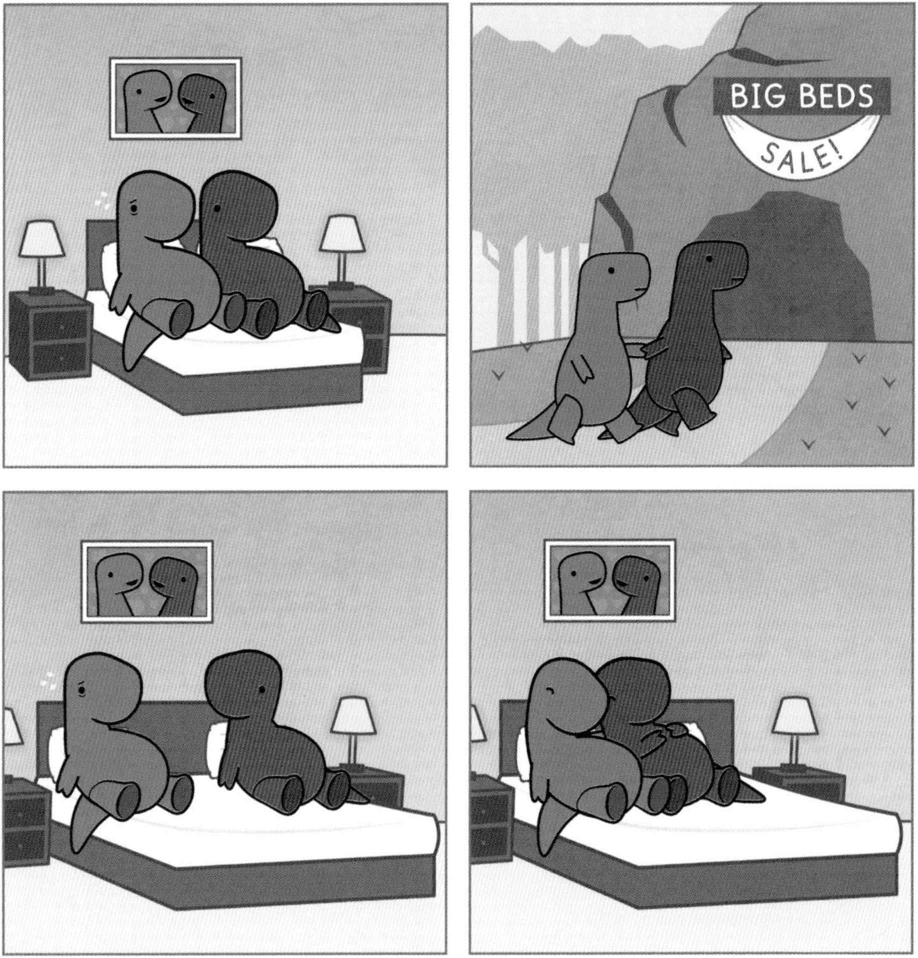
BIG BEDS
SALE!

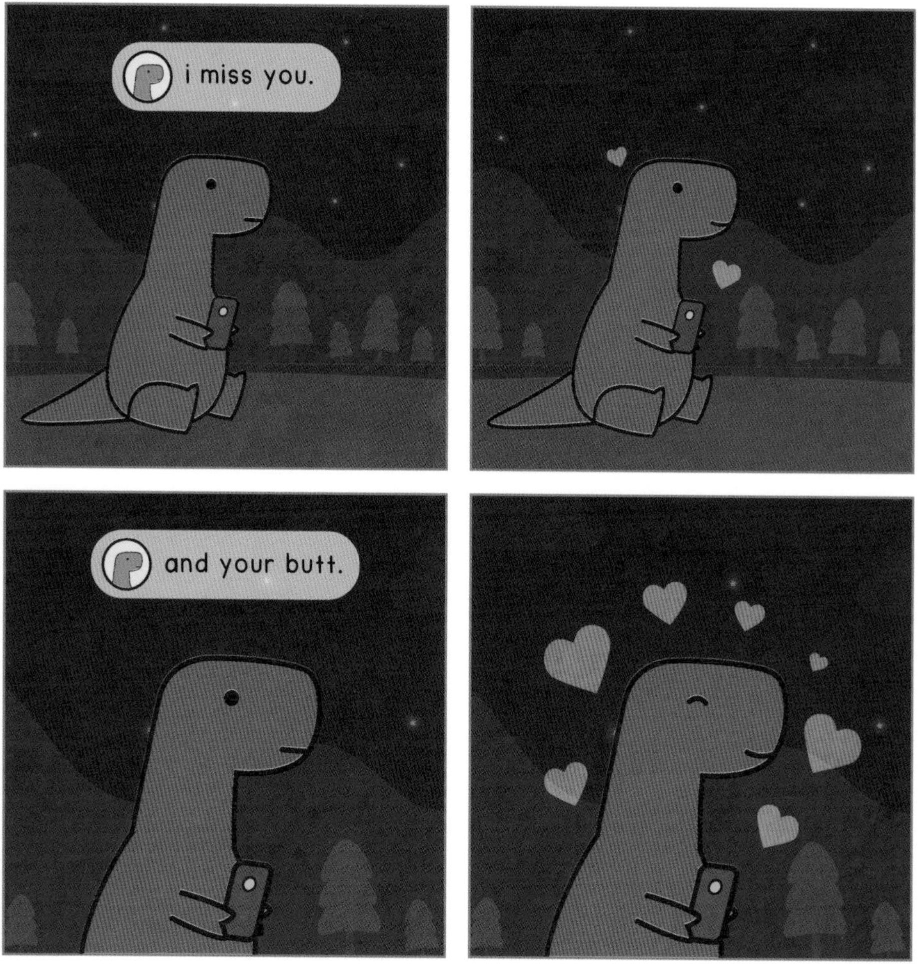
i miss you.
and your butt.

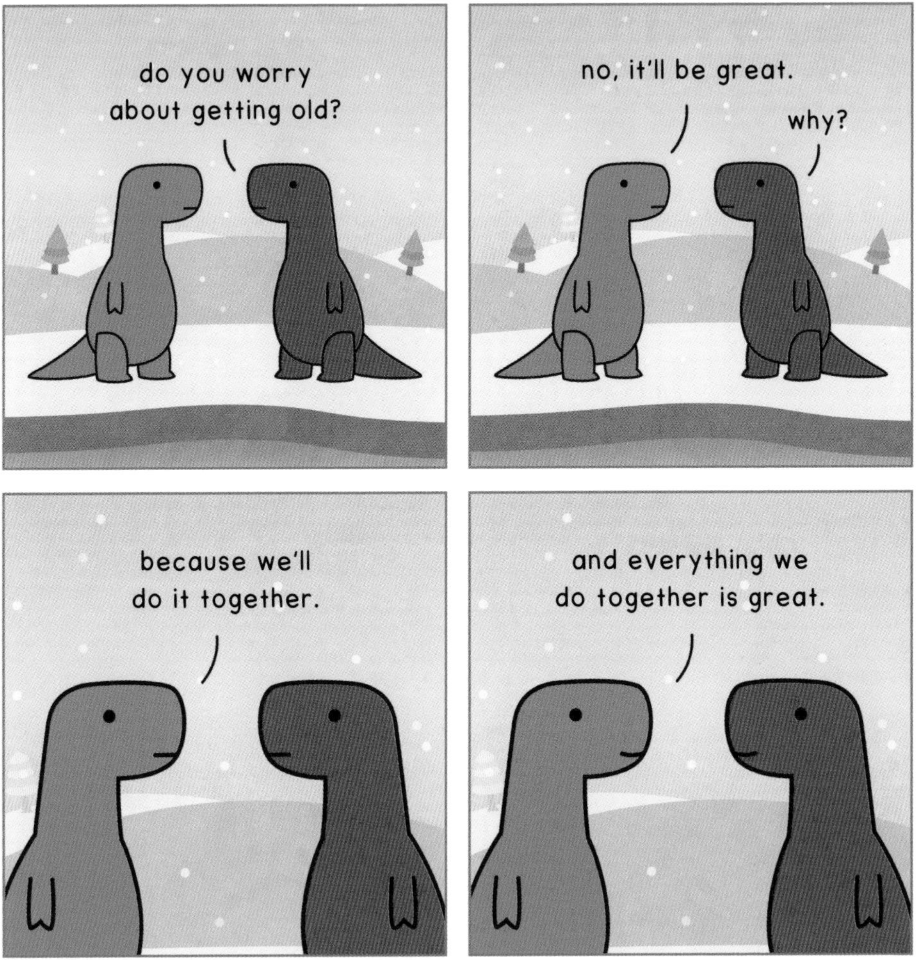
do you worry
about getting old?
no, it'll be great.
why?
because we'll
do it together.
and everything we
do together is great.

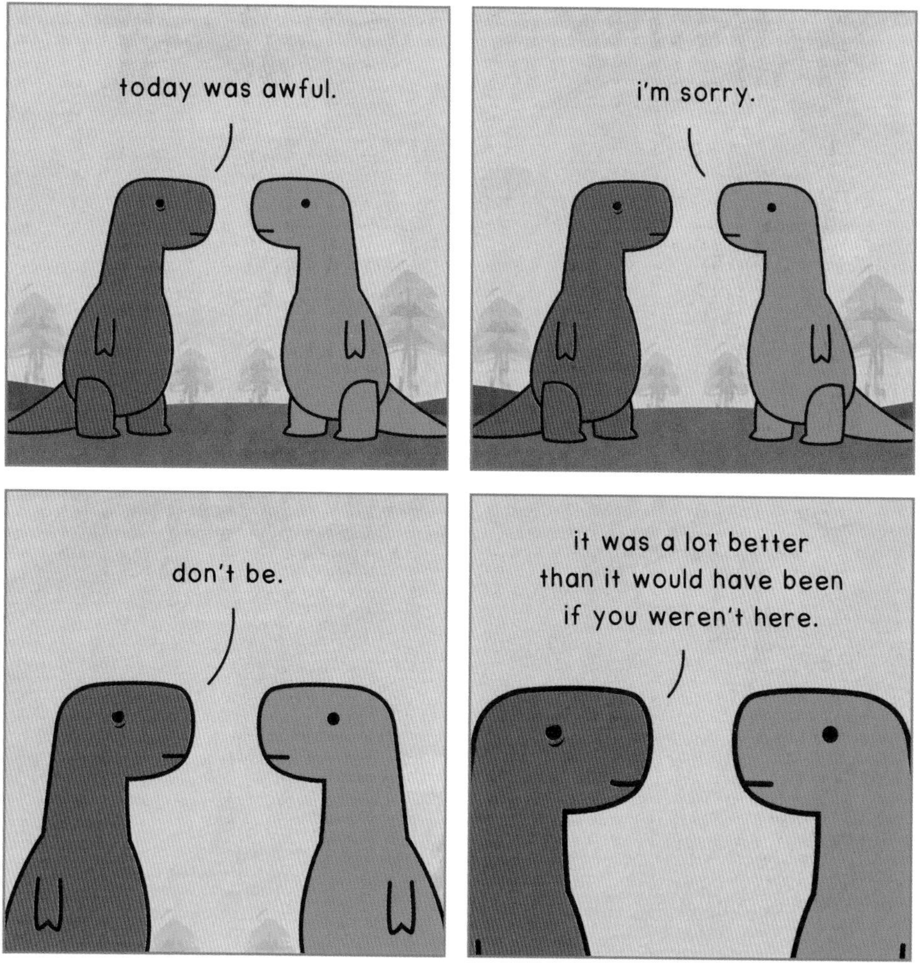
today was awful.
i'm sorry.
don't be.
it was a lot better than it would have been if you weren't here.

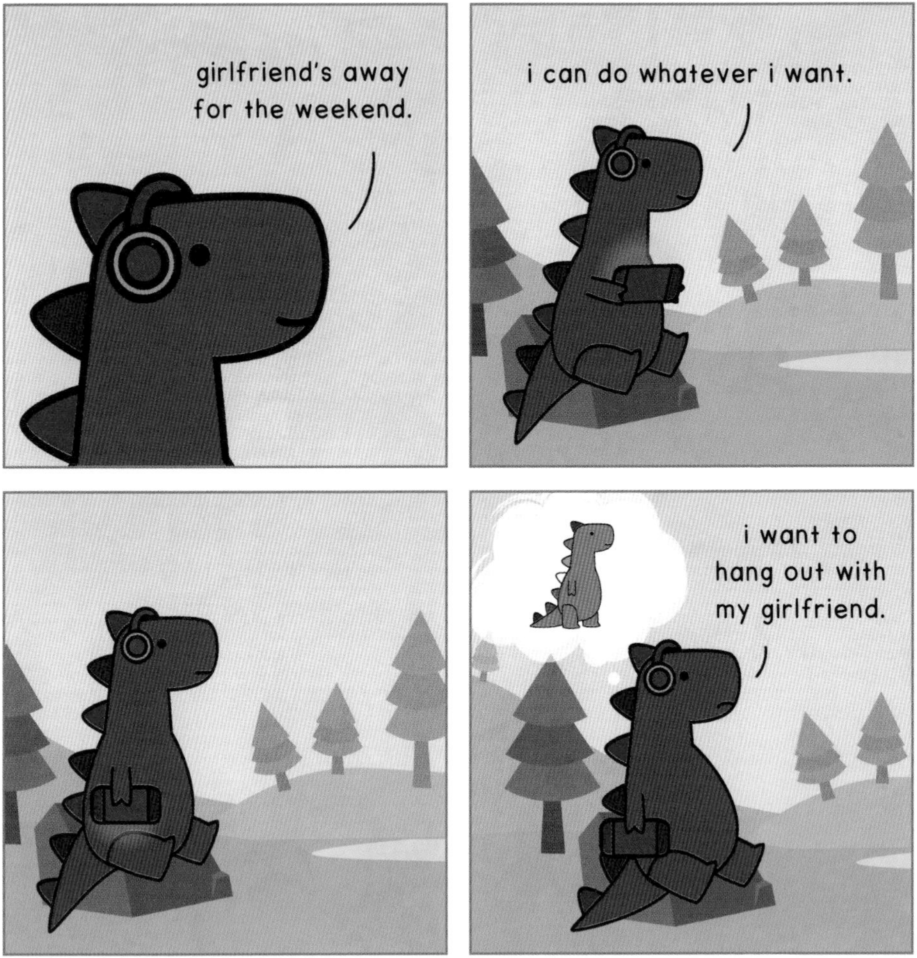
girlfriend's away
for the weekend.
i can do whatever i want.
i want to
hang out with
my girlfriend.

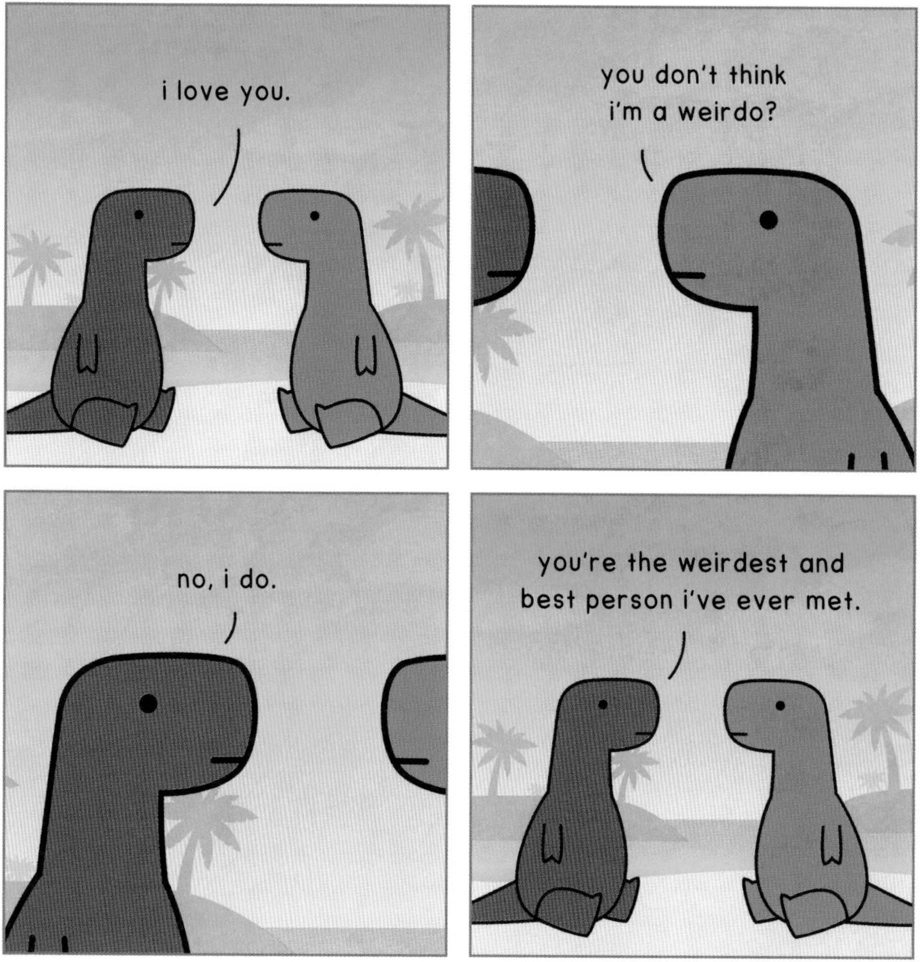
i love you.
you don't think i'm a weirdo?
no, i do.
you're the weirdest and best person i've ever met.

yourself

the friend it's easy
to forget

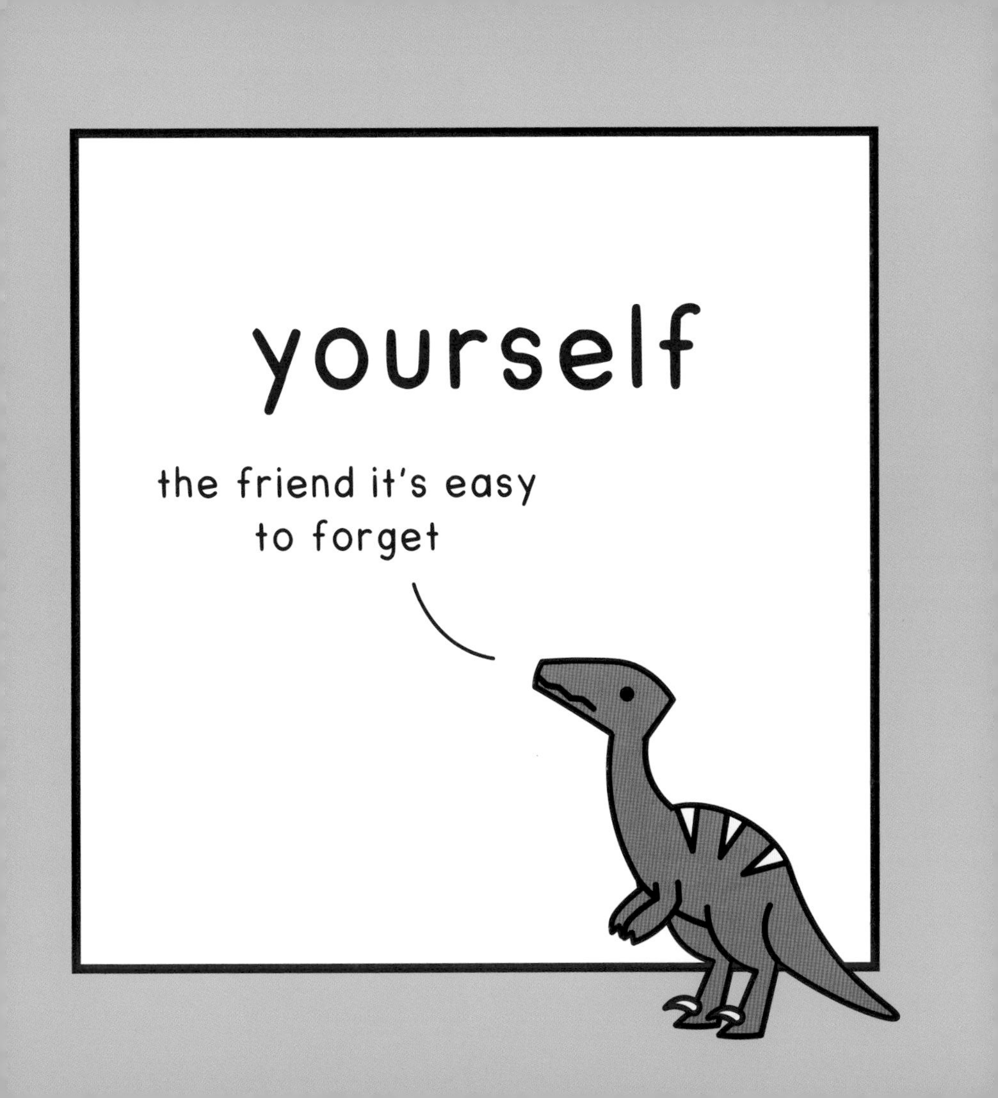

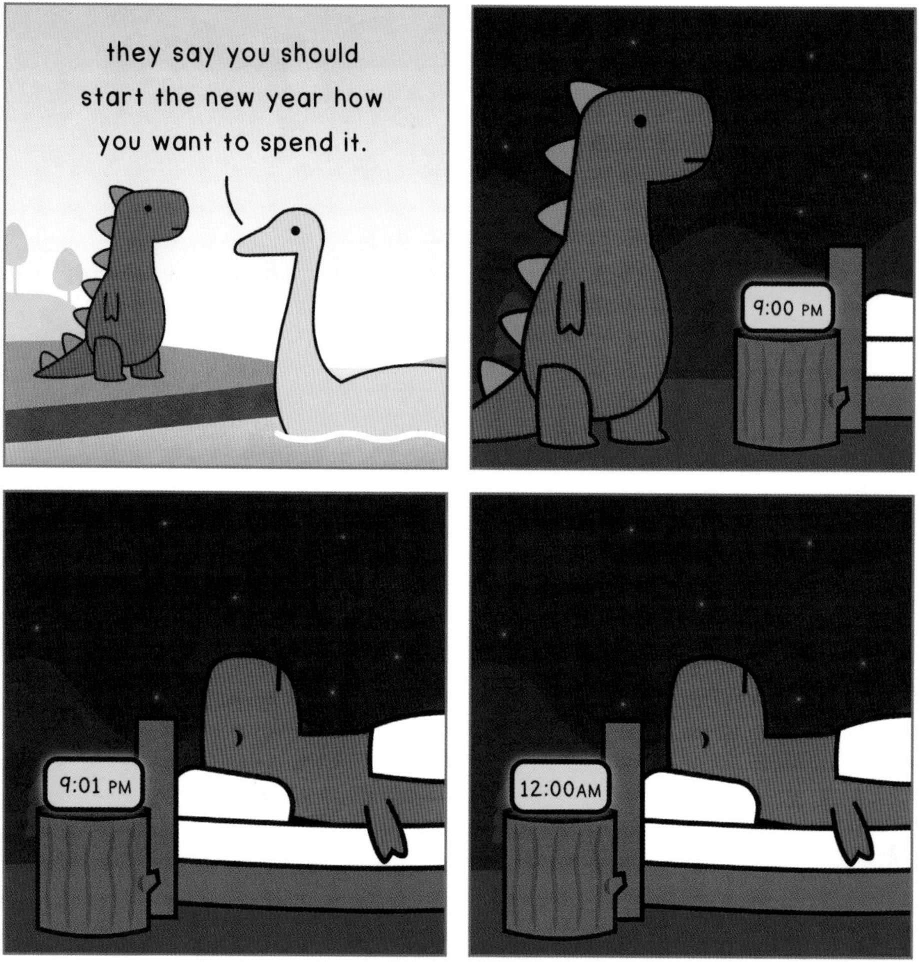
they say you should start the new year how you want to spend it.
9:00 PM
9:01 PM
12:00AM

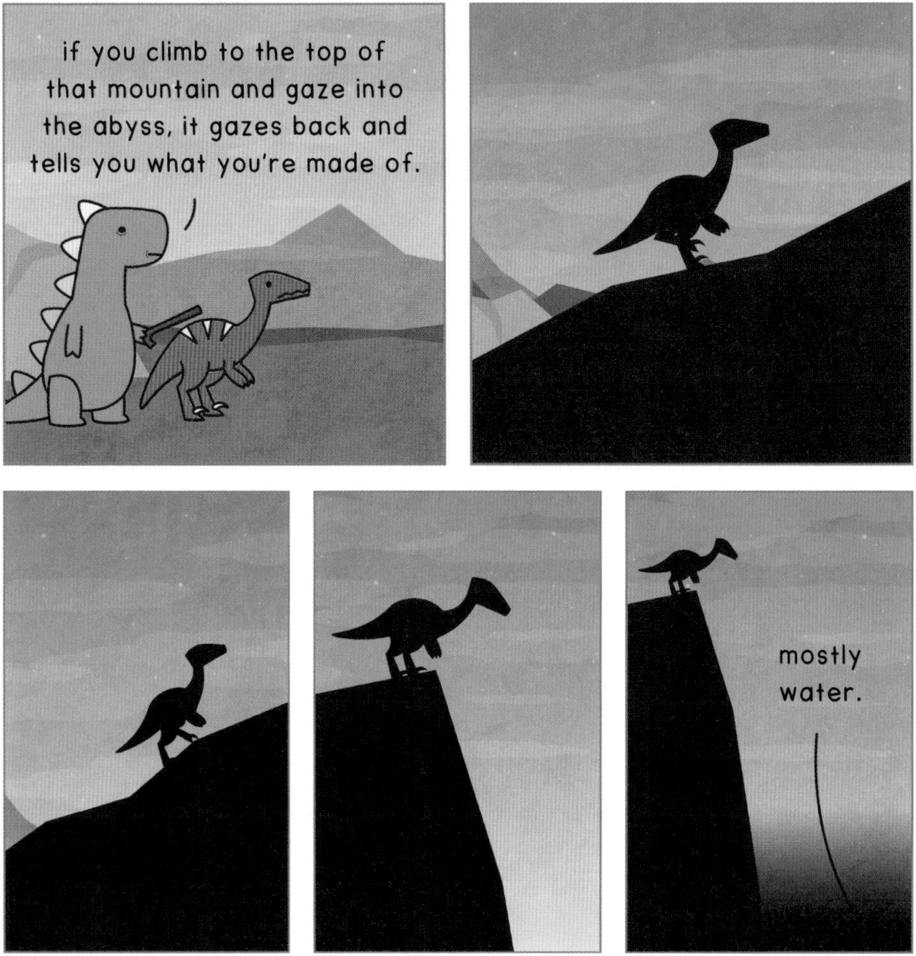
if you climb to the top of that mountain and gaze into the abyss, it gazes back and tells you what you're made of.
mostly water.

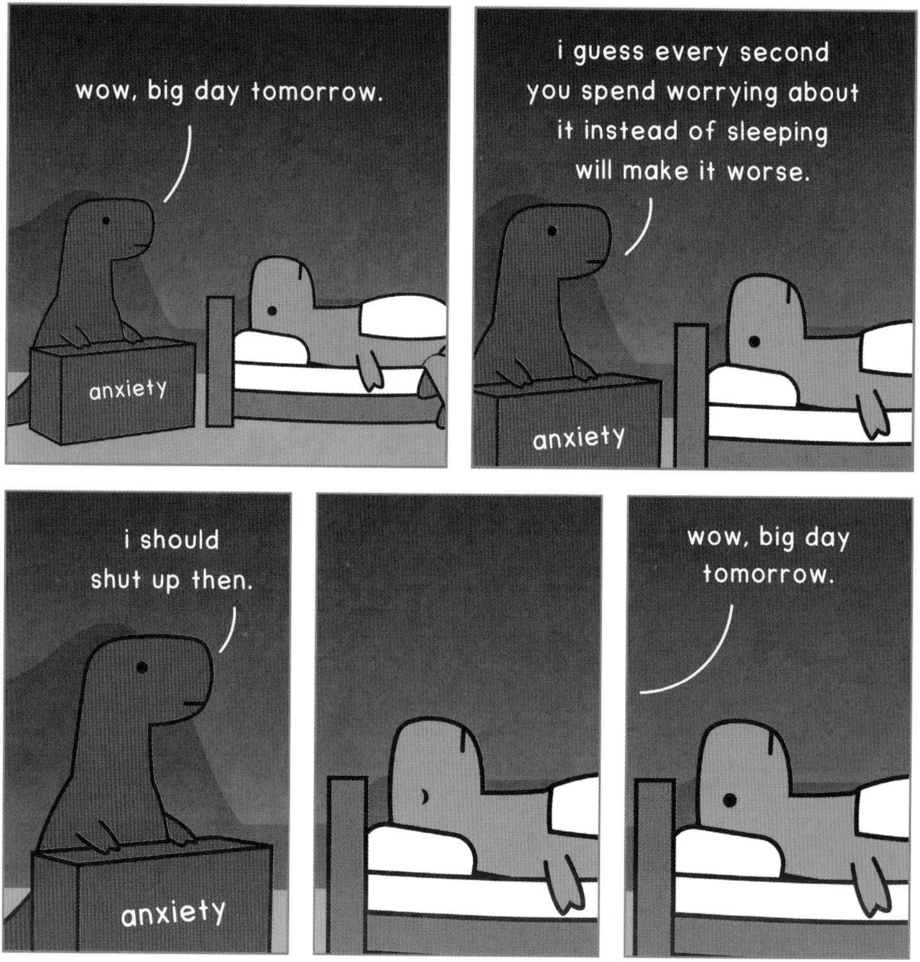
wow, big day tomorrow.
anxiety
i guess every second you spend worrying about it instead of sleeping will make it worse.
anxiety
i should shut up then.
anxiety
wow, big day tomorrow.

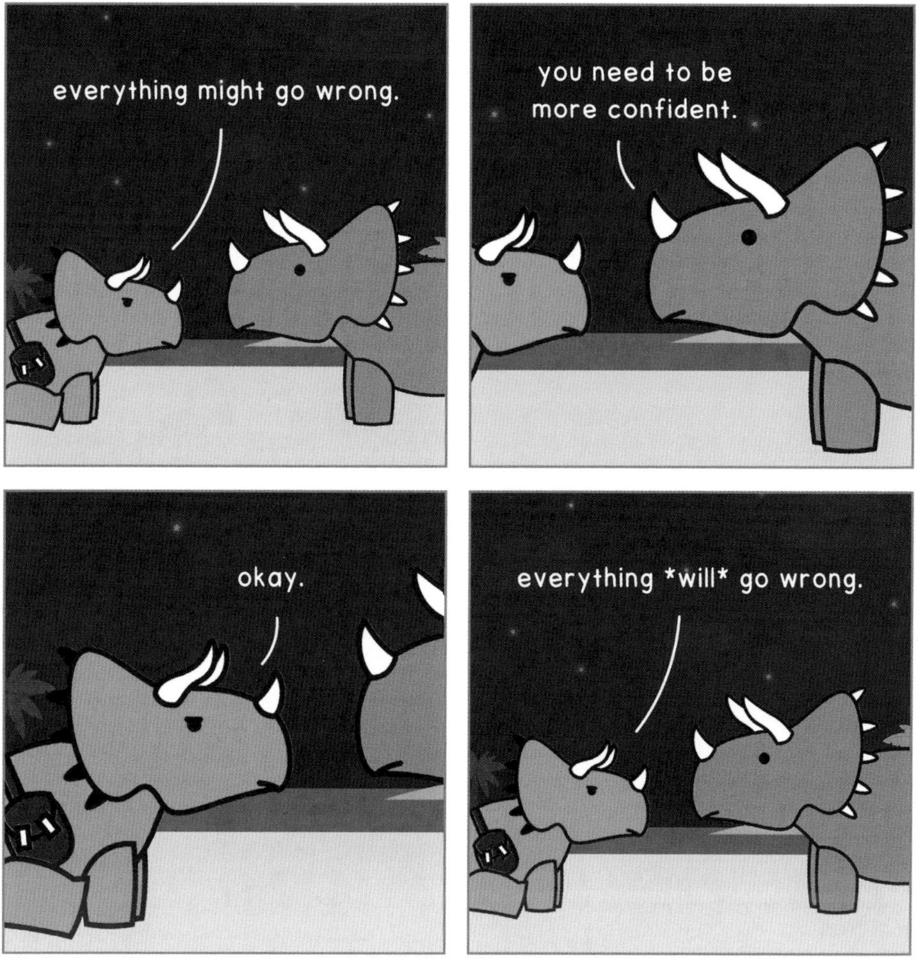
everything might go wrong.
you need to be more confident.
okay.
everything *will* go wrong.

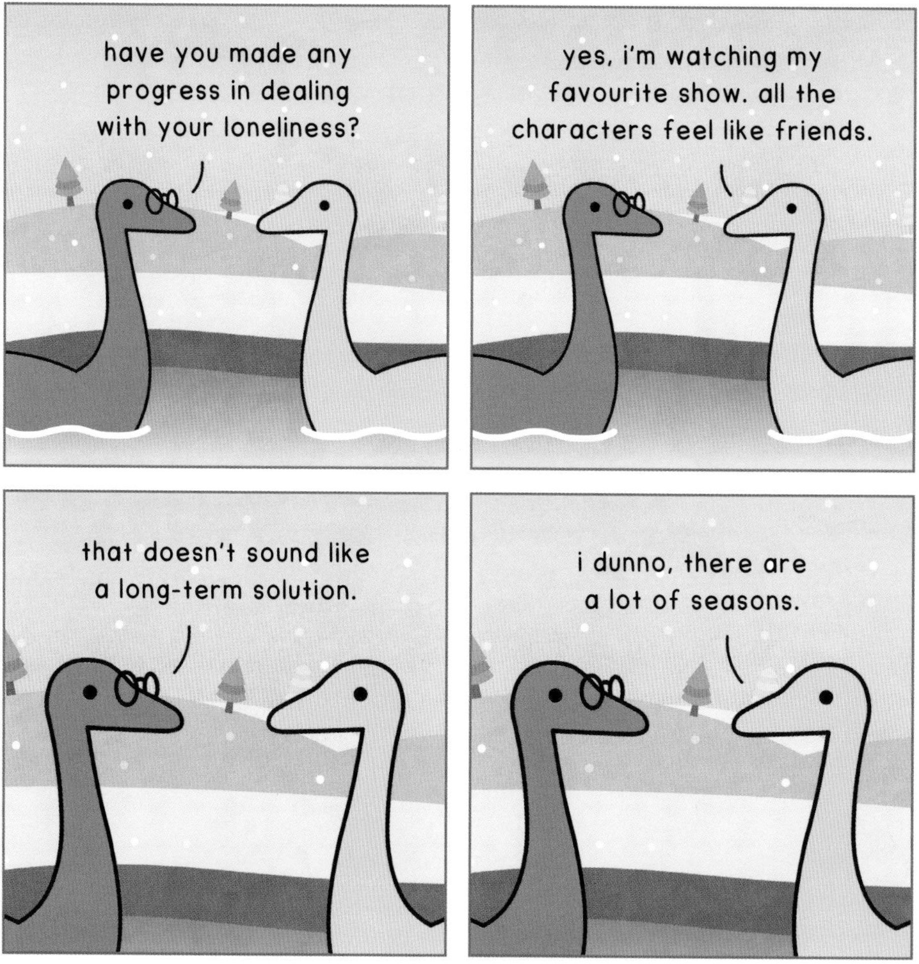
have you made any progress in dealing with your loneliness?
yes, i'm watching my favourite show. all the characters feel like friends.
that doesn't sound like a long-term solution.
i dunno, there are a lot of seasons.

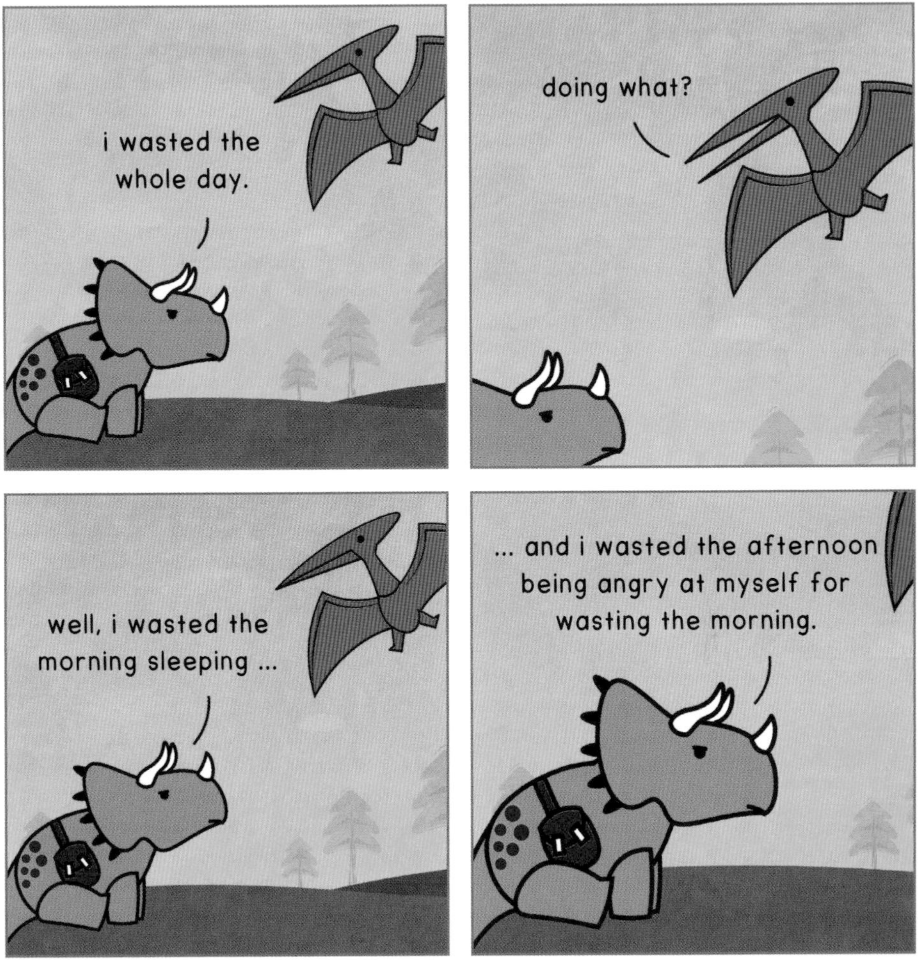
i wasted the whole day.
doing what?
well, i wasted the morning sleeping ...
... and i wasted the afternoon being angry at myself for wasting the morning.

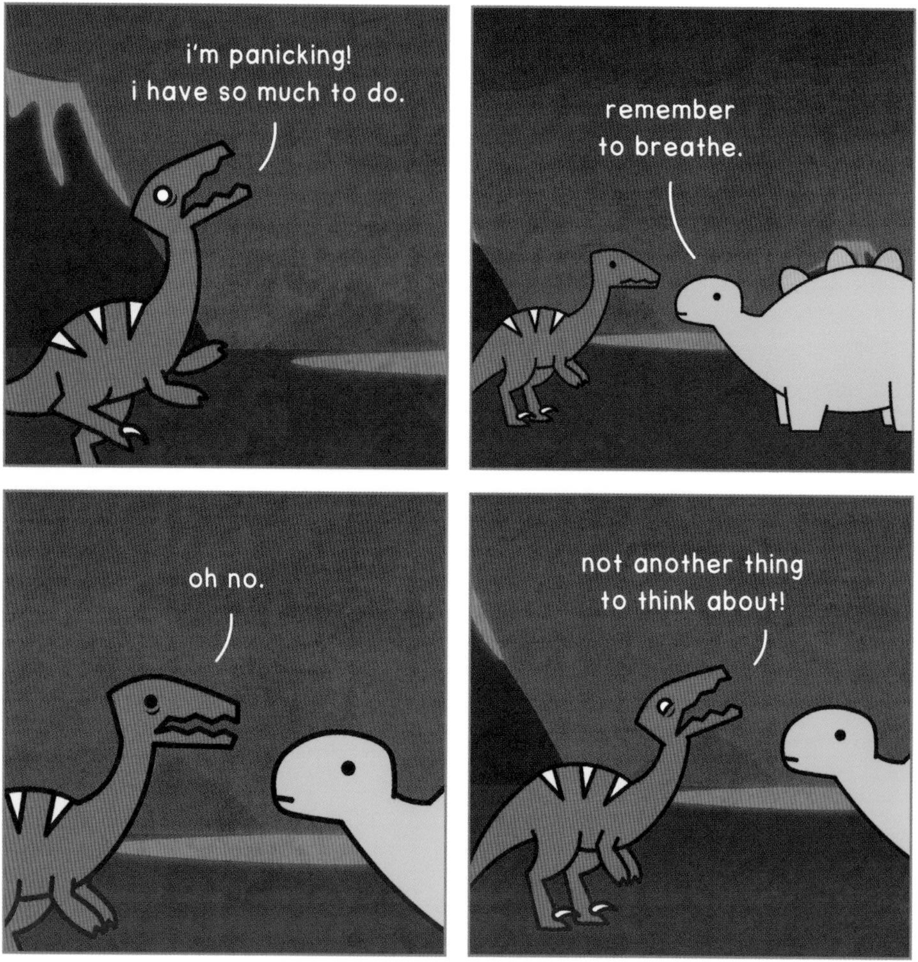
i'm panicking!
i have so much to do.
remember
to breathe.
oh no.
not another thing
to think about!

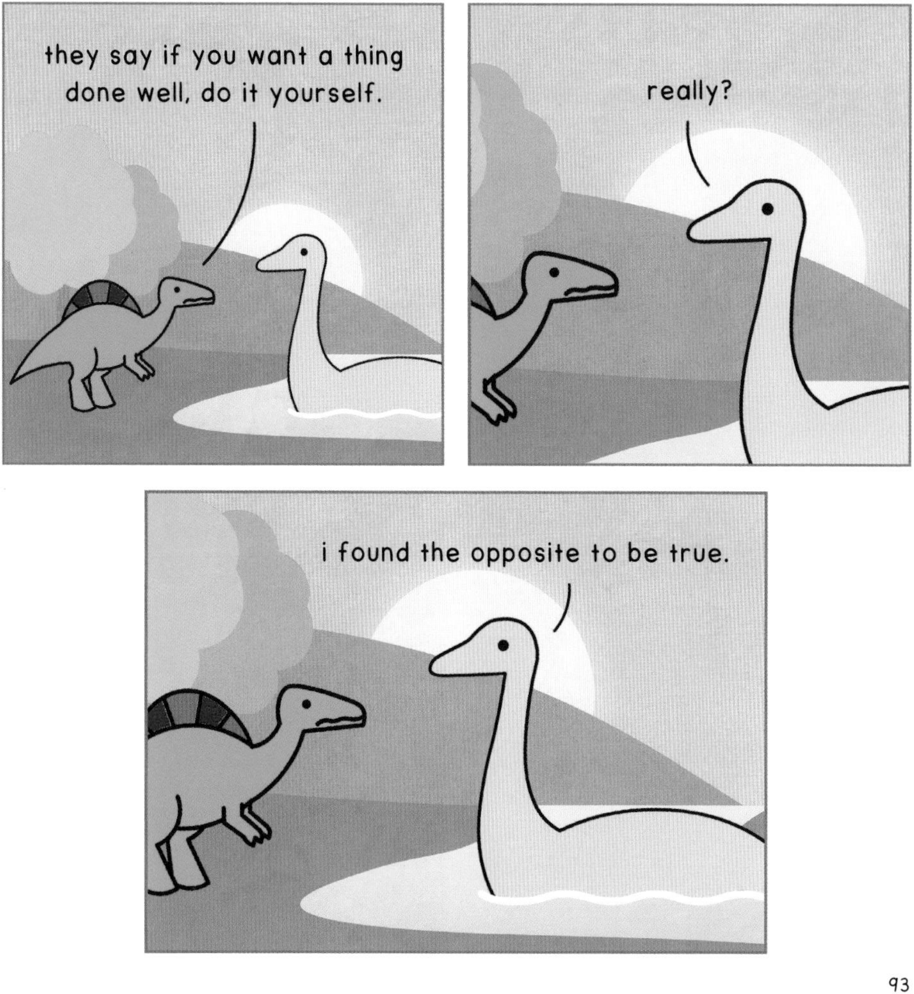
they say if you want a thing done well, do it yourself.
really?
i found the opposite to be true.

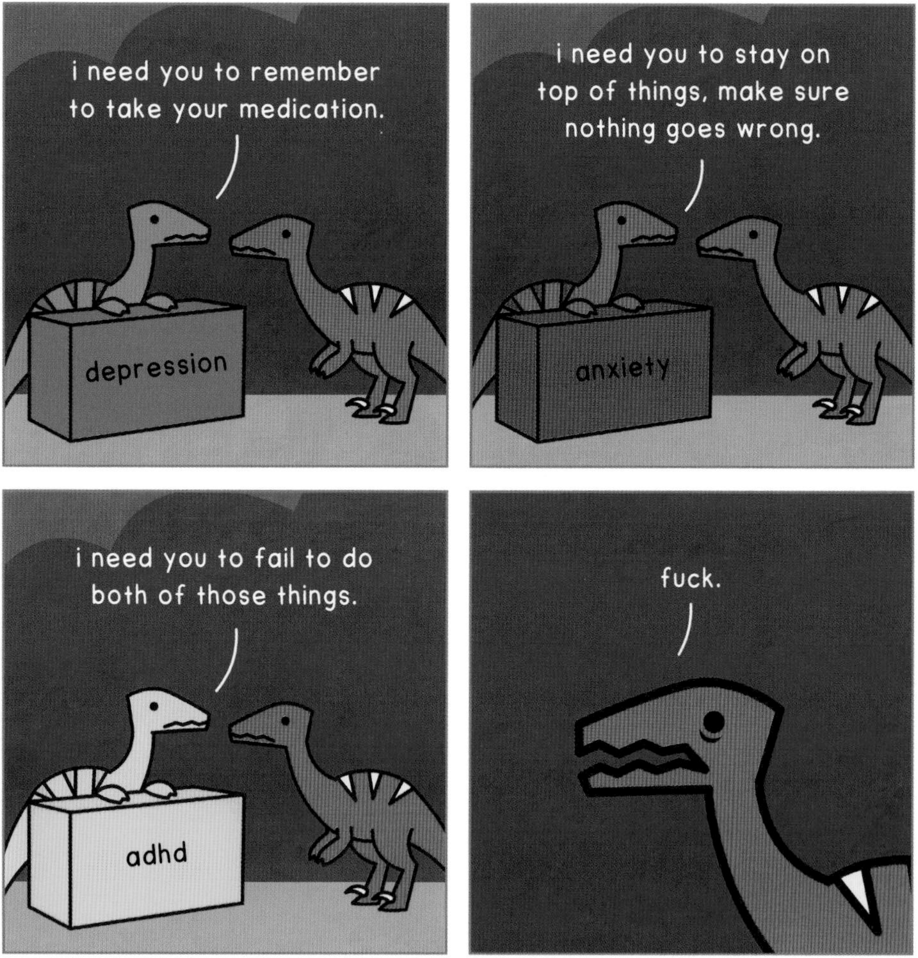
i need you to remember to take your medication.
depression
i need you to stay on top of things, make sure nothing goes wrong.
anxiety
i need you to fail to do both of those things.
adhd
fuck.

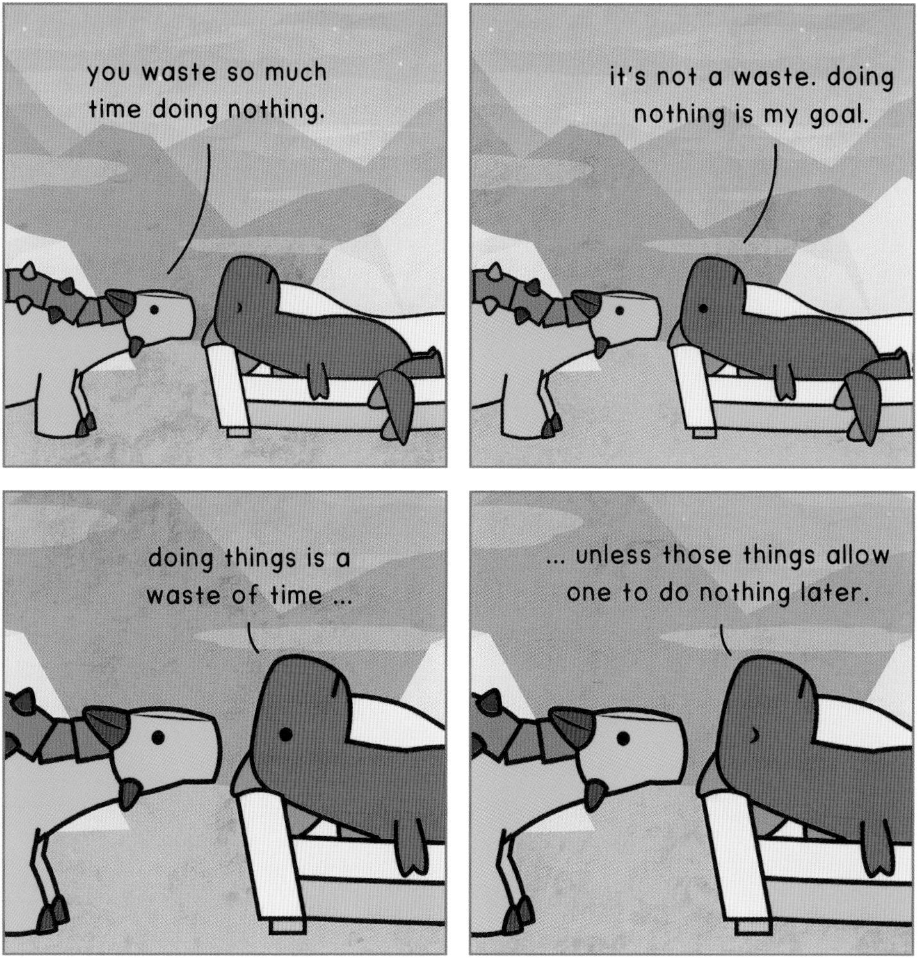
you waste so much time doing nothing.
it's not a waste. doing nothing is my goal.
doing things is a waste of time ...
... unless those things allow one to do nothing later.

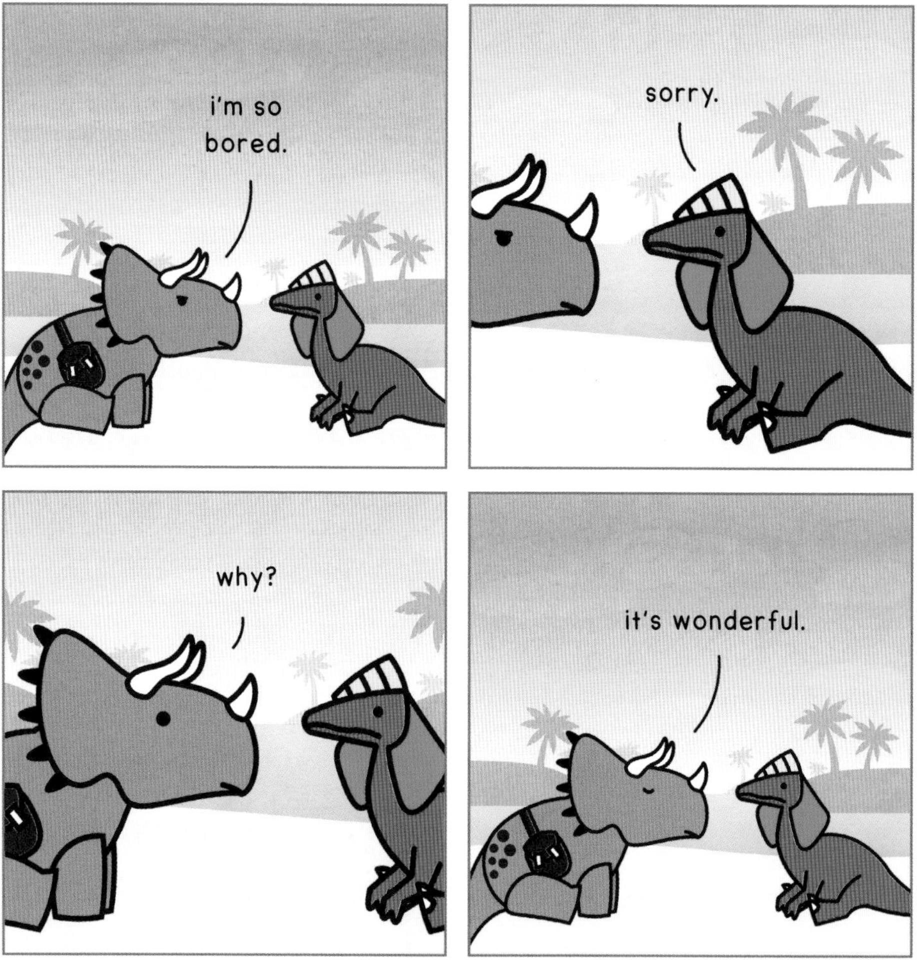
i'm so bored.
sorry.
why?
it's wonderful.

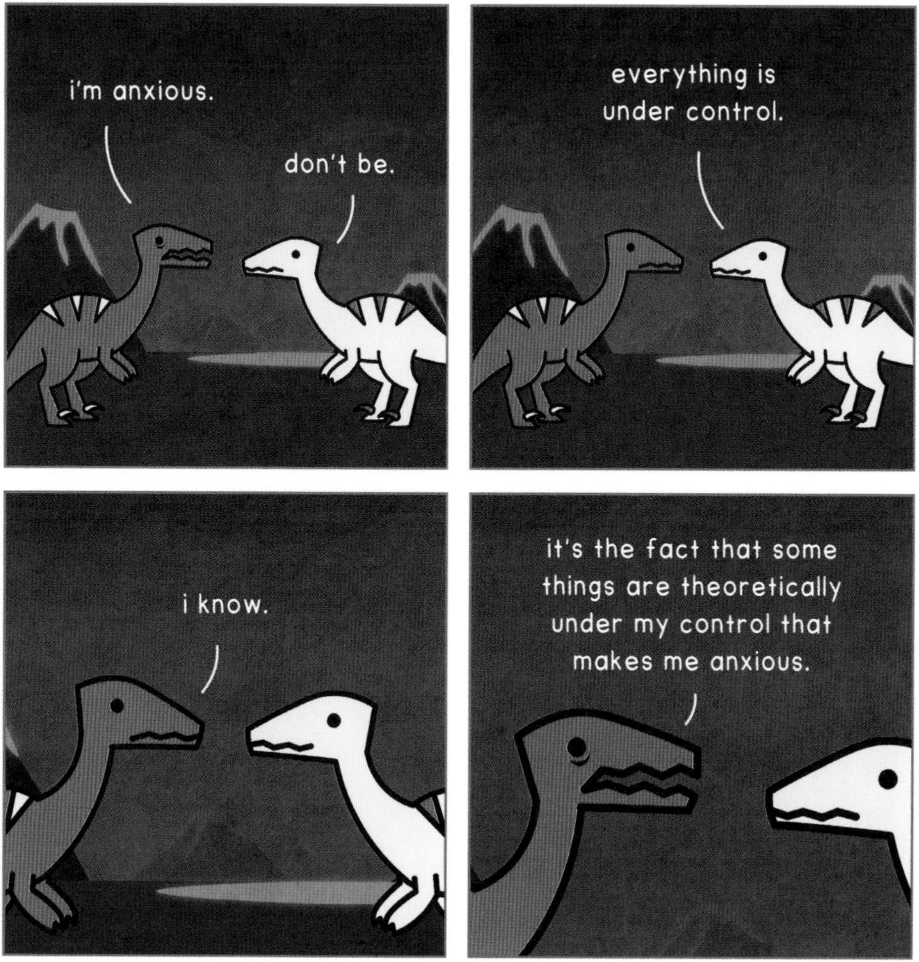
i'm anxious.
don't be.
everything is under control.
i know.
it's the fact that some things are theoretically under my control that makes me anxious.

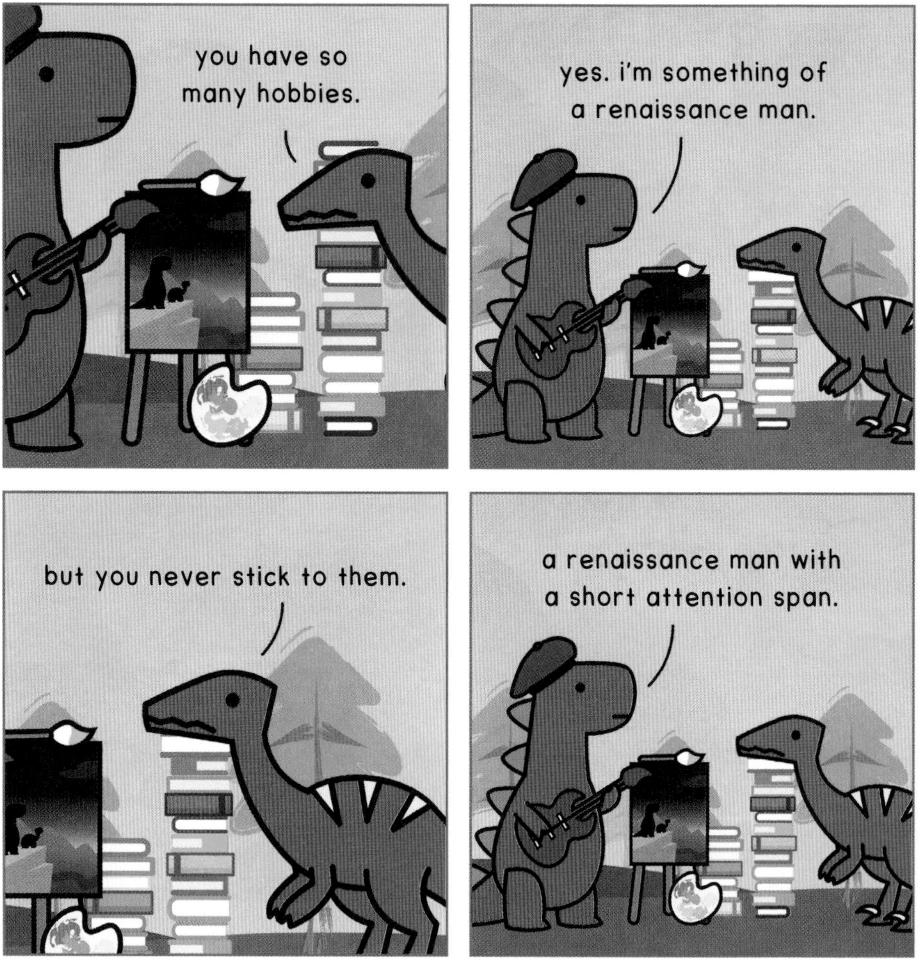
you have so many hobbies.
yes. i'm something of a renaissance man.
but you never stick to them.
a renaissance man with a short attention span.

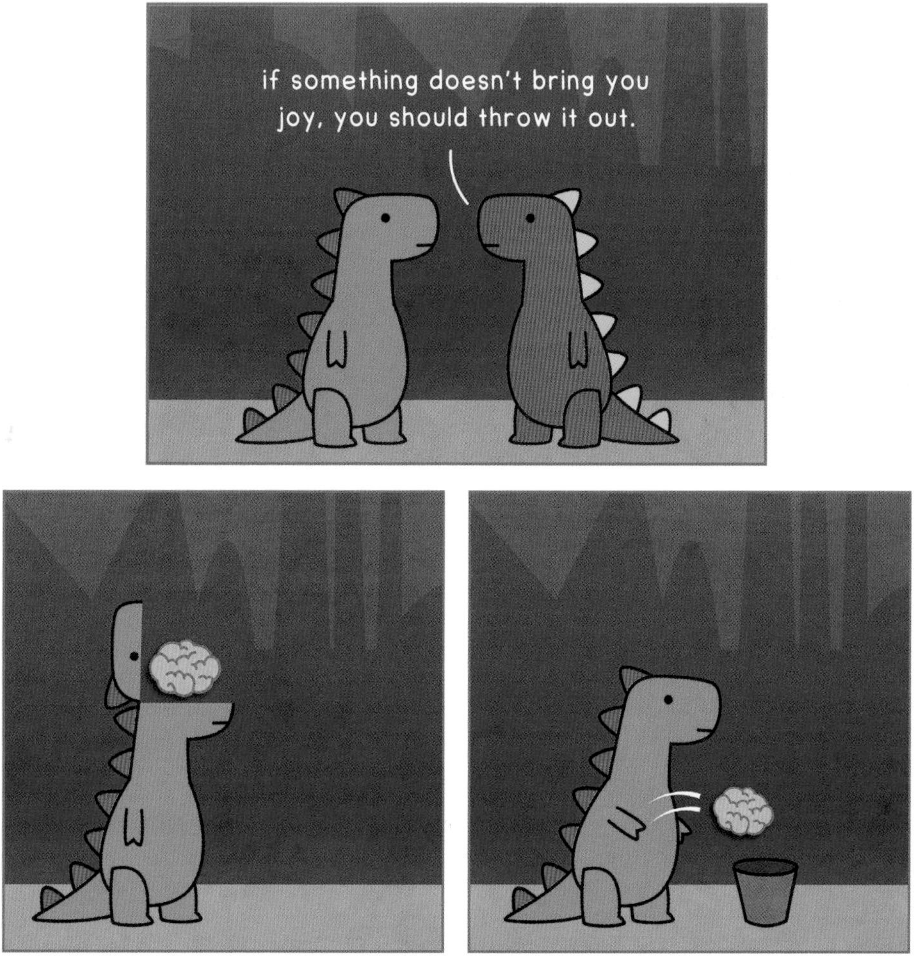
if something doesn't bring you joy, you should throw it out.

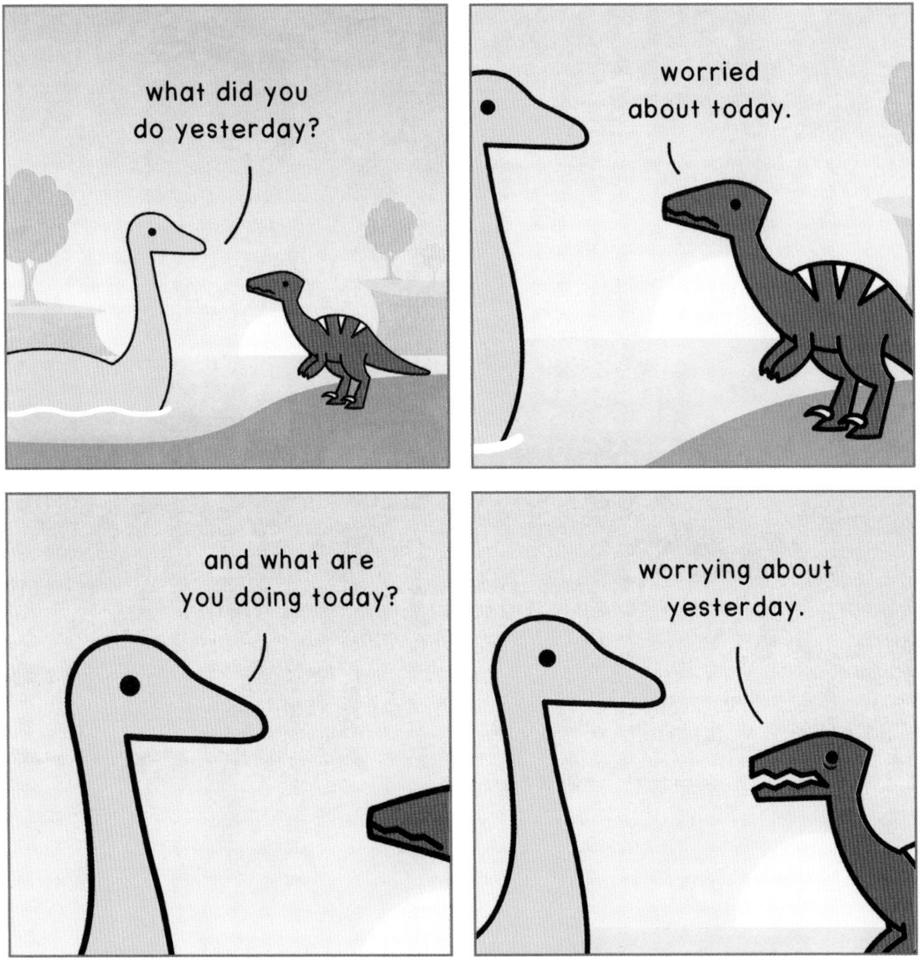
what did you do yesterday?
worried about today.
and what are you doing today?
worrying about yesterday.

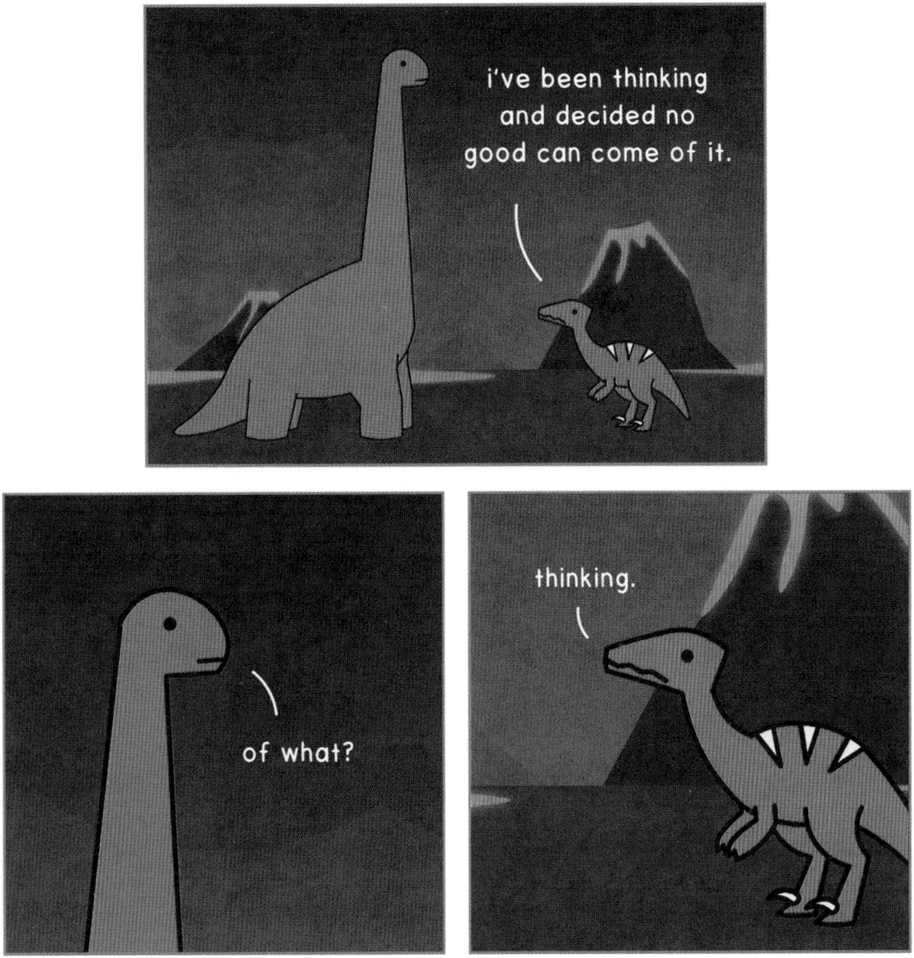
i've been thinking and decided no good can come of it.
of what?
thinking.

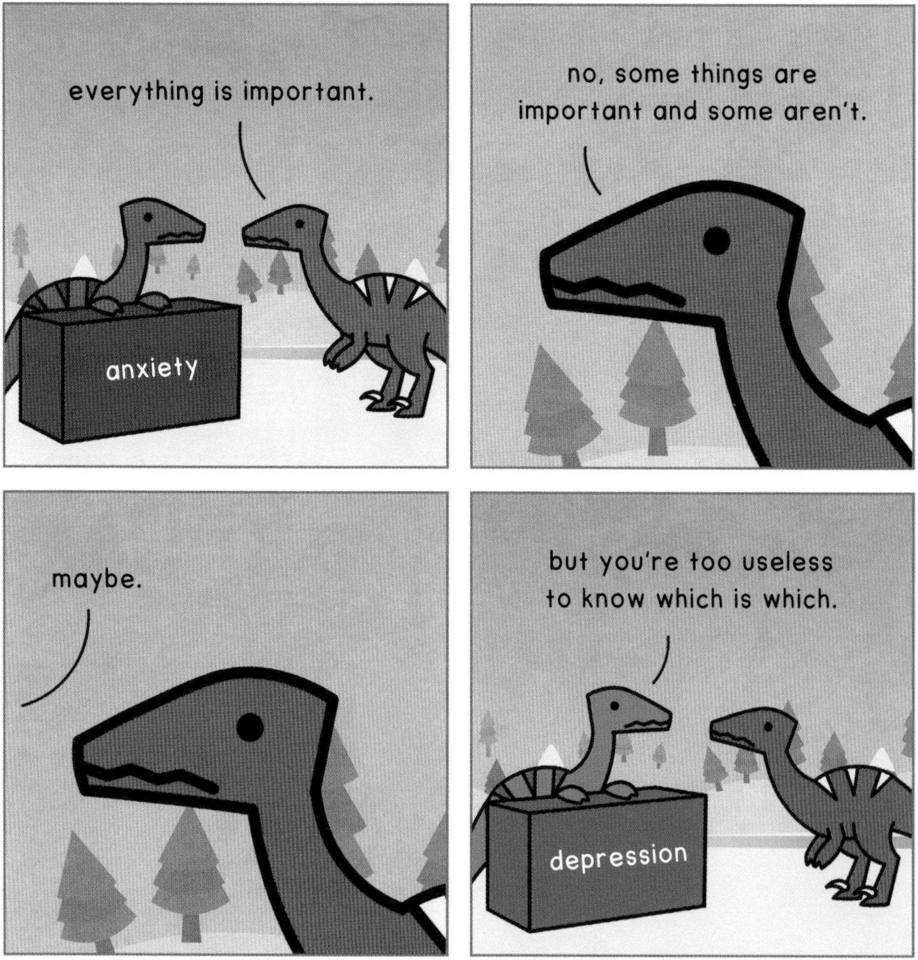
everything is important.
anxiety
no, some things are important and some aren't.
maybe.
but you're too useless to know which is which.
depression

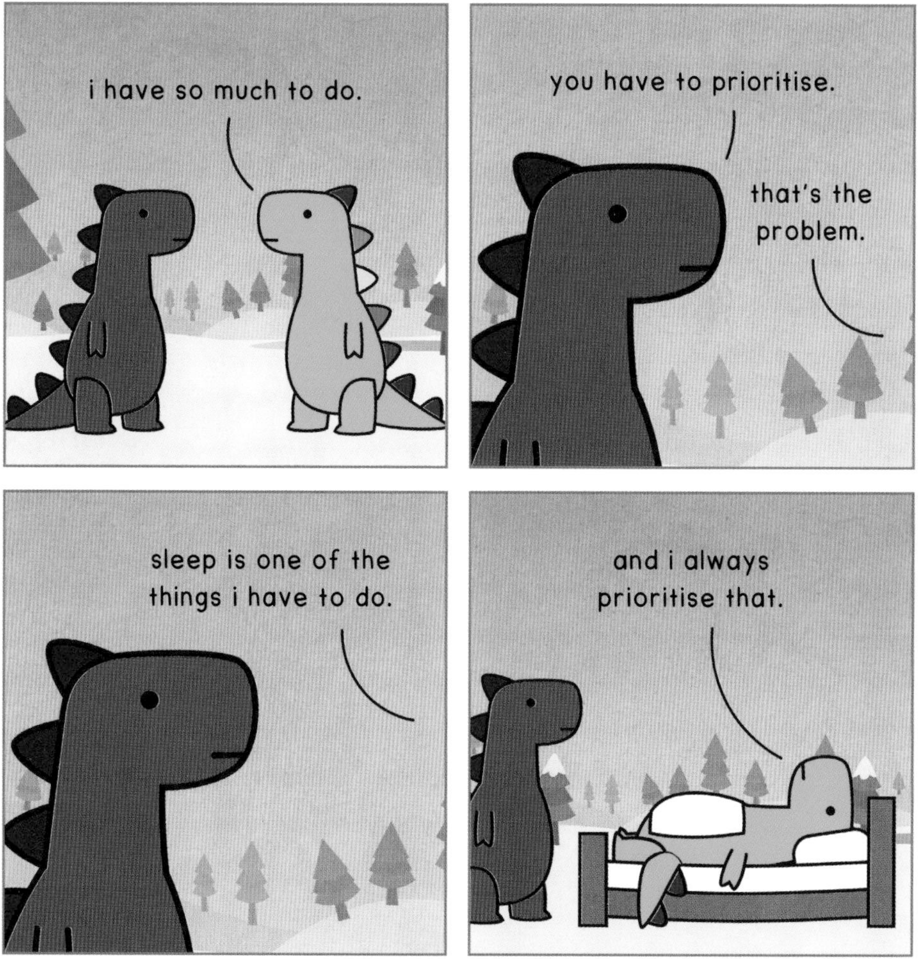
i have so much to do.
you have to prioritise.
that's the problem.
sleep is one of the things i have to do.
and i always prioritise that.

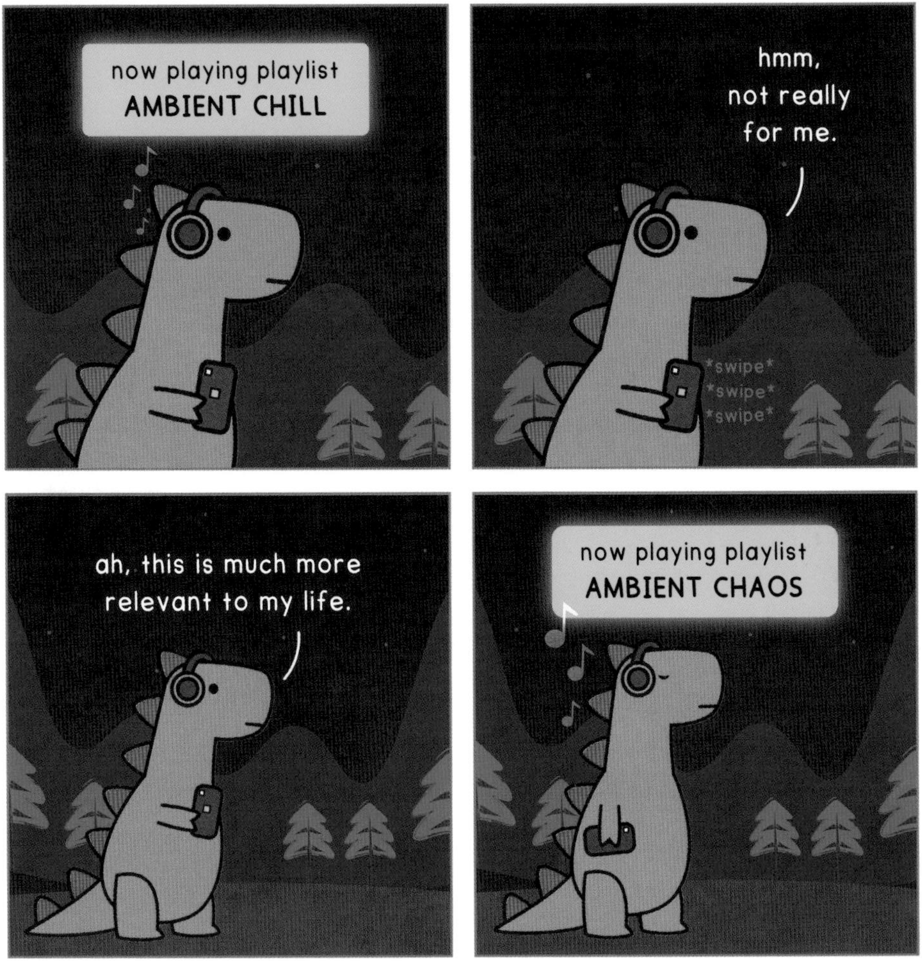
now playing playlist
AMBIENT CHILL
hmm, not really for me.
swipe
swipe
swipe
ah, this is much more relevant to my life.
now playing playlist
AMBIENT CHAOS

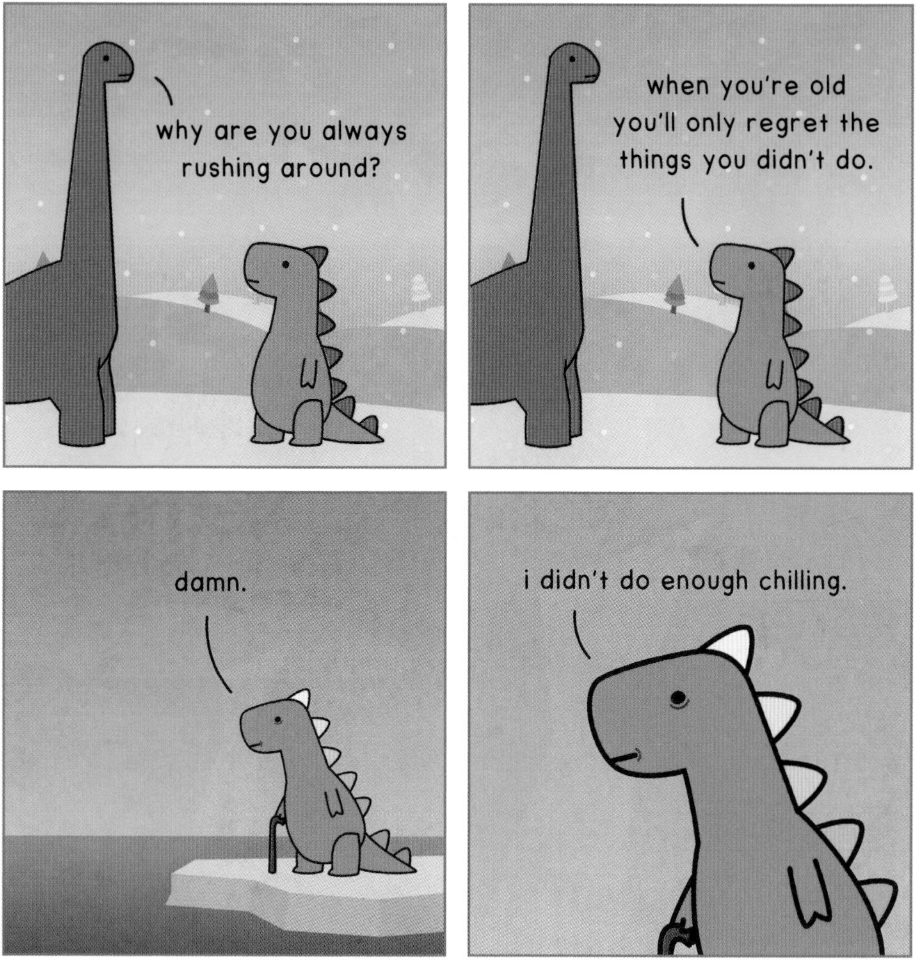
why are you always rushing around?
when you're old you'll only regret the things you didn't do.
damn.
i didn't do enough chilling.

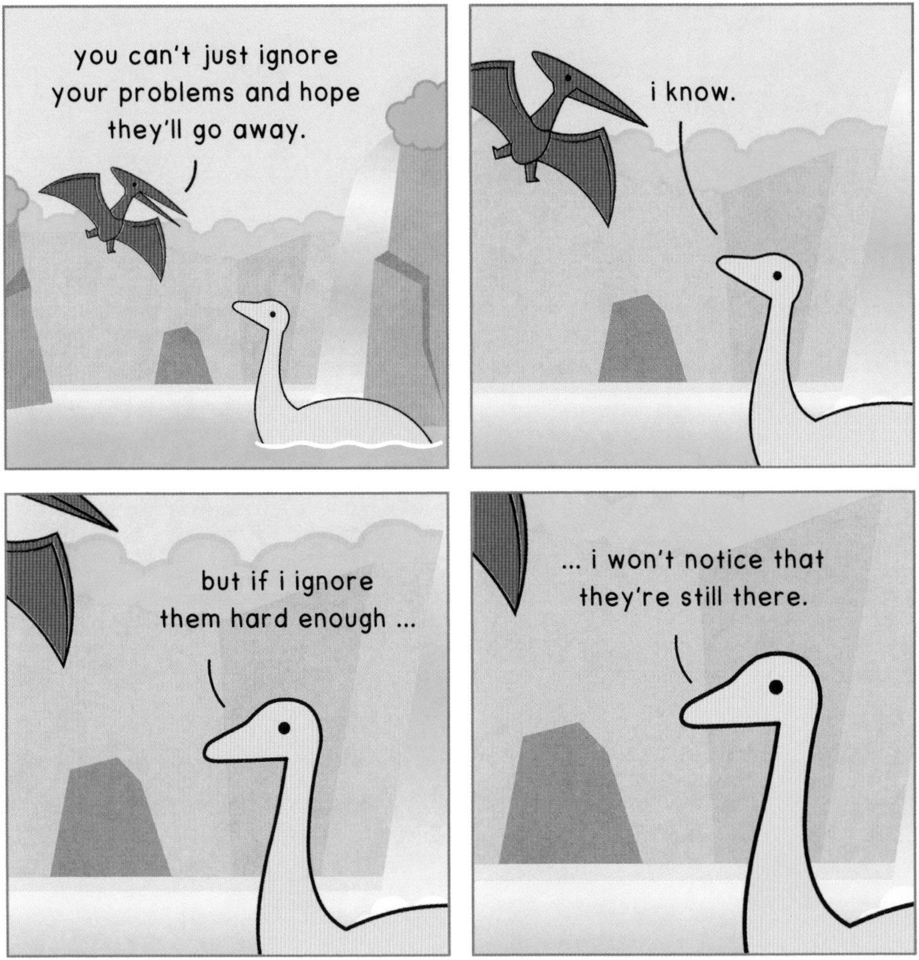
you can't just ignore your problems and hope they'll go away.
i know.
but if i ignore them hard enough ...
... i won't notice that they're still there.

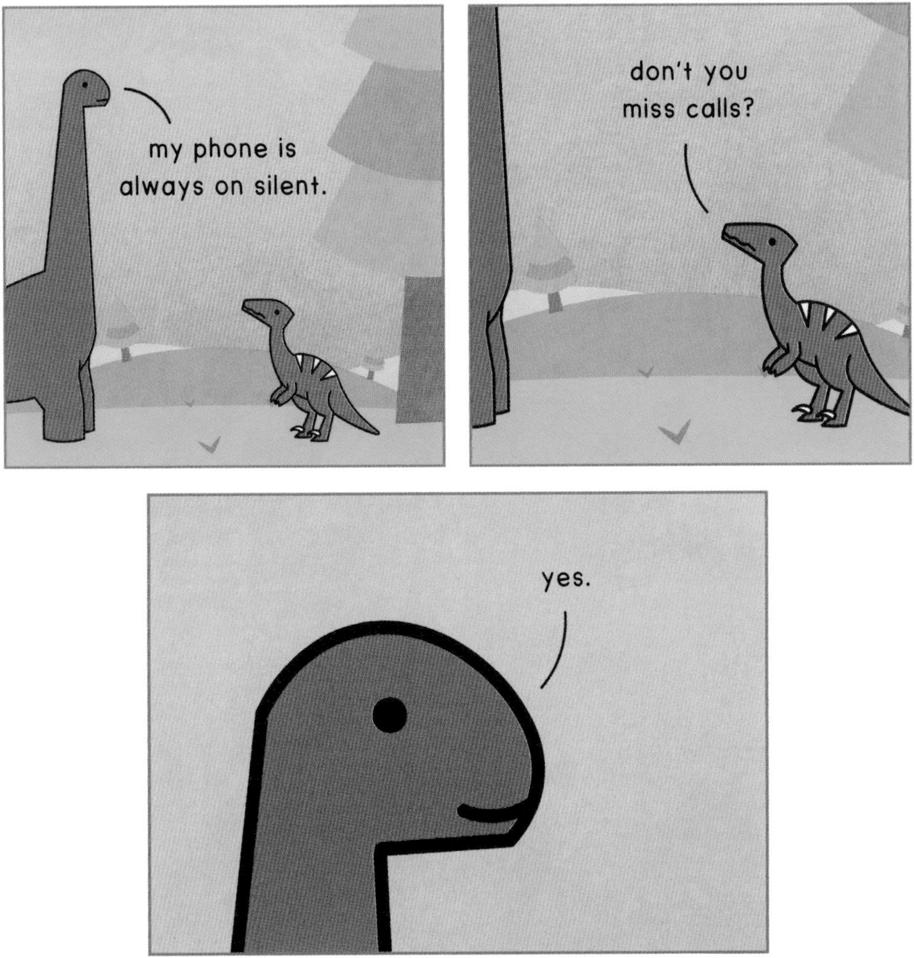
my phone is always on silent.
don't you miss calls?
yes.

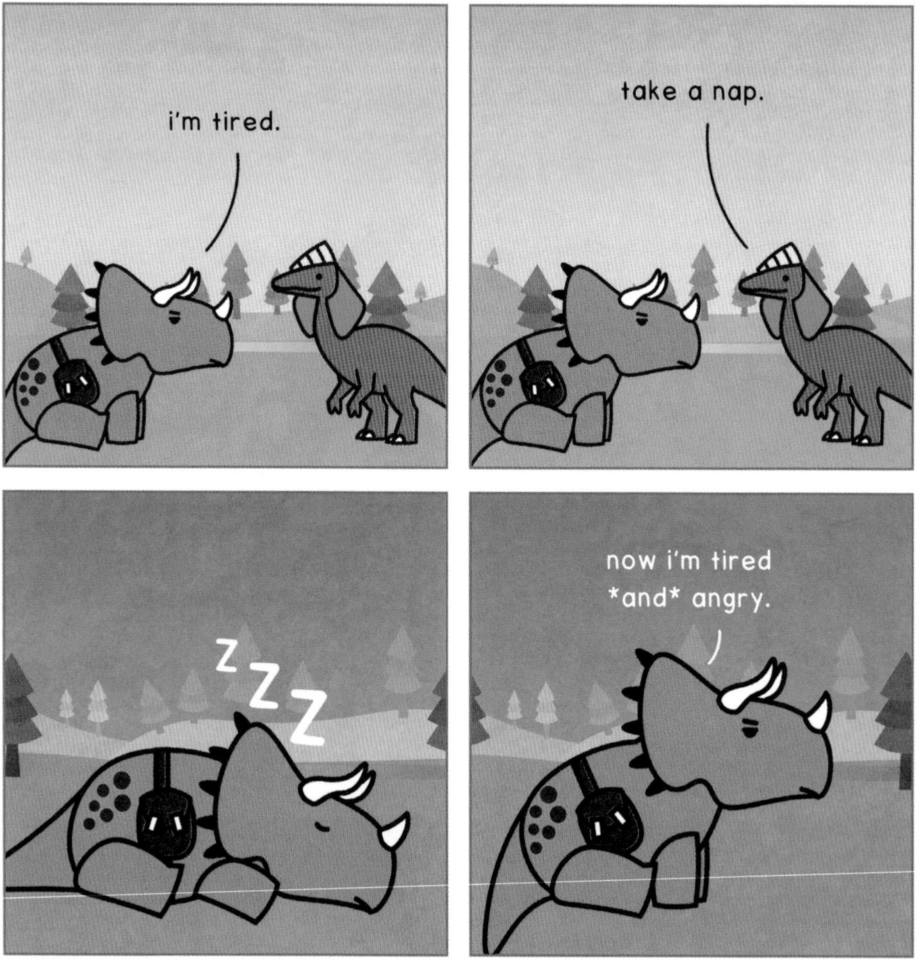
i'm tired.
take a nap.
Z Z Z
now i'm tired *and* angry.

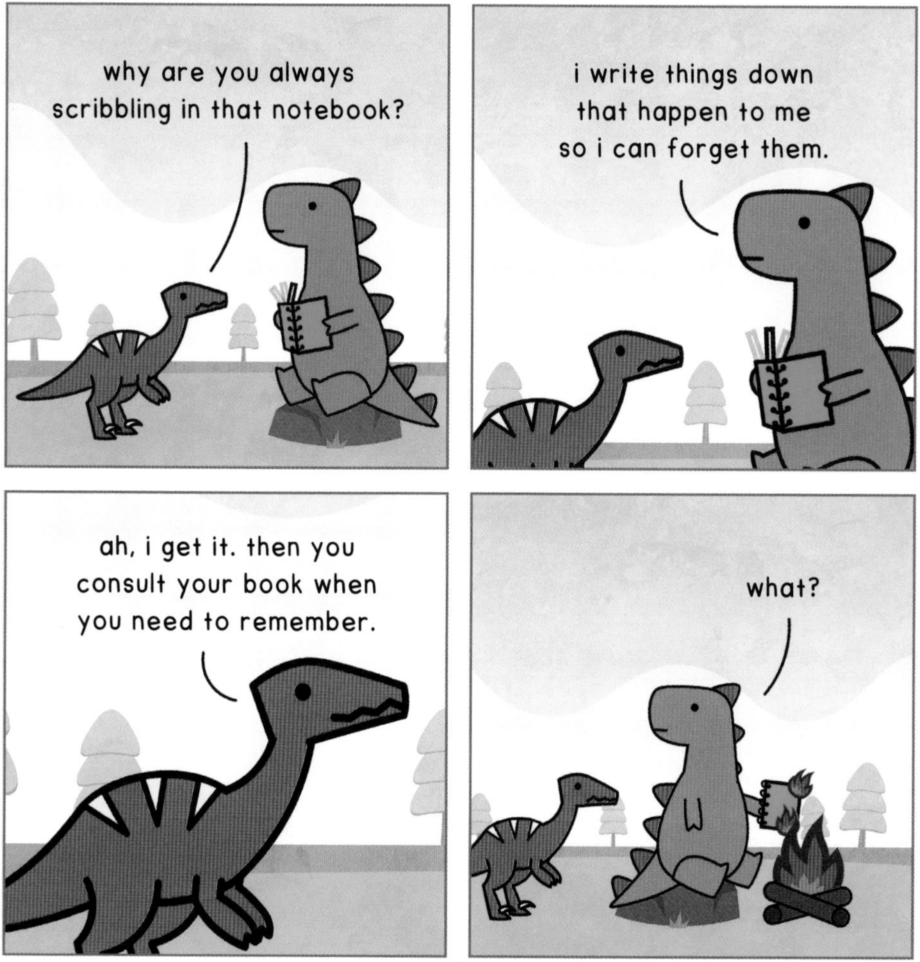
why are you always scribbling in that notebook?
i write things down that happen to me so i can forget them.
ah, i get it. then you consult your book when you need to remember.
what?

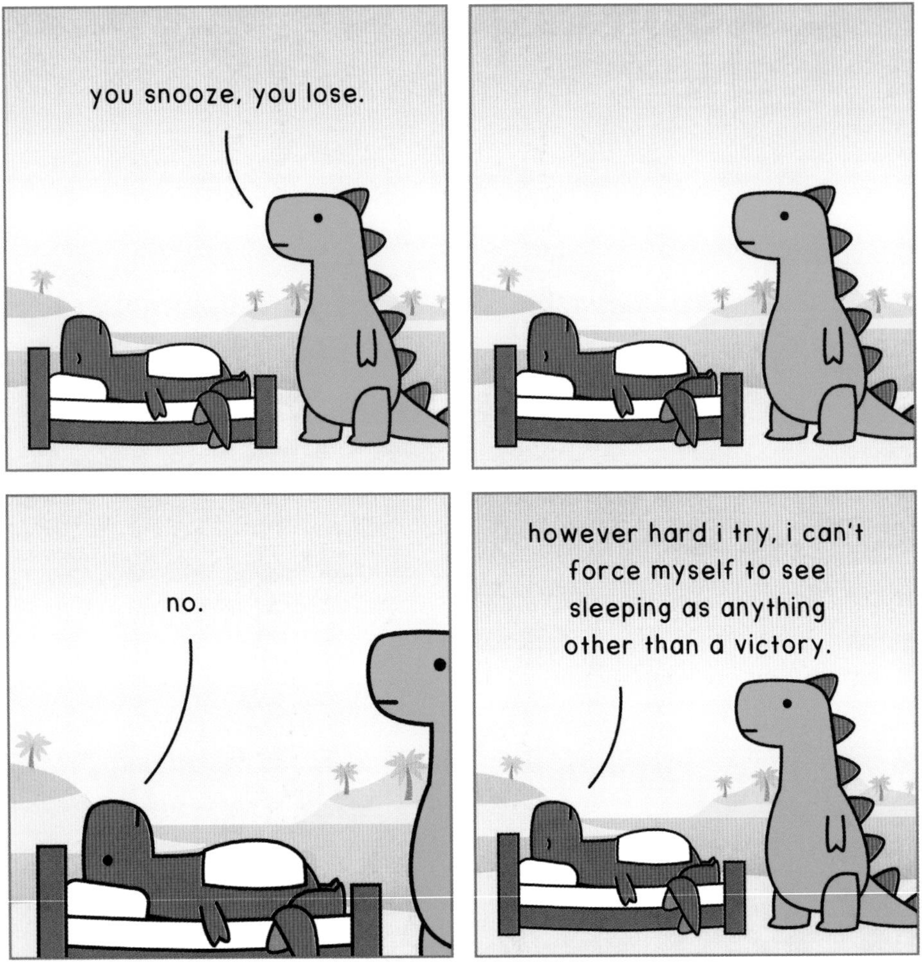
you snooze, you lose.
no.
however hard i try, i can't force myself to see sleeping as anything other than a victory.

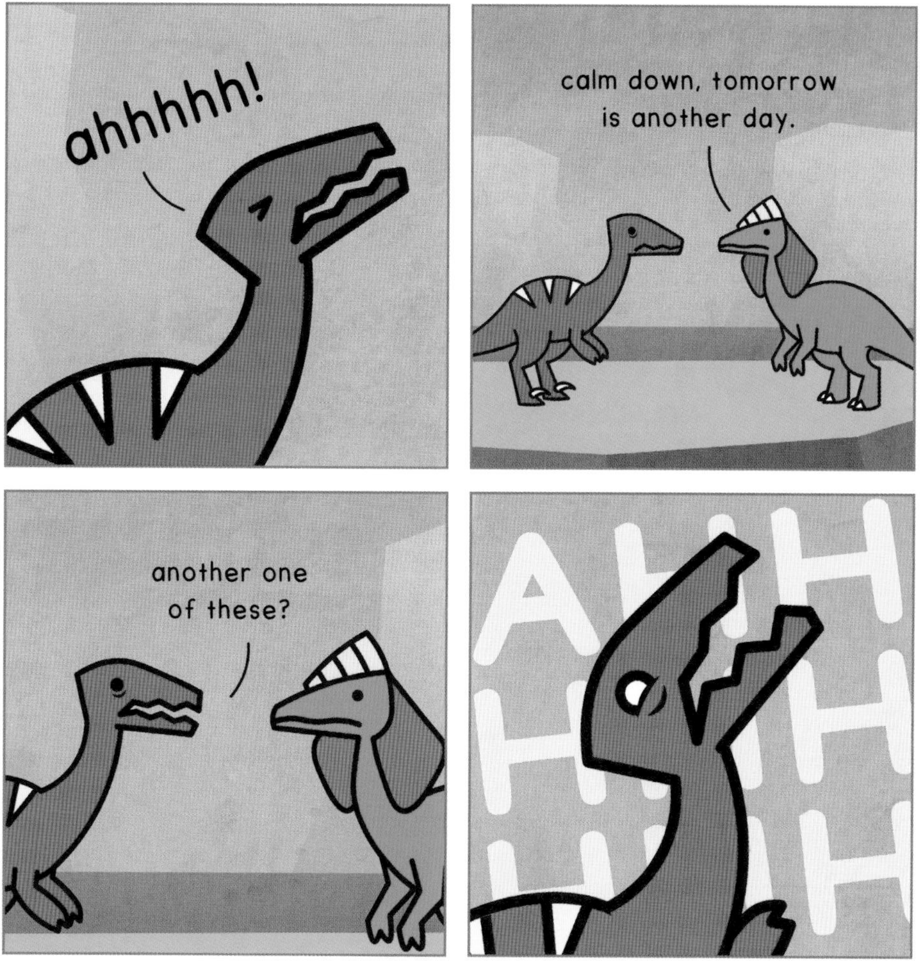
ahhhhh!
calm down, tomorrow is another day.
another one of these?

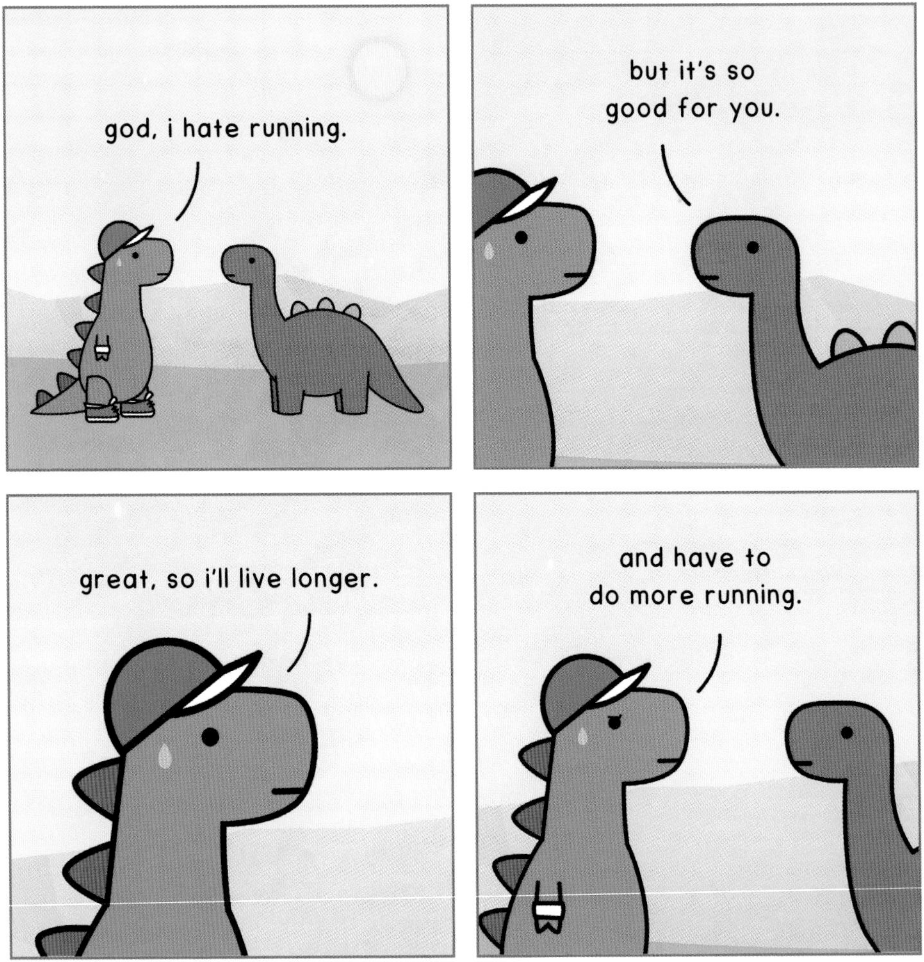
god, i hate running.
but it's so good for you.
great, so i'll live longer.
and have to do more running.

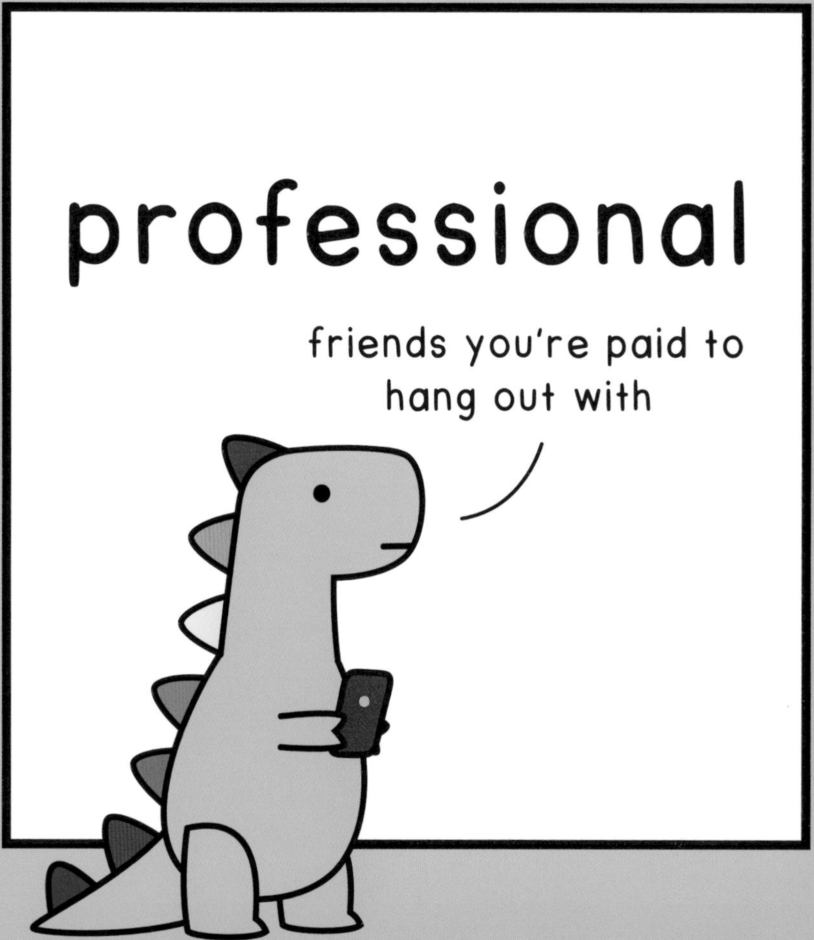
professional
friends you're paid to hang out with

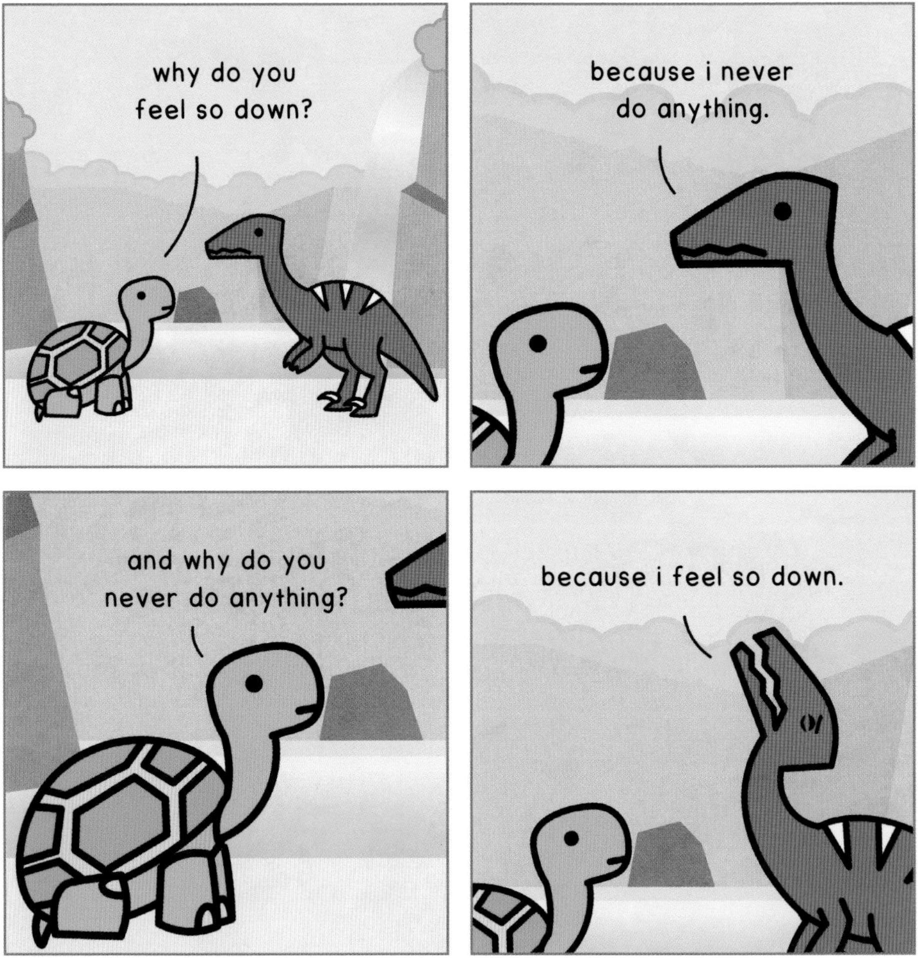
why do you
feel so down?
because i never
do anything.
and why do you
never do anything?
because i feel so down.

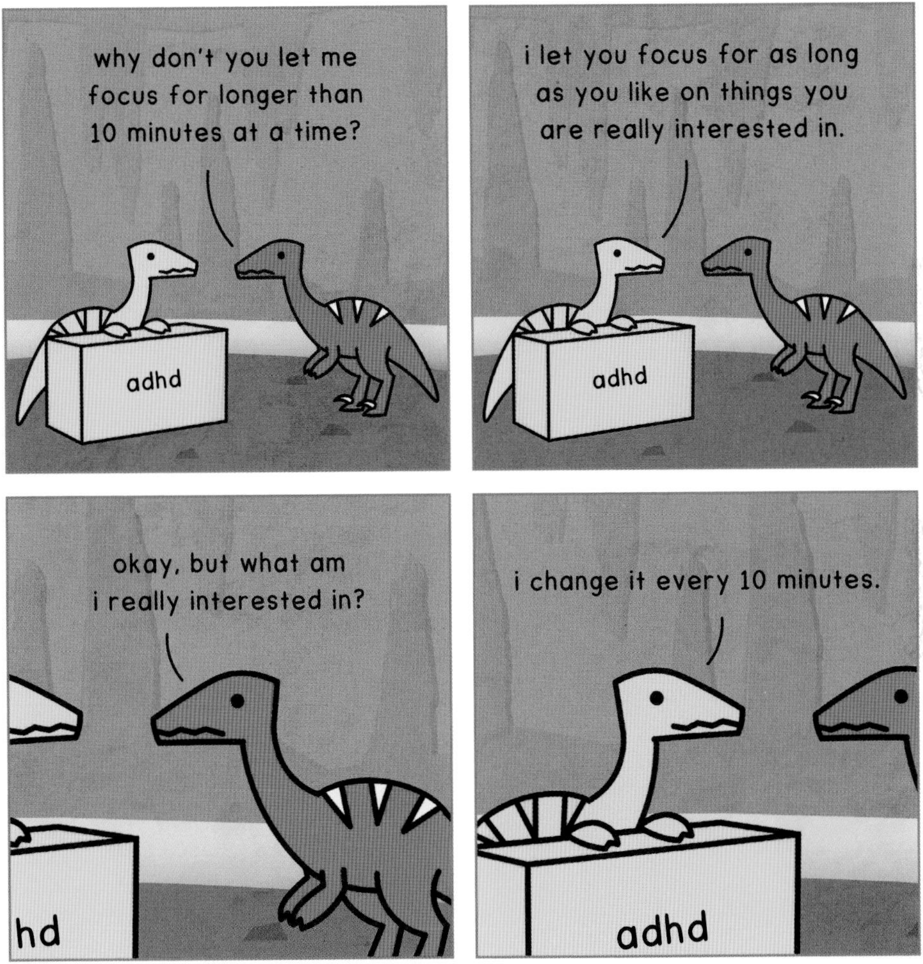

why don't you let me focus for longer than 10 minutes at a time?
adhd
i let you focus for as long as you like on things you are really interested in.
adhd
okay, but what am i really interested in?
hd
i change it every 10 minutes.
adhd

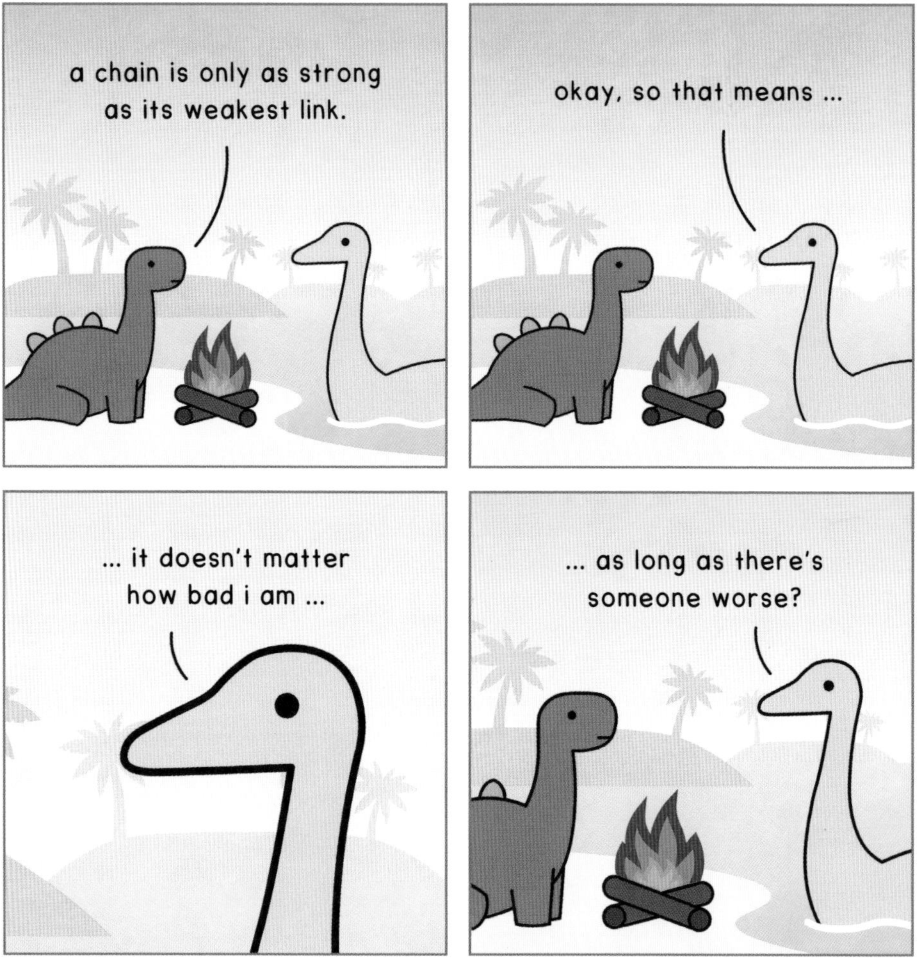
a chain is only as strong as its weakest link.
okay, so that means ...
... it doesn't matter how bad i am ...
... as long as there's someone worse?

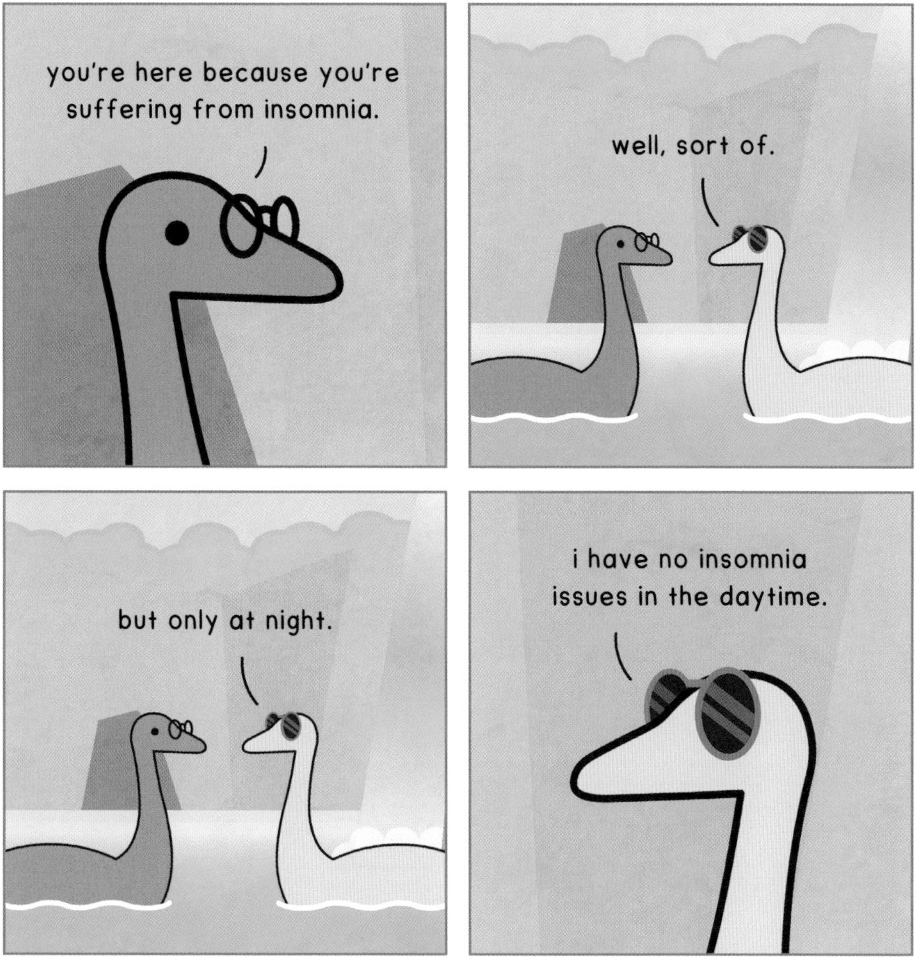
you're here because you're suffering from insomnia.
well, sort of.
but only at night.
i have no insomnia issues in the daytime.

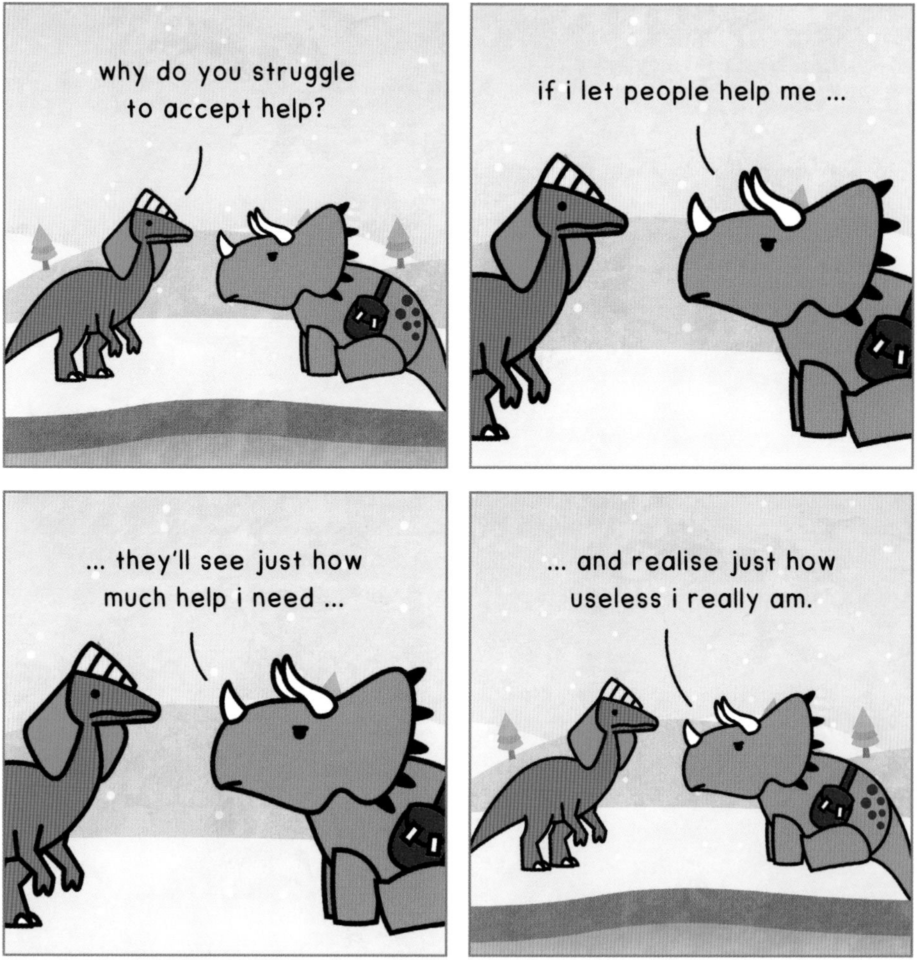
why do you struggle to accept help?
if i let people help me ...
... they'll see just how much help i need ...
... and realise just how useless i really am.

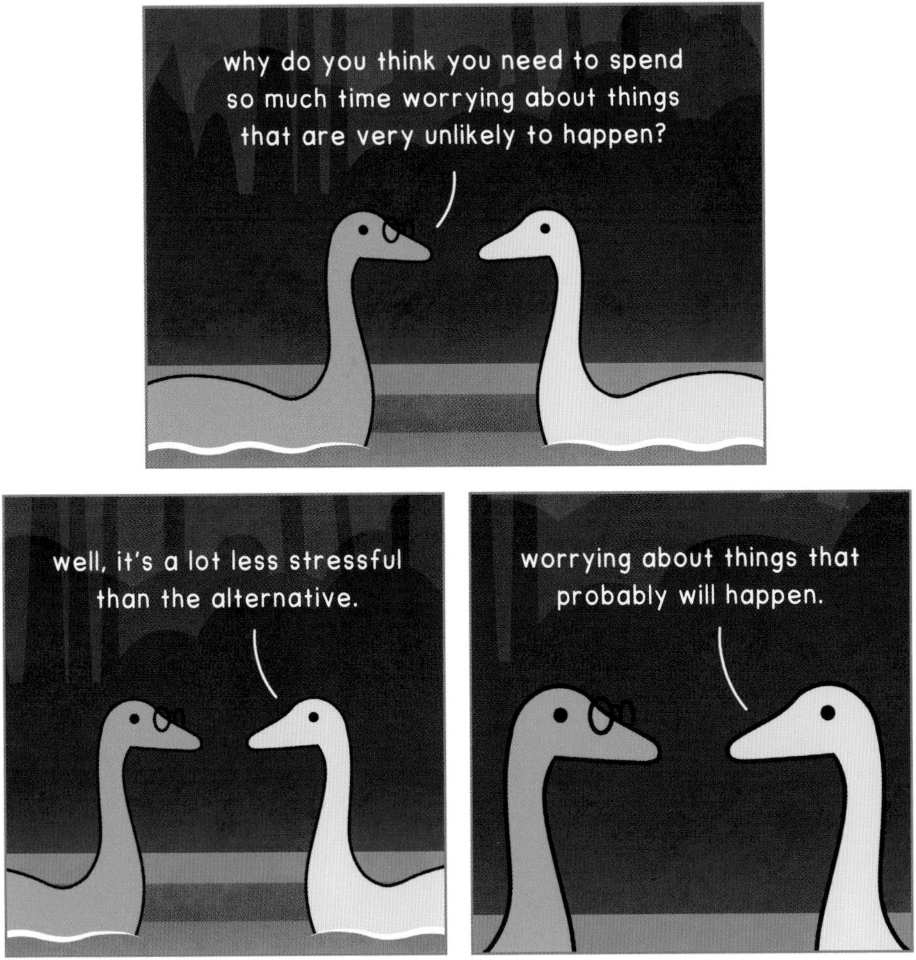
why do you think you need to spend so much time worrying about things that are very unlikely to happen?
well, it's a lot less stressful than the alternative.
worrying about things that probably will happen.

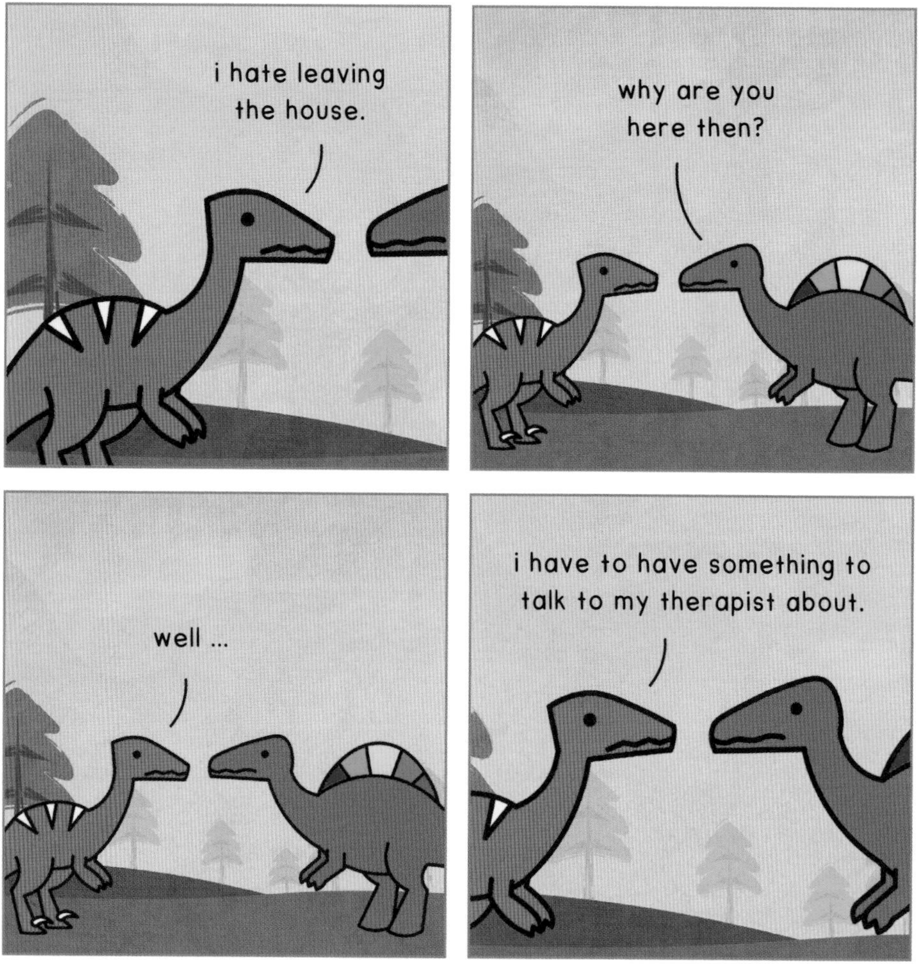
i hate leaving the house.
why are you here then?
well ...
i have to have something to talk to my therapist about.

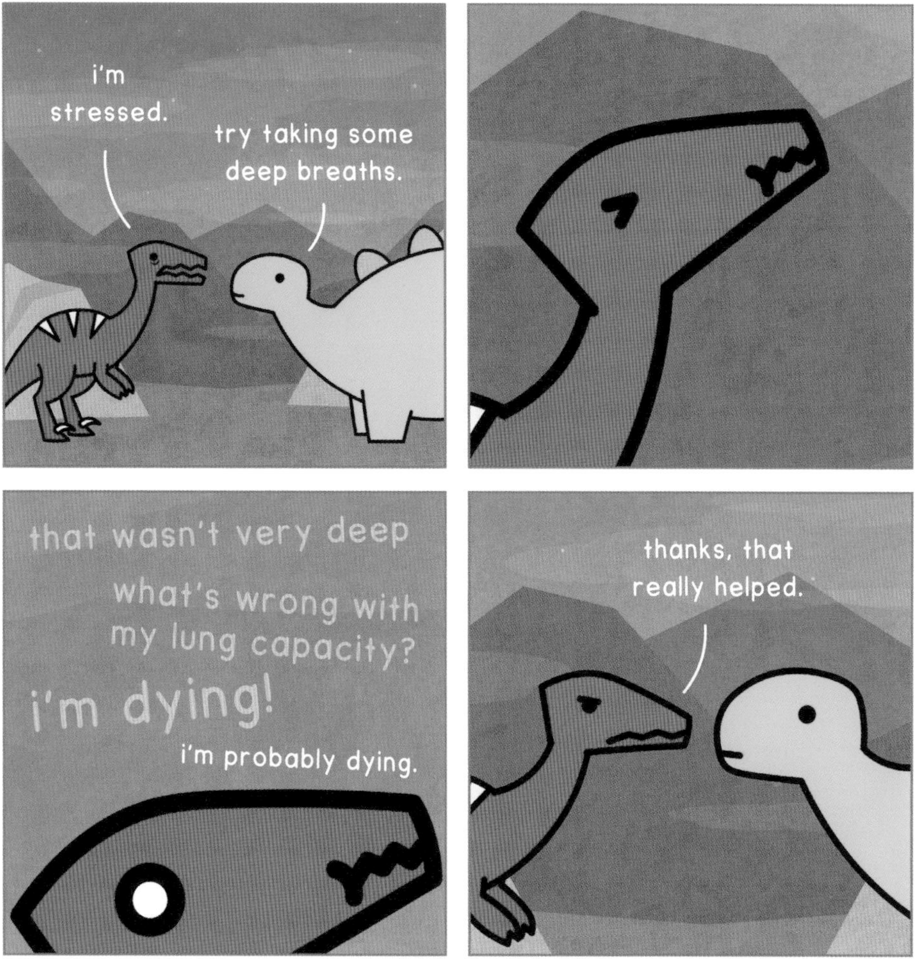
i'm stressed.
try taking some deep breaths.
that wasn't very deep
what's wrong with my lung capacity?
i'm dying!
i'm probably dying.
thanks, that really helped.

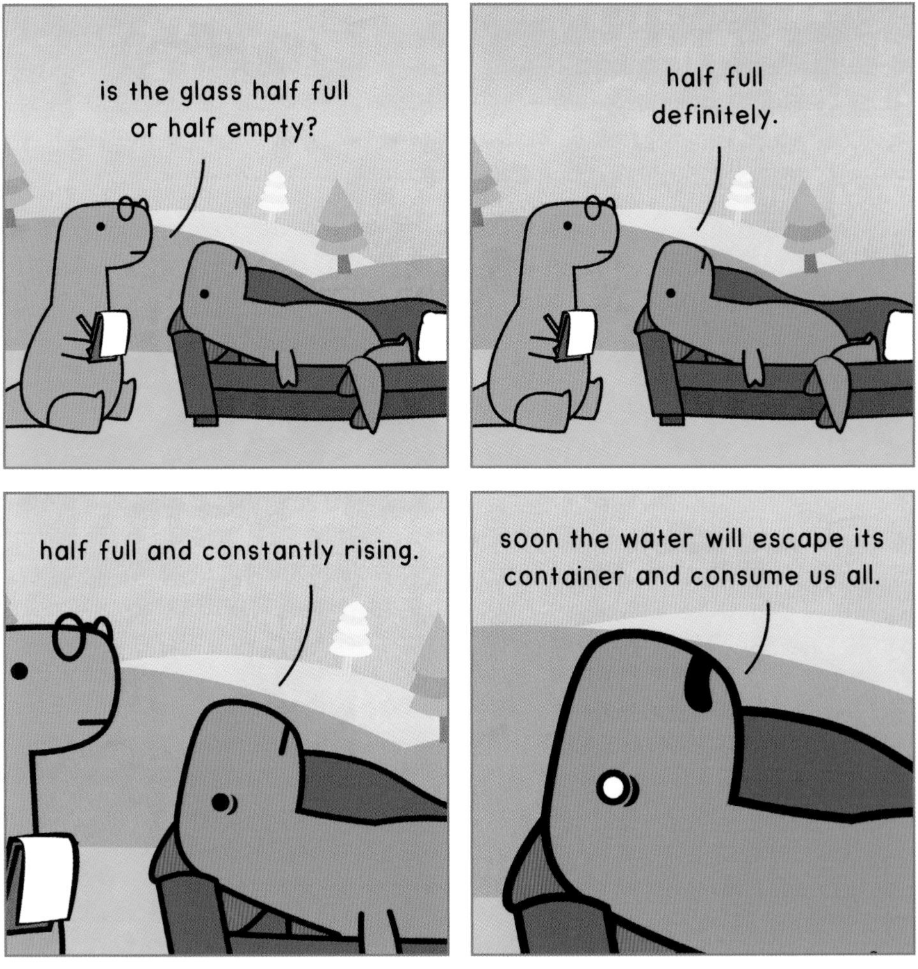
is the glass half full
or half empty?
half full
definitely.
half full and constantly rising.
soon the water will escape its
container and consume us all.

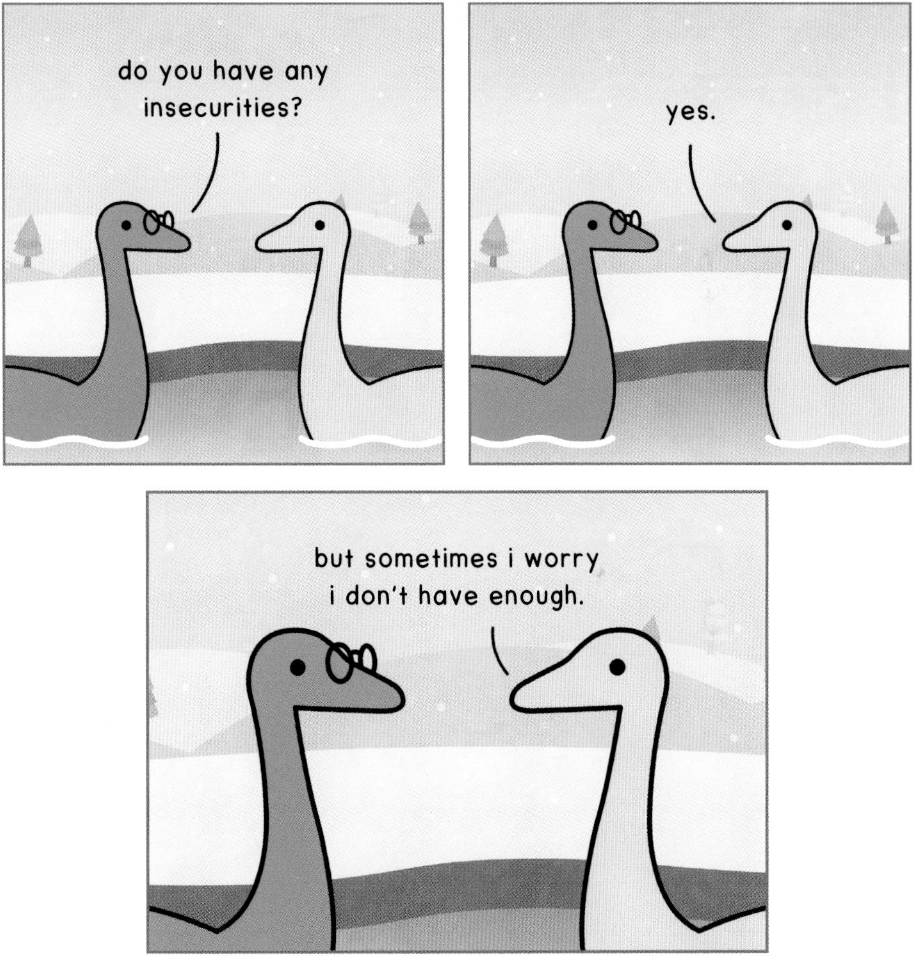
do you have any insecurities?
yes.
but sometimes i worry i don't have enough.

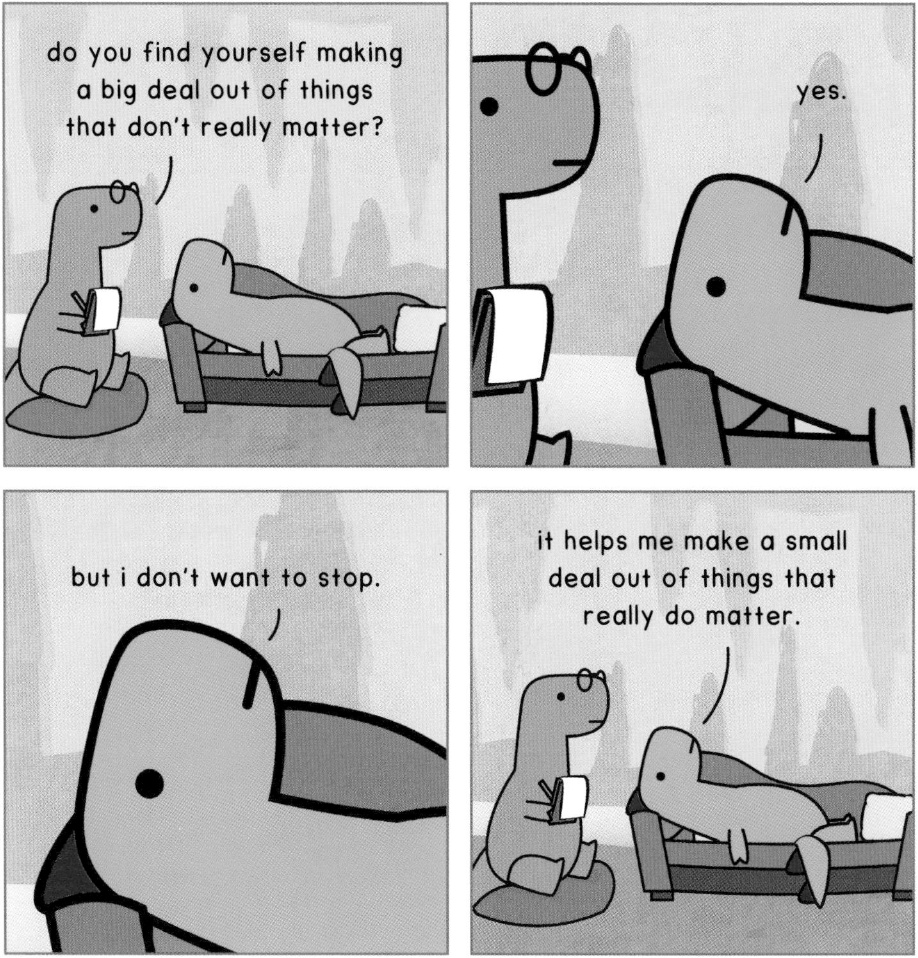
do you find yourself making a big deal out of things that don't really matter?
yes.
but i don't want to stop.
it helps me make a small deal out of things that really do matter.

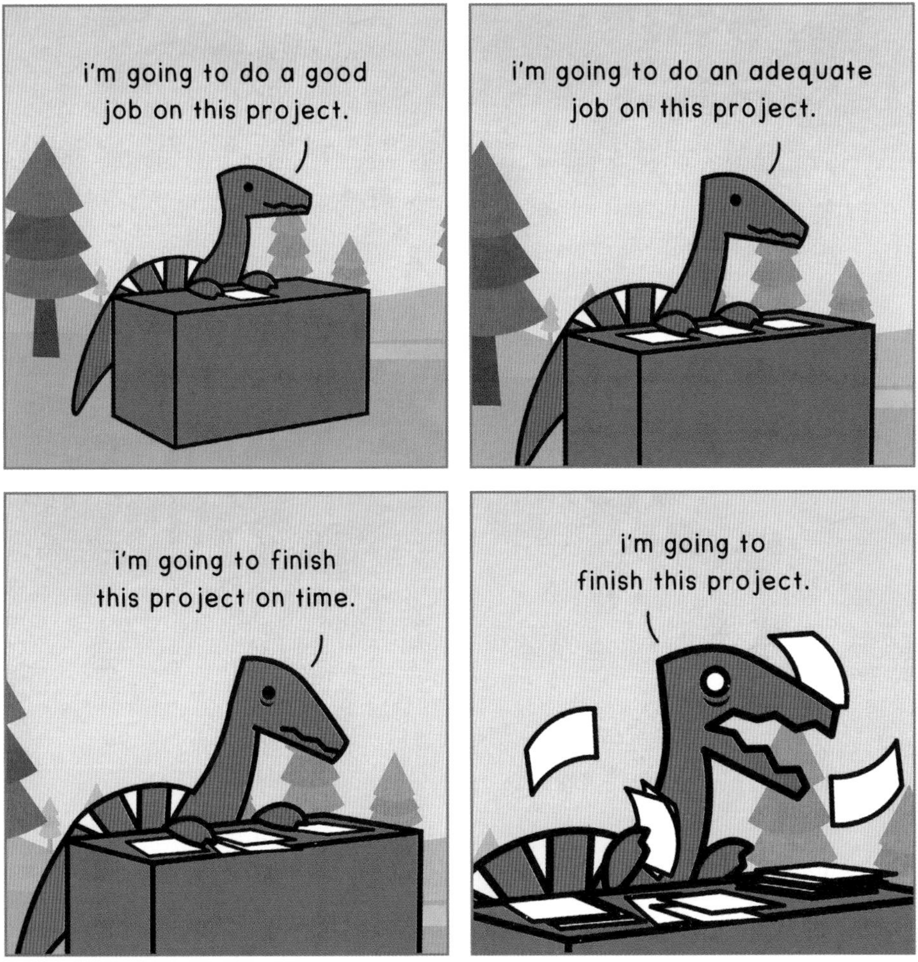
i'm going to do a good job on this project.
i'm going to do an adequate job on this project.
i'm going to finish this project on time.
i'm going to finish this project.

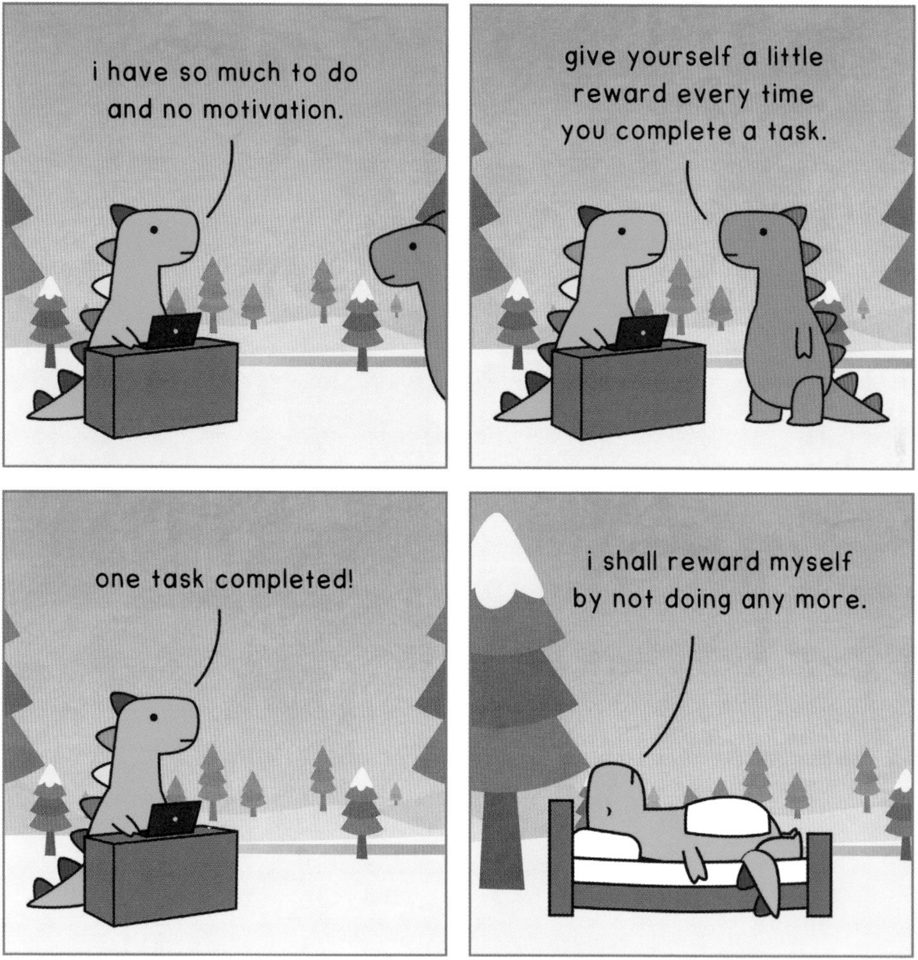
i have so much to do and no motivation.
give yourself a little reward every time you complete a task.
one task completed!
i shall reward myself by not doing any more.

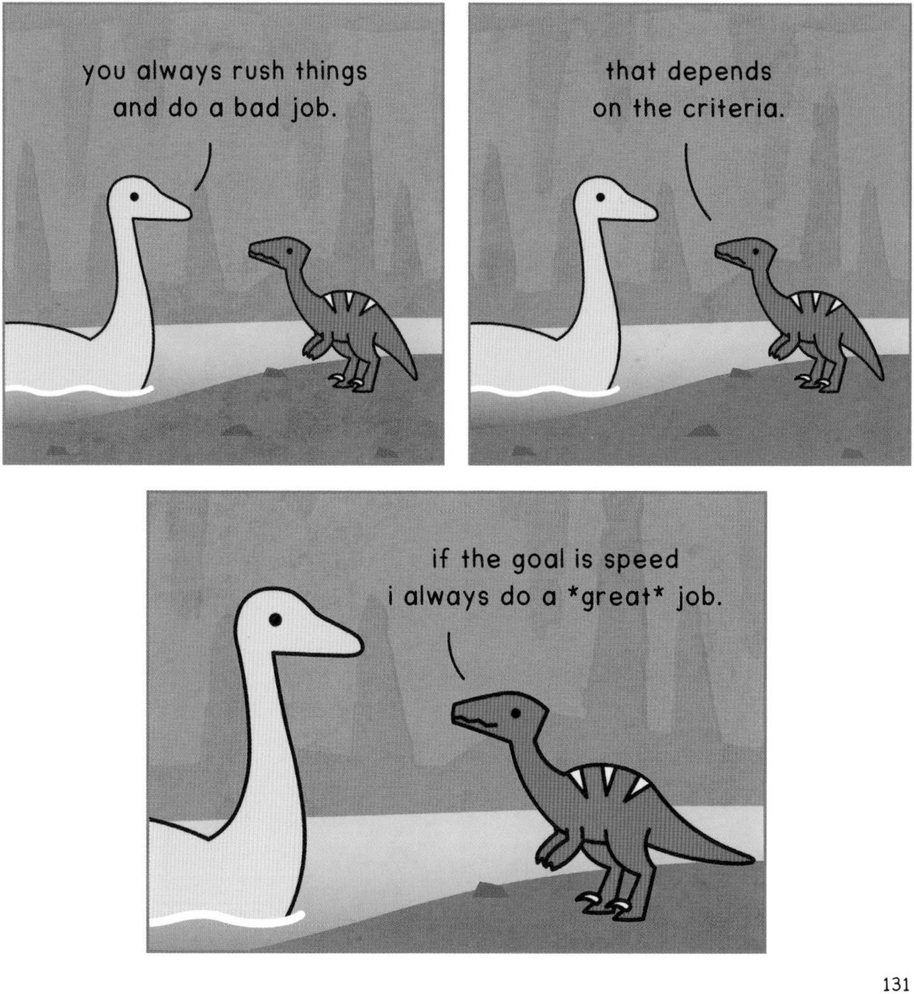
you always rush things and do a bad job.
that depends on the criteria.
if the goal is speed i always do a *great* job.

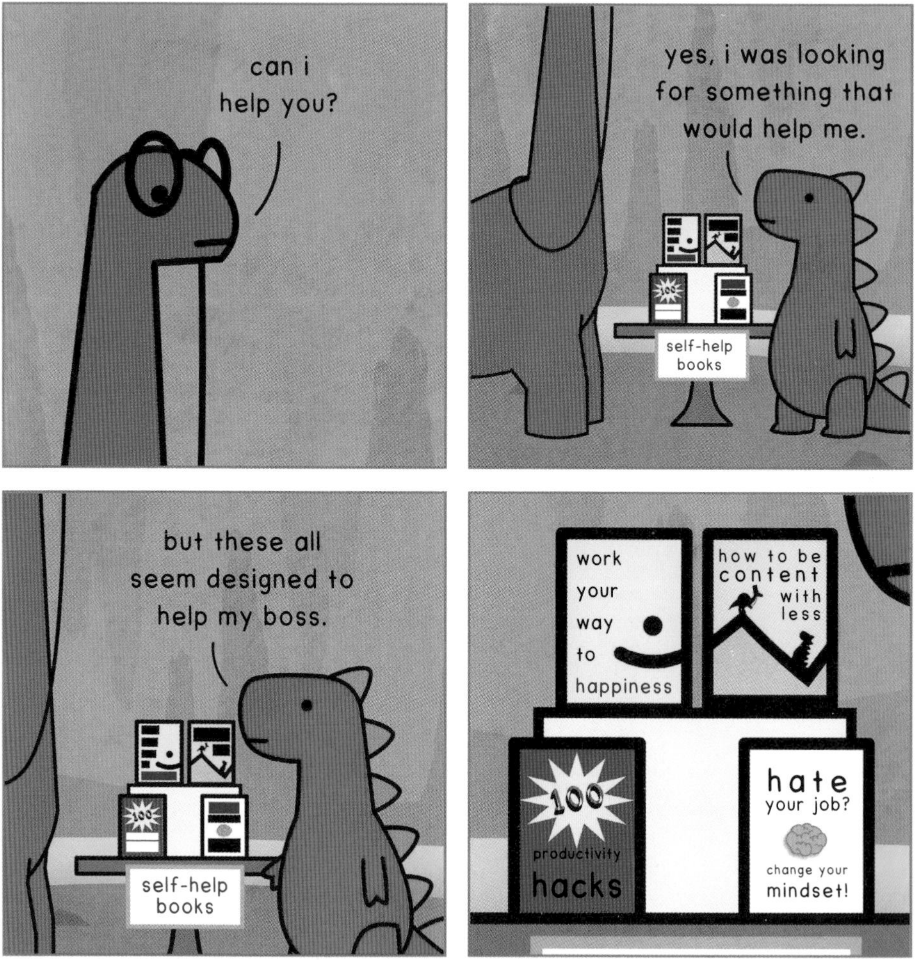
can i help you?
yes, i was looking for something that would help me.
self-help books
but these all seem designed to help my boss.
self-help books
work your way to happiness
how to be content with less
100 productivity hacks
hate your job? change your mindset!

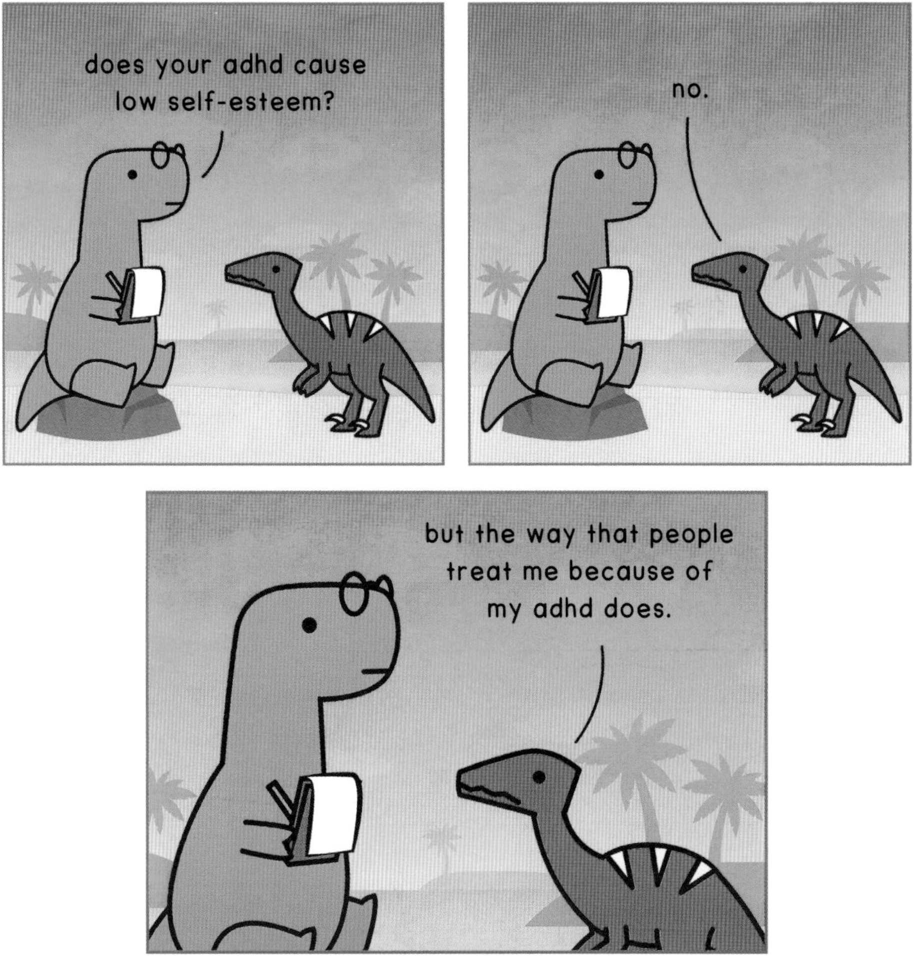
does your adhd cause
low self-esteem?
no.
but the way that people
treat me because of
my adhd does.

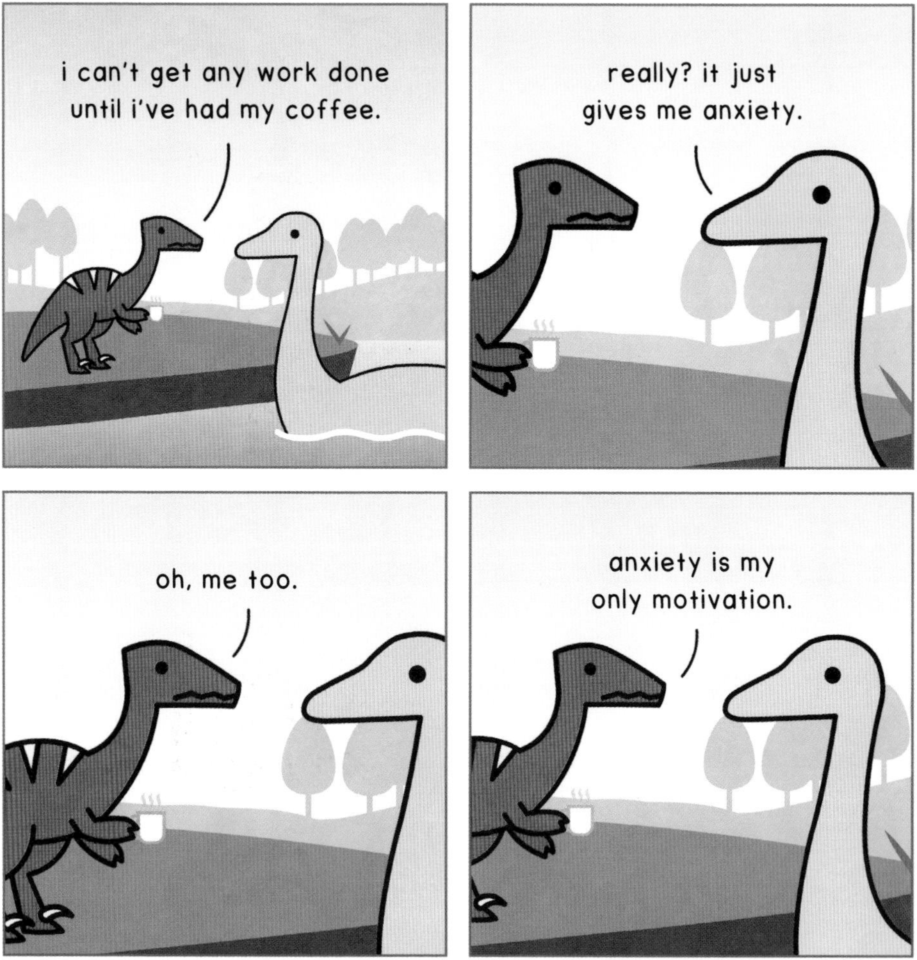
i can't get any work done until i've had my coffee.
really? it just gives me anxiety.
oh, me too.
anxiety is my only motivation.

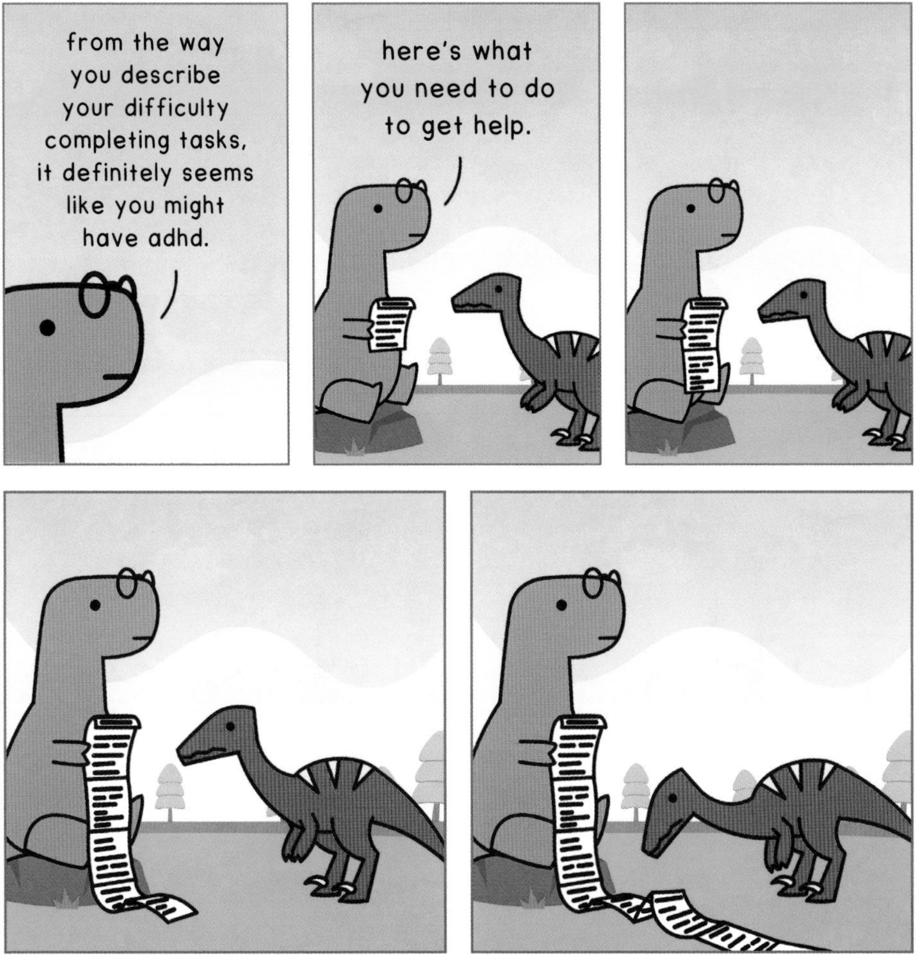
from the way you describe your difficulty completing tasks, it definitely seems like you might have adhd.
here's what you need to do to get help.

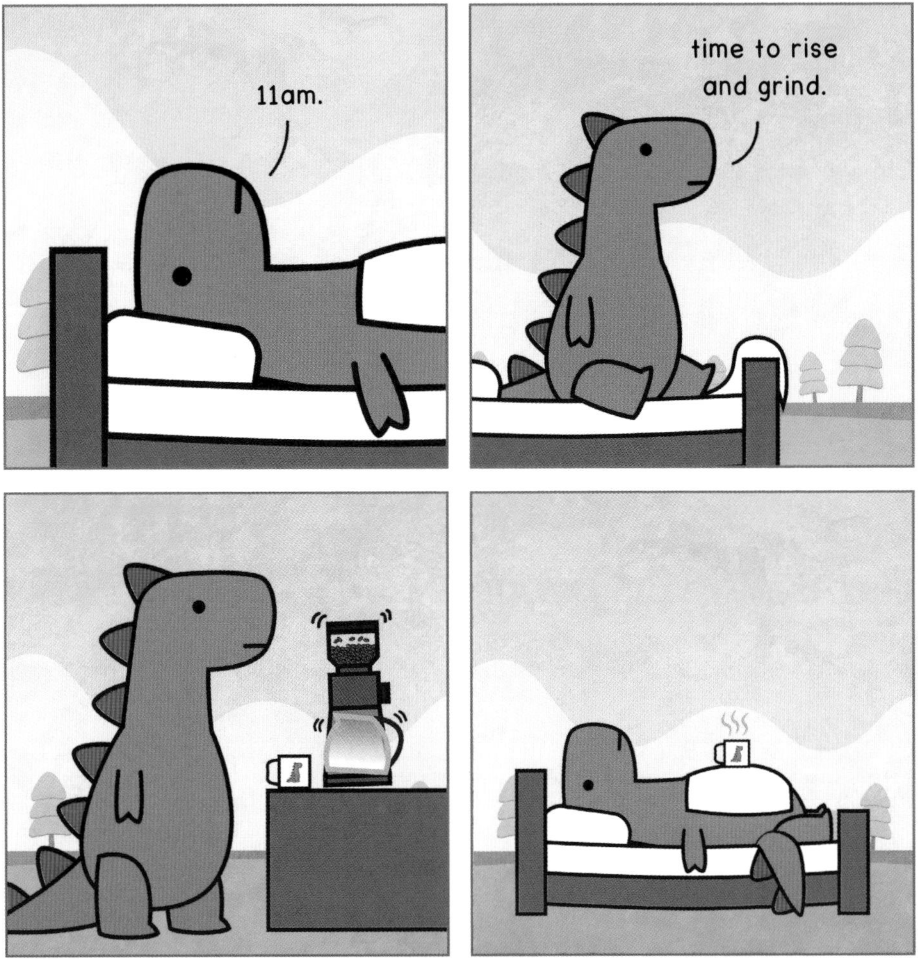
11am.
time to rise and grind.

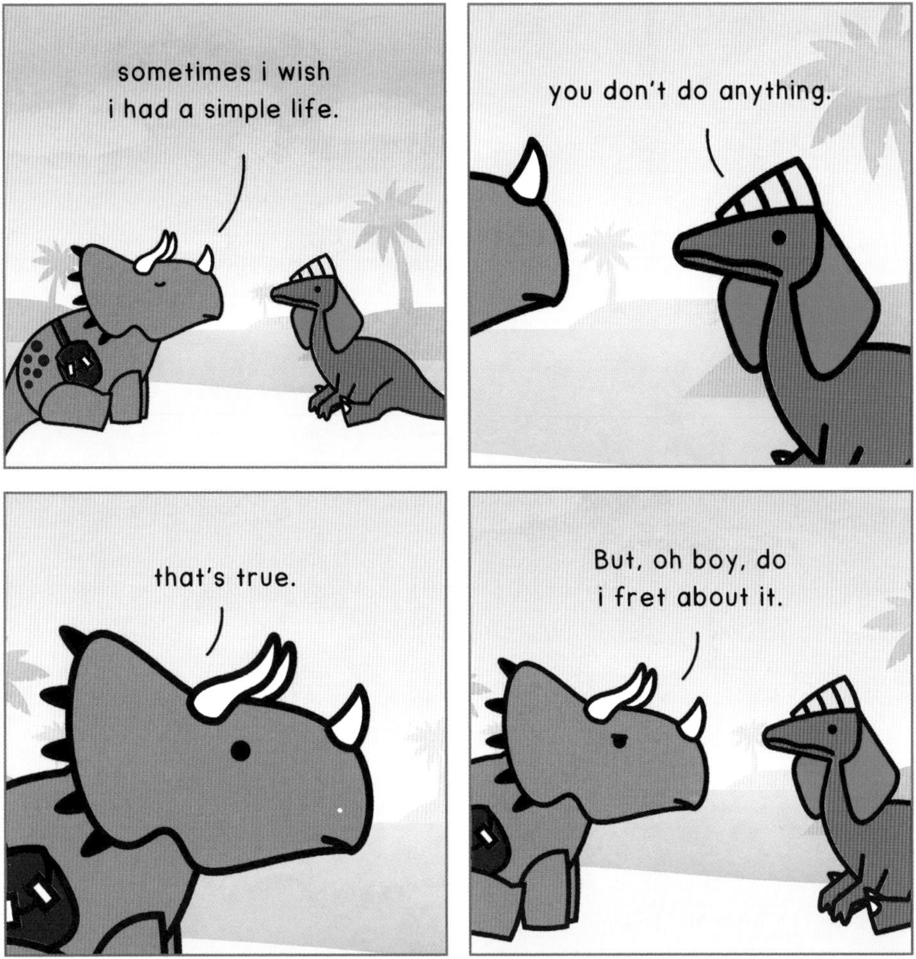
sometimes i wish
i had a simple life.
you don't do anything.
that's true.
But, oh boy, do
i fret about it.

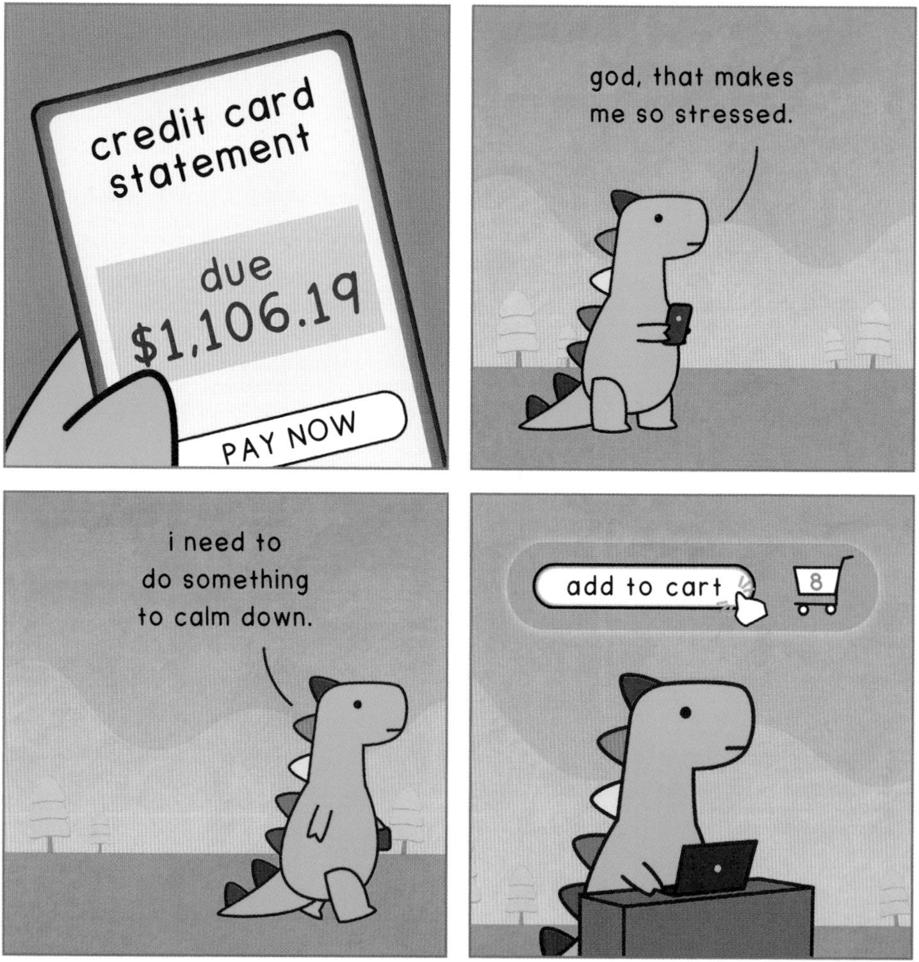
credit card statement
due $1,106.19
PAY NOW
god, that makes me so stressed.
i need to do something to calm down.
add to cart
8

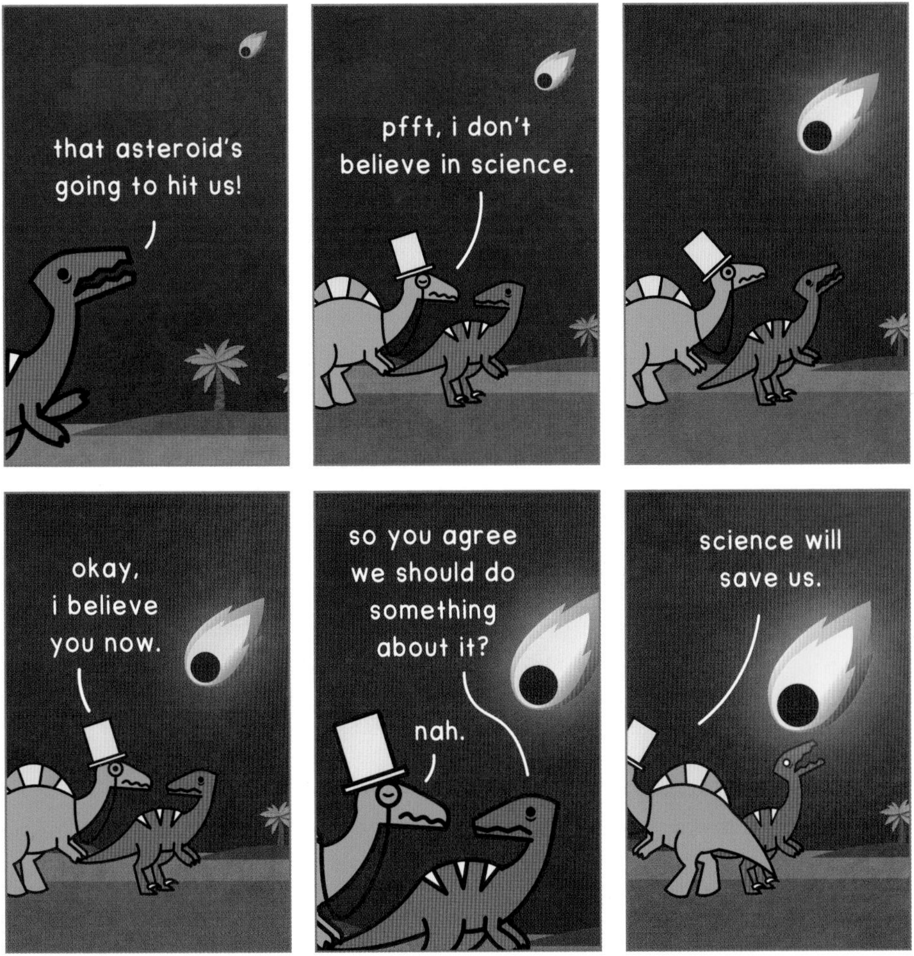
that asteroid's going to hit us!
pfft, i don't believe in science.
okay, i believe you now.
so you agree we should do something about it?
nah.
science will save us.

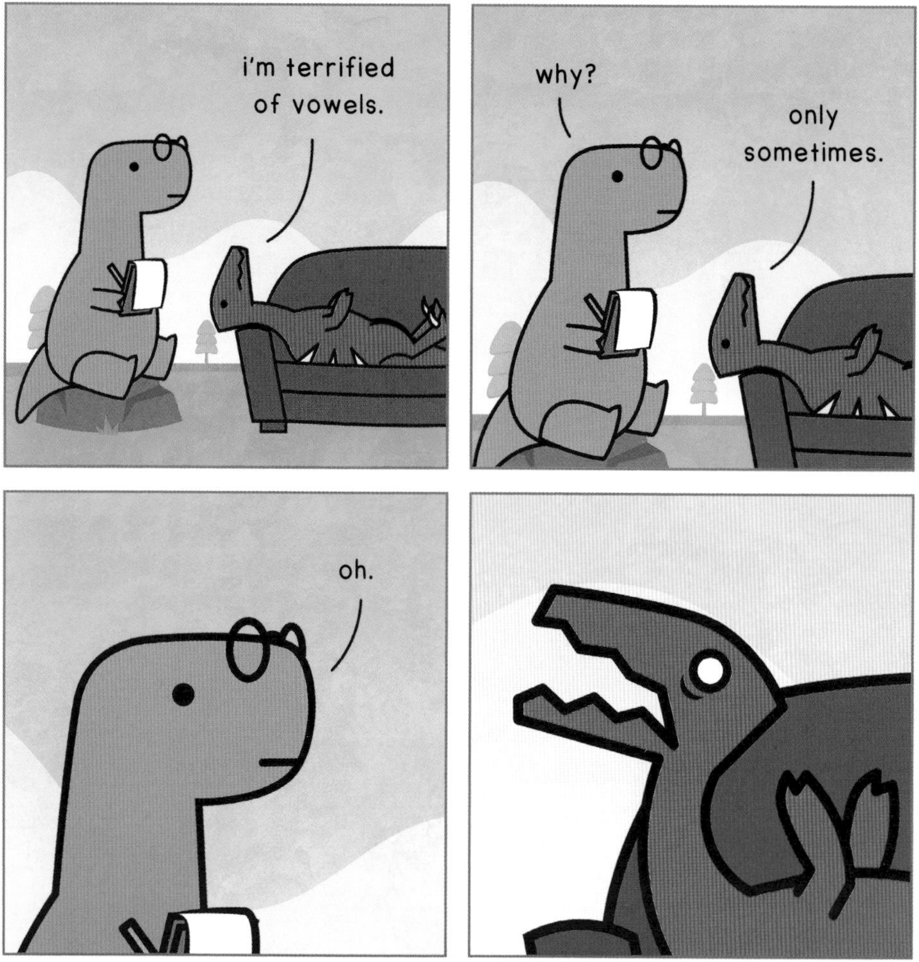
i'm terrified of vowels.
why?
only sometimes.
oh.

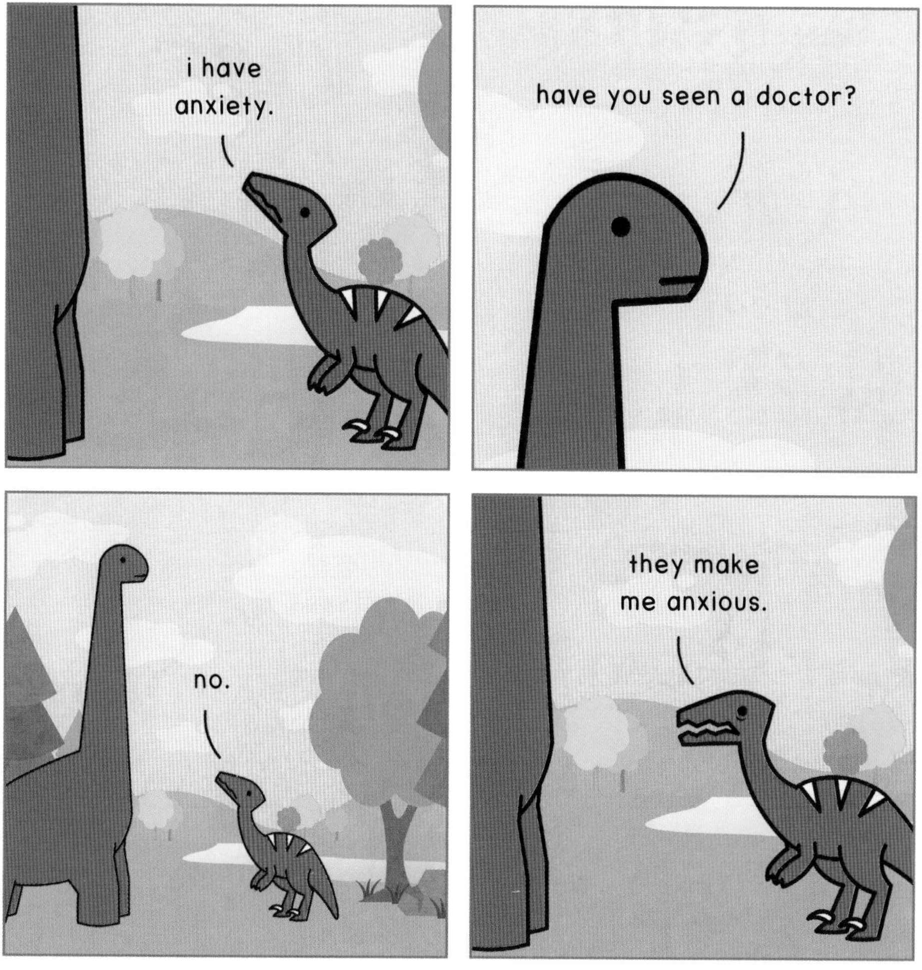
i have anxiety.
have you seen a doctor?
no.
they make me anxious.

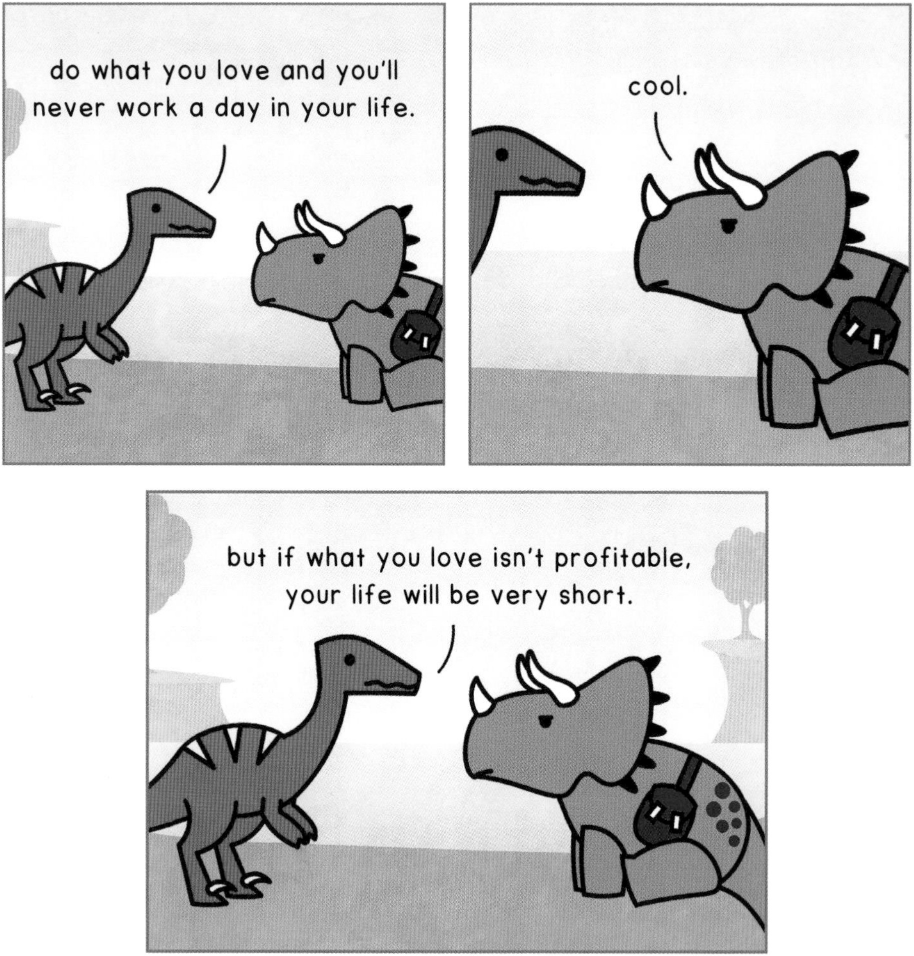
do what you love and you'll never work a day in your life.
cool.
but if what you love isn't profitable, your life will be very short.

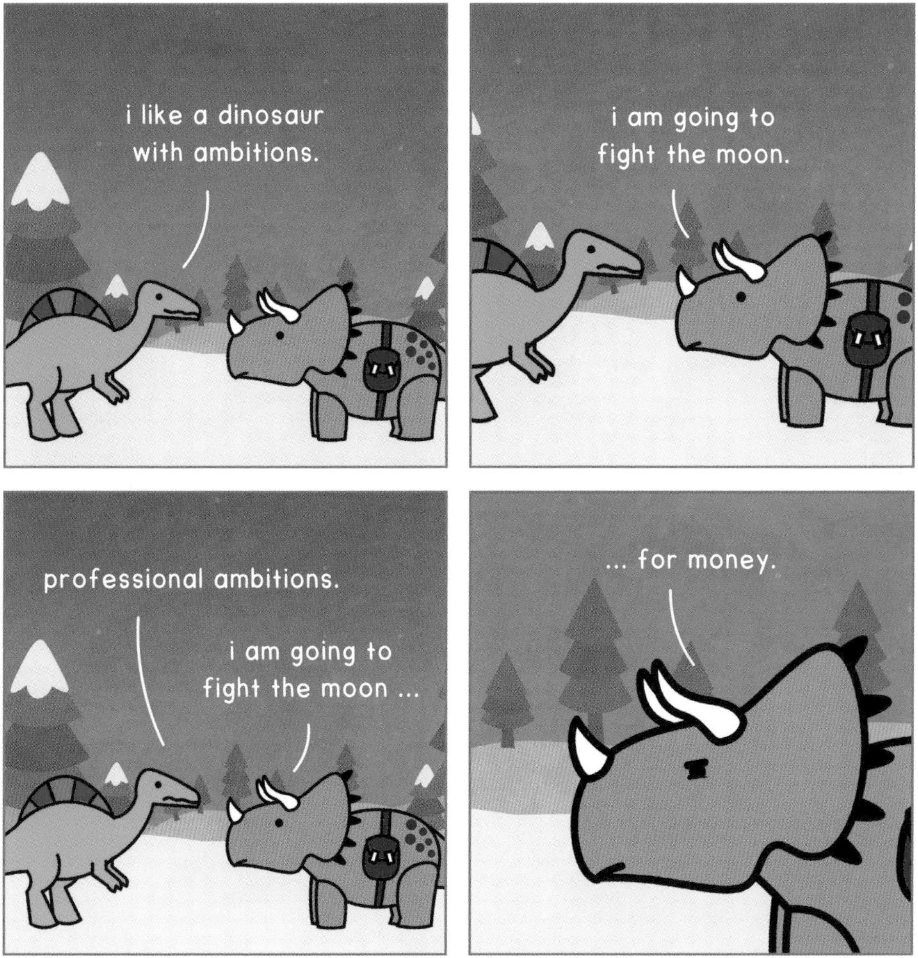
i like a dinosaur
with ambitions.
i am going to
fight the moon.
professional ambitions.
i am going to
fight the moon ...
... for money.

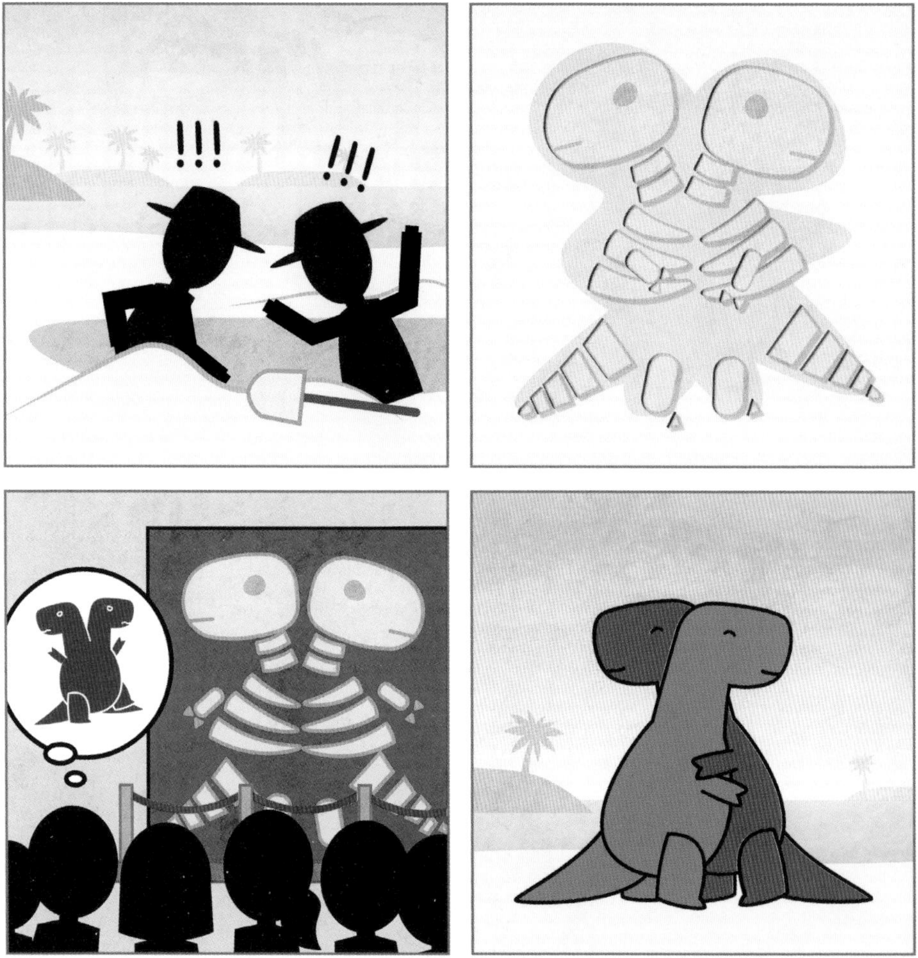
!!!
!!!